LEAPFROGGING
TO POLE-VAULTING

PRAISE FOR THE BOOK

'More than ever before, the world needs radical yet sustainable transformation. This captivating book, through its impressive assured innovation framework, shows the way forward for achieving this daunting task. A must-read.'

—Ratan Tata
Former chairman, Tata Sons, and chairman, Tata Trust

'Raghuanth and Ravi in this book provide a rich perspective on today's global challenges and the inevitable need for a holistic transformation to ensure a better future. This is all stitched together through engaging case studies, which makes it an interesting read.'

—N.R. Narayana Murthy
Founder, Infosys Ltd

'As the world and especially India embrace unprecedented opportunities, pole-vaulting will be a central strategy. This book is a masterpiece that lays down an innovative roadmap for fundamental transformation. Lofty thinking, compelling vision!'

—Mukesh Ambani
Chairman and managing director, Reliance Industries

'This book is full of interesting insights and suggestions for achieving bold yet sustainable transformative solutions. Its strategies for creating 'pole-vaulting' leaders are especially relevant for companies today. It's an easy read that radiates optimism about building a sustainable future.'

—Anand Mahindra
Chairman and managing director, Mahindra & Mahindra Ltd

'Mashelkar and Pandit walk the talk! Respect for others, open-mindedness and humility are traits anyone would notice when interacting with the authors. Their model asks the same from us—respect the planet and its people, be open-minded to rapidly changing technology and attitudes, and do your work with all humility.'

—Vijay Kelkar
Chairman, National Institute of Public Finance and Policy, New Delhi

'This is a riveting piece of writing with inspiring data substantiated by transformative case studies. The invaluable lessons must be adopted by every developing economy to break free from economic status quo that emanates from eminently discardable obsolete policies. A must-read for entrepreneurs, policymakers and every individual who seeks to be relevant in the changing world, where sustainability is the lifeline of our future.'

—Kiran Mazumdar-Shaw
Chairman and managing director, Biocon Limited

'The book provides a provocative yet powerful thesis, which will enrich courses on technology management, public policy for inclusive development and bringing about social change. I have no doubt that this book will convert the most cynical and pessimistic person into a hopeful participant in meaningful and transformative pole-vaulting social and technological engagements.'

—Anil Gupta
Founder, Honeybee Network, SRISTI and National Innovation Foundation

'Rapid yet sustainable transformation is the need of the hour to create a better world, but for this we need some radical game-changing solutions. The authors of this engaging book suggest a powerful pole-vaulting metaphor to achieve precisely this by going over the wall of obstacles, by setting the bar at heights that are in sync with our high aspirations. An inspiring book.'

—Professor Muhammad Yunus
2006 Nobel Peace Prize winner

'Mashelkar and Pandit provide a realistic view of the problems of the future and provide an optimistic vision of how they can be overcome. Turning from reacting from fear—leapfrogging—to planning to overcome seemingly insurmountable barriers—pole-vaulting—provides a pathway to the future. Their solutions are appropriate for both the developed and developing world.'

—Professor Robert Grubbs
2005 Noble Prize winner in Chemistry

'To be a success you have to aim to clear the high bar of aspirations. For that, you need a coach. Mashelkar and Pandit's book is the ideal coach, encouraging you and teaching you to clear the high bar in a giant leap powered by human ingenuity—our only inexhaustible resource.'

—Alan Finkel
Chief Scientist, Australia

'Leapfrogging, R.A. Mashelkar and Ravi Pandit tell us, is not enough. We must pole-vault. Leapfrogging means jumping to safety, while pole-vaulting means exceeding the bar through daring innovation. Today's global society must pole-vault to sustainable development, that is, to a world that is prosperous, socially inclusive and environmentally sustainable. This wonderful book, by two of India's most illustrious and knowledgeable engineers and innovators, is an invaluable primer on how we can pole-vault to the future we want by building bold, breakthrough technologies that rapidly reach unprecedented scale.

'As the book's exciting narrative and vivid examples makes clear, India is already on this path, with breakthrough innovations carrying India's 1.4 billion people into a new age of shared prosperity and environmental sustainability. There are, of course, huge challenges, risks and tasks ahead. This book will provide invaluable inspiration and guidance for success, especially for the new generation of innovators, entrepreneurs and leaders who will soon lead the way.'

—Jeffrey D. Sachs
Special advisor to UN Secretary-General, and professor, Columbia University

LEAP FROGGING to POLE-VAULTING

RAGHUNATH MASHELKAR
RAVI PANDIT

A special thank you to Meeta Kabra. She added lustre to this book with her passion for perfection and unbound creativity, ceaselessly challenging us to raise the bar!

PENGUIN

VIKING

An imprint of Penguin Random House

VIKING

USA | Canada | UK | Ireland | Australia
New Zealand | India | South Africa | China

Viking is part of the Penguin Random House group of companies
whose addresses can be found at global.penguinrandomhouse.com

Published by Penguin Random House India Pvt. Ltd
4th Floor, Capital Tower 1, MG Road,
Gurugram 122 002, Haryana, India

First published in Viking by Penguin Random House India 2018

ISBN 9780670089956

Cover design by Falguni Gokhale
Typeset in Sabon by Manipal Digital Systems, Manipal
Printed at Replika Press Pvt. Ltd, India

www.penguin.co.in

Dedicated to the two ladies
who stood behind me through thick and thin—
my mother, Anjani, and my wife, Vaishali
—Raghunath Mashelkar

Dedicated to my parents, Aai and Dada,
and my wife, Nirmala—
I am where I am because of you
—Ravi Pandit

CONTENTS

LEAPFROGGING TO POLE-VAULTING
THE BEGINNING OF A
CONVERSATION

This book emanates from lessons from the books of our own lives.

Our individual experiences, beliefs and common passion to make technology work for the betterment of society have been the driver of this book.

We both come from different backgrounds. One of us, Raghunath Mashelkar, was born in a poor family, walked barefoot to school, studied under street lights and completed all levels of education in India, including his PhD, thanks entirely to scholarships.

He was strongly influenced by a huge scarcity of resources in both his personal life as well as in his studies and research. But the combination of extreme scarcity and great aspiration led him to create the 10x principle that reverberates throughout the book. Extreme scarcity implies doing things ten times cheaper, and great aspiration means doing them ten times better.

On the other hand, Ravi Pandit had the benefit of studying at one of world's best institutes—the Massachusetts Institute of Technology (MIT)—which taught him that every problem can be solved through cutting-edge science and technology for the betterment of the world. He believes that it is incumbent upon each one of us to play one's part in improving our universe. The limitless power of technology to do good and the conviction that the golden age is ahead of us—and not behind us—is also the result of this influence. MIT also lays a strong emphasis on *doing*, with a great focus on engineering and technology, and not just pure science—a proclivity towards action and not just towards thought, creativity and analysis.

Thoughts mature over time and become refined by the experiments one does and the experiences one gathers. We have been fortunate that we were able to 'play' with our thoughts and chisel and refine them through the institutions with which the two of us have been involved.

Mashelkar returned to India in 1976 at the age of thirty-three, at a time when the Indian brain drain was the norm, and the best talent left the country, never to return! He joined National Chemical Laboratory as a polymer scientist, became its director and then went on to become the director general of the Council of Scientific and Industrial Research (CSIR), which has a chain of forty national laboratories. The radical yet sustainable transformation that CSIR achieved under his leadership is now rated by some leading experts as among the top ten achievements of Indian science and technology, because CSIR demonstrated how technology with affordable excellence can create a better India.

Ravi Pandit quit his well-paying job in the US the day his educational loans were repaid and returned to India with a goal to build an organization that could make a difference. He co-founded KPIT Technologies, whose motto is 'Technologies for a Better World'. More specifically, KPIT is engaged in the transformation of the world of mobility, a world which is at the cusp of a generational change. Ravi has been passionate about green, smart and safe mobility and he has led KPIT Technologies to the forefront of global changes that are recreating this new world. Ravi considers all his colleagues at KPIT who share his passion as co-authors of this book.

Mashelkar and Pandit got the opportunity to engage professionally when Mashelkar joined KPIT's board of directors, radically changing the pace of technology and the pursuit of innovation at the organization. Mashelkar also chaired the KPIT Innovation Council, established eight years ago. This council nurtured the spirit of innovation to an extent that it is now blossoming through the extraordinary technologies that are being brought into fruition. Initiatives like '*Chhote* [Young] Scientists' and 'KPIT Sparkle' have taken the power of scientific thought and the passion for innovation far beyond the boundaries of the company. This has strengthened the belief that the power of the social mind and the might of technology will promise a tomorrow radically better than the past!

However, technology is merely an instrument for change. The bigger picture beyond technology pertains to a profound confluence of our thoughts from diverse streams. There is a thought embedded in our culture which sees humans and the sentient and the insentient universe around us as an expression of the one and only supreme life-force, by whatever name we may call it. This thought creates a thread of oneness across everything around us, teaching us that we and our environment are all bound together, and that one cannot survive without the other. It teaches us that humanity is not merely sitting atop the world, which we can rummage around in and ravage at will, but that we are actually one element amongst everything around us, all of which is so closely connected. This core belief is further reinforced by the new scientific discoveries that have unravelled the common bond amongst all sentient things. These discoveries also show that there is only a thin, almost imperceptible, line that stands between the sentient and the inert.

And this thought has made us look at the world in a different way. What do we see when we look around us? We see ourselves surrounded by many challenges. The deterioration of the environment is alarming. News from across the world of declining living standards of the lower-to-middle-income population is disturbing. And, of course, we are all concerned about the ways in which we use fossil-fuel energy and the rapidly rising quantity needed for development.

As bleak as the current situation seems, we see many opportunities for a fundamental shift in the way in which we live and 'develop'. Hidden in the problems of this world are also the seeds of exciting transformations which can make the world a far more sustainable and liveable place.

This book is about converting much-needed hope into reality, with optimism. Our optimism is not just 'techno-optimism'. It offers a manifesto for the future. Better still, like any good engineer, we have reduced a paralysing mass of problems into a formula: 3,4,7.

And what is this '3,4,7 formula'? The formula comprises:
- 3Es, namely: Energy, Environment and Employment;
- 4 elements of STEP, namely: Society, Technology, Environment and Policy and;
- 7 elements of ASSURED Innovation, 'ASSURED' standing for: Affordability, Scalability, Sustainability, Universality, Rapidity, Excellence and Distinctiveness.

Our framework emphasizes the need for urgent action that can help make a radical yet sustainable transformation. The core idea of 'pole-vaulting' as opposed to 'leapfrogging' is the only way forward that expresses the deeply felt need for speed, considering our keen awareness of the fact that time is running out fast.

We feel that our pole-vaulting metaphor is the need of the hour. Its message is being proactive not reactive; setting the bar at extraordinary heights, not jumping to safety, like a frog does due to a fear of predators, but pole-vaulting over the walls of seemingly insurmountable obstacles, the size of the pole being the size of the aspiration.

This book has been made possible by the significant contributions of many. While it would be impossible to acknowledge everyone, we have attempted to list out a few without whose inputs and insights the book wouldn't have been what it is now.

We would like to gratefully acknowledge the perceptive insights of Dr Vijay Kelkar on the art and science of public policy. Dr Kelkar has the extraordinary ability to lucidly set forth some of the most complex thoughts. The chapter on social engagement draws on Mr Anand Karandikar's insights. The authors hold his work in the field of social transformation in very high regard.

The book also draws on the experience gained at Janwani, which provided an excellent laboratory for experiments in social change. This has been a journey over half a decade, with many learnings, some disappointments and a great deal of satisfaction. Our colleagues at Janwani, especially Vishal Jain, Kishori Gadre and Saroj Badgujar, deserve special mention. We would like to mention the significant contribution of Vishwesh Pavnaskar for the hard work and great diligence in the collection of data sources.

Finally, grateful thanks are also due to Sanid Patil, Chitralekha Yadav, Sushil Borde, Shrikant Deo and Makarand Phadke, who directly or indirectly kept adding exponential value over the years, both to the book and our thought processes.

Last but not the least, Falguni Gokhale and Meeta Kabra have been so special that they have been acknowledged separately in a distinctive manner.

This book is for everyone who cares for the plants and animals around us, for the air we breathe and the water we drink—for this generation and the next. We hope to spark off productive dialogue around issues critical to each one of us. Let the conversation begin!

Raghunath Mashelkar
Ravi Pandit

ONE

The World at a Crossroads

It was the best of times, it was the worst of times,
It was the age of wisdom, it was the age of foolishness,
It was the epoch of belief, it was the epoch of incredulity,
It was the season of light, it was the season of darkness,
It was the spring of hope, it was the winter of despair.

—Charles Dickens, *A Tale of Two Cities*

What could be said of the eighteenth century is true again now. Today the world stands at the cusp of great change—change driven by as many unprecedented opportunities as extraordinary challenges.

We produce far more food than we ever have in human history. However, some societies waste enormous amounts of food while many sleep hungry every night—and not necessarily only in poor countries. On the one hand our farmers cannot make ends meet, and on the other our agricultural practices cause an almost unbearable strain on our natural resources, such as fresh water and the quality of our soil. Yet, on the horizon we see newer technologies

1

that will ensure much larger agricultural production using far fewer people. Moreover, these technologies, in the form of automation, robotics and analytics, will ensure that smaller amounts of water are used in farming with lowered use of chemical fertilizers too, thus reducing pollution.

Contrary to what our headlines might lead us to believe, over the past five to six decades, our world has seen a period of unprecedented peace and prosperity. Millions and millions of people have risen above the poverty line, lead longer and healthier lives, and have reached higher levels of literacy and education. Today we travel better; we are connected across the globe, and we have many more means of entertainment. The new e-commerce and retailing trends are leading to fewer malls and better inventory management but, unfortunately, less employment too. At the same time, we are sitting on an environmental time bomb. The rate of increase in carbon dioxide in the earth's atmosphere is threatening to push global temperatures beyond the precipice, to the extent that we could see the collapse of human civilization in just a few generations. As a matter of fact, we can already hear its march, in the changing rhythm of the seasons, cataclysmic storms and diminishing biodiversity. We see the potential of space travel and the possibility of making the human race inhabit multiple worlds. At the same time we are unsure whether our present and only world will continue to be habitable.

There is a possibility that all the dull, dirty and dangerous work will be delegated to robots, while human beings will employ themselves in only creative and fulfilling work. The coming generations might need to work only a few hours every week, spending the rest of their time following their passions. But it is also possible that this new wave will leave millions of people behind—having rendered them unemployed and unemployable. And here again, the footsteps are audible. In developed countries such as the USA, large chunks of the population have seen their standards of living drop over the past few decades. They are staring at the prospect of their children being condemned to a lower quality of life than their own.

We use energy that is environmentally harmful, finite in supply and dangerously concentrated in the hands of a few. On the demand side our energy requirements are shooting up, especially because of the rising standard of living in the developing world. It is heartening, though, to see the potential for new technologies that can provide clean, infinite and limitless energy to all, at affordable prices.

These contradictions have us positioned in a unique situation. The direction in which we place our next steps will determine the future of the human race and the earth that we call home. These times call for a thorough understanding of the root of our problems. This is also a time to reflect on the levers that can change the course of mankind.

At this juncture we need to assess our progress and arrive at solutions to counter its negative impacts. At the same time, we believe this progress should be available to humanity at large and not just to a privileged few. To address larger issues effectively, incremental solutions will not be sufficient. Inclusive, long-lasting solutions are the need of the hour. We need disruptions that will help us pole-vault, for frog leaps are just not good enough.

No solution can be effective if the problems are not understood thoroughly. An extensive study of the larger problems the world faces today—poverty, poor health, food and water scarcity, climate change, poor education, political instability, technology-driven unemployment, to name a few—has convinced us that there are three all-encompassing issues at the crux of the most imminent problems of the world. They are the 'three Es' of Energy, Environment and Employment: the 3Es.

Today's imposing challenges: The 3Es

Energy: Consumption of energy is the very essence of life. Global issues such as poverty, health, food and water scarcity, and even political instability can be traced back to the tug of war between demand and supply of traditional sources of energy.

Environment: Almost every action we take impacts the environment around us. Our collective callous attitude towards nature has taken its toll on the diversity of species, which comes full circle back to us. We will die if our flora and fauna become extinct, species by species.

Employment: A declining rate of global income and replacement of humans with technology are the results of technology-driven innovations in lieu of job-driven innovations. Also, economic progress is not translating into progress for all.

Sure, the problems are many. They are growing in number and size. And they are growing fast. But so is our creativity in finding solutions. Through various examples in the coming chapters, we will see that every problem is, after all, only an opportunity in disguise. Also, innovative solutions are not just about technology. Solutions can come in a variety of forms, from disruptive business models or processes and game-changing operational structures or distribution channels, to a completely unconventional look at policy and regulation.

The four levers—in STEP with each other

Fortunately or unfortunately, solutions do not exist in silos.

Executable ideas require the support of four levers. Each of these levers, in its individual capacity, can make or break a solution. However, only when they work in tandem do we see true impact.

Technology: We are unlikely to see successful solutions to any of our big problems without technology. Solutions that use technology effectively will keep up with changing times while also standing the test of time.

Policy: A bold, consistent and enabling regulatory environment with adequate government support will be imperative for driving positive change.

Social engagement: On most occasions, change in policy is not initiated by governments. It is the people at large who come together to push policymakers into doing what's good for society.

Economic model: Only a solution that makes economic sense to all stakeholders involved will survive.

There is a logical sequence to the order in which these four levers are to be engaged. However, each lever is equally important, and to reaffirm this equality we have disregarded the logical sequence and changed the order in which the levers are represented in the acronym for our four-lever framework—STEP—to represent Social Engagement, Technology, Economic Model and Public Policy. These levers have to work in STEP with each other and not as steps one after the other.

In our experience, any viable solution has to satisfactorily address the three fundamental problems of energy, environment, and employment. Viable solutions will require creative, transformative innovations. To convert the 'power of ideas' into the 'power of execution', an innovation has to be an 'ASSURED Total Innovation'. This requires the solution to have seven contributing and confluent attributes; the intention is to overcome the disadvantages of old-school thought processes through some basic tenets. Here's a quick glance at the importance of these aspects.

The key: ASSURED Total Innovation

A: *Affordability* is required to create access for everyone across the economic pyramid, especially for those at the bottom.

S: *Scalability* assumes that solutions ought to make a significant impact on issues related to the 3Es, but cannot if they reach and benefit only a handful of people. Bigger problems need true and meaningfully inclusive solutions.

S: *Sustainability* is a call for not only economic but also environmental and social sustainability. As per our framework's requirement, transformational solutions have to be environmentally sustainable at their heart. These solutions will also have to adapt to varying, complex local needs to stay relevant in the long haul. This sensitivity is inevitable for solutions to be sustainable socially. Moreover, we will need a long-term view towards economic sustainability. New solutions often receive financial impetus from government agencies. However, the solutions cannot be called sustainable if they stay economically dependent on such a push, forever.

U: *Universality* implies user-friendliness with an intention to be inclusive. It is imperative that new solutions respect the capabilities and skill levels of the end user.

R: *Rapidity* has many facets to it, and all of them are to do with the sense of urgency. So imminent are the problems of energy, environment and employment that we need solutions—yesterday! In addition, newer technology is taking us towards solutions that give quicker results—faster airplanes, instantaneous medical results with speedier healing and swift data transfer being just a few examples. Speed is also required for a solution to stay competitive.

E: *Excellence* is not merely having an innovation that we think is excellent. We define an innovation as excellent only when it is affordable excellence. That is, the innovation doesn't compromise on quality or features just because it has to be affordable. In fact, it aims to strike a balance between quality and affordability.

D: *Distinctiveness* can be thought of as accumulative disruption. Innovators cannot stop after creating their initial solution. Instead, they have to keep improving on the current version for it to stay relevant.

These seven attributes will indeed require a shift in the thought process of all stakeholders. We believe this transformation of mindset is imperative to go from leapfrogging to pole-vaulting.

The required turnarounds are a combination of moving from 'jugaad' (stop-gap, make-do hack jobs) to systematic innovation; from 'best practices' to 'next practices'; from incremental to disruptive innovation; and from singular to holistic innovation. With these attributes in mind, we will be able to achieve ASSURED Total Innovation.

This book provides a model to face the challenges posed by the 3Es using the STEP levers while achieving the criteria of ASSURED Total Innovation that are necessary for ultimate success. We would like to emphasize that this is not just a theoretical model but one which we have used successfully in our practical endeavours. In fact, we contend that the framework is not only applicable to businesses but can also be used by NGOs, by institutions such as universities and hospitals, and by government initiatives.

From this bird's-eye view, we will take you deeper into the complex interplay between these parameters. While discussing them individually, we will allude to real-life examples from a wide spectrum of industries including, but not limited to, agriculture, health and education. Further, to provide a complete picture, we will apply the model to some major industries. For instance, we will address the automotive and transportation industries— which are the lifeblood of every economy and are amongst the largest contributors to employment, the GDP (Gross Domestic Product) and environmental damage across the world. Another phenomenon central to civilization today is urbanization. We will take a look at how the levers work together to create effective solutions to one problem area in the management of cities—solid waste management.

Through the book, you will notice references from both the developing and the developed world. You might wonder why a problem that relates to Africa is explained, and is followed by a description of a solution from America. We strongly believe that what is happening in developed nations today at a macro level—both favourable and not—is the shape of things to come in developing nations.

At the same time, many references here focus on India even though the proposed model is applicable across the board. As it stands today, India is a good representation of the global population in transition. Indian population is one-sixth of the world. What applies to India is arguably applicable to the population of China—making it applicable to one-third of humanity. Just a few steps behind India and China are the populations of Africa, South America and South East Asia—another one-third of world population. Solutions that are good for two-thirds of the planet are certainly a good starting point for worldwide application.

Our endeavour in this book will follow the path of our real-life efforts—to explore, develop and present a model for futuristic solutions, which shifts gears from 'leapfrogging' to 'pole-vaulting'.

From leapfrogging to pole-vaulting

Why is it so important to move from leapfrogging to pole-vaulting?

The Cambridge Dictionary defines leapfrogging as 'making improvements to your position by going past other people quickly or by missing out some stages'. Dictionary.com defines it as 'an advance from one place, position, or situation to another without progressing through all or any of the places or stages in between'.

These definitions seemed conventional and did not really capture why a frog leaps. Scientific studies show that frogs leap because they are afraid of predators. The only objective of the leap is to land in a place or to cover a distance that keeps the frog safe. So, leapfrogging for a frog is a response to an external stimulus and not to an internal trigger, safety being the only goal.

If we were to apply this metaphor to corporate behaviour towards innovation, the logic seems rather unsatisfactory. Should a company only innovate because it is afraid of a competitor? Should it go only as far as is sufficient to keep the business safe? Thereafter, should the company leapfrog again, to another safe place, only when the threat from a competitor starts lurking large?

We feel that for true transformation, one has to look far beyond leapfrogging. Transformational changes need extraordinary aspiration that aims for exponential achievement.

Thereby arose a new, more apt metaphor—pole-vaulting. First and foremost, by definition, pole-vaulting requires you to go over a bar. In innovation, such bars are set by one's limited aspirations or by the perceived limitations of current technologies. The higher the bar, the higher the ambition. The bars in pole-vaulting are also assigned based on limited imagination. Minds that dare always want to stretch these limits to what at first might appear unattainable.

The inspiring inscription on the Lamme Medal of the Institute of Electrical and Electronics Engineers, USA, says it all: 'The engineer views hopefully the hitherto unattainable.' In that spirit, pole-vaulting can not only view the unattainable but also achieve the seemingly unattainable.

Unlike leapfrogging, which is instant and reactionary, pole-vaulting requires preparation. The higher the kinetic energy of the pole-vaulter, the higher is the height they can aim for. The kinetic energy that propels the pole-vaulter over the bar varies directly and exponentially with their velocity. When the pole-vaulter starts to run, the velocity is zero. When they approach the bar, this velocity is at its highest. Rapid acceleration is the key. Such acceleration can be achieved when the speed of thought matches the speed of action.

The pole too plays a vital role. It has to be strong but flexible to make the vault powerful. In a corporate world, the pole is the supporting talent, technologies and tools.

However, the question still remains: Why does one need to go from leapfrogging to pole-vaulting?

A shift away from leapfrogging and approaching innovations with an attitude of a pole-vaulter will take us towards progress in the true sense of the word. A 10 per cent increase in performance is an incremental innovation. It is easy. You are doing what everyone is doing, but only slightly better. A 100 per cent increase in performance in a short time is more difficult. It requires innovation at another level. This is, still, leapfrogging. When this increase is 1000 per cent however, a 10x improvement, it is then that we are talking of transformational innovation, progress in its true sense. This is what we would call pole-vaulting. We need a 10x change in the demands of ourselves as a community of innovators, creators, sellers, buyers and policymakers.

It is time we stop being happy with a 20 per cent reduction in price, but instead look at twentyfold price improvement. This is not unachievable. Such aspirations have led to unimagined cost reductions. For instance, until ten years ago an ECG machine used to cost around $10,000.* When an innovative mind, Rahul Rastogi, applied himself, a $70 version was developed that made ¢8 tests possible. This is not all. This machine is portable and can be used in the remotest corners of the world.[1]

Similarly, a business challenged itself to make high-speed, 4G Internet available at ¢10 per GB, with free voice calls, for a billion people, and did it—that is Jio in India. Only when we set ourselves such lofty aims are today's successes—such as 1 billion Aadhaar registrations in India—conceivable.

This book is all about pole-vaulting towards a new future, a future that is radically and not just marginally different, a future that is radically transformed and is yet sustainable. And this has to be achieved notwithstanding all the formidable obstacles, either perceived or real. We capture the essence of the pole-vaulting innovation processes, products and people, which has made the seemingly impossible, possible.

Environment, energy and employment pose stiff challenges, but they also offer momentous opportunities for bold change. To make the most of these opportunities, we must reject inadequate, timid solutions. Timid solutions include digging deeper wells in response to running out of water. Timid solutions include scrambling to squeeze incrementally more oil from the planet in response to diminishing reserves. Timid solutions include desperate economic policies, which confer neither dignity nor security, in response to plummeting living conditions. We believe that as a global community it is time to let go of such knee-jerk, stop-gap solutions in lieu of inclusive, long-term ones.

The urge in our efforts, over the years, is guided by the ancient desire of our forefathers, as described in a prayer for the universe:

ॐ सर्वे भवन्तु सुखिनः
सर्वे सन्तु निरामयाः ।
सर्वे भद्राणि पश्यन्तु
मा कश्चिद्दुःखभाग्भवेत् ।।
ॐ शान्तिः शान्तिः शान्तिः

Om, may all be happy,
may all be free from illness.
May all see what is auspicious,
may no one suffer.
Om peace, peace, peace.[2]

This leading philosophy of happiness and well-being for all is a part of our mature culture. As expressed in this Sanskrit verse, we wish for the entire world a healthy and pain-free existence—physically, mentally and emotionally. We look forward to the moulding of a world in which all of humanity can be happy. We wish to see the good that people can do. We pray that the entire human race may lead a life of peace and harmony.

Our real-life efforts so far have been driven by the spirit of progress, prosperity and peace for all; we are not content with the progress of just an advantaged handful. This book is a logical step taking forward this belief—that the world is a better place only if it is a better place for all.

---

* Since most of the sources that we pulled our data from had amounts in US Dollars, we have taken USD as the main currency through the book. A local currency has been used when the base source has used that currency. On most occasions, this currency has been converted to USD to make comparisons easy. In other cases, we have left this conversion out because it is not relevant to the point under discussion. The local currency–USD conversion has been made at the exchange rate prevalent on the 31 March of the relevant financial year, as per the Reserve Bank of India's official website. In some cases, the conversion has been applied at $1: 65 (the rounded-off conversion rate as on 31 March 2018). These numbers have been further rounded off, on a case-to-case basis.

TWO

The 3Es
Today's Imposing Challenges

Be it your morning Twitter feed or the newspaper, the top page greets you with headlines similar to:

World News	South Africa	USA	Brazil
'Crude's top hedge fund manager says oil at $300 not impossible' *—Economic Times*, 30 Apr 2018[1]	*'Icebergs could be tugged from Antarctica to drought-hit Cape Town to ease water crisis'* *—Japan Times*, 1 May 2018[2]	*'Automation could kill 73 million U.S. jobs by 2030'* *—USA Today*, 28 November 2017[3]	*'Brazil's lawmakers renew push to weaken environmental rules'* *—Nature*, 30 April 2018[4]

And yet, scroll down further or turn to page 7 of your newspaper and you smile with hope:

World News	India	Germany	Haiti
'Solar PV and wind are on track to replace all coal, oil and gas within two decades' —*Conversation*, 6 April 2018[5]	*'Around 6,000 Aurangabad villages being trained to tackle drought'* —*Times of India*, 25 February 2018[6]	*'German government predicts one million new jobs for next year'* —*Local*, 25 April 2018[7]	*'Solar Startup Brings Renewable Energy To Haitian Businesses'* —*Forbes*, 30 April 2018[8]

These examples only fortify our belief: for every problem, there is a solution waiting to be found. Challenges mask opportunities that are yet to be unveiled. This contrast is evident across the globe.

Consider India. The juxtaposition of problem and promise is stark. Wealth lives alongside poverty. Excitement about India's technological progress, human capital and potential as a knowledge economy is tempered by concerns about the country's quality of education and the employability of its people. Even as we celebrate the growth of awareness about India's environmental heritage, the country's environment itself degrades like never before. Unsurprisingly, this is not unique to India. Each region in the world is suffering environmental degradation, only the circumstances and conditions are different. However, the factors that affect a nation and its people are strikingly similar across the world.

A deeper look at any major negative news item reveals that almost every one of them has its roots in one of the following three areas—energy, environment or employment, the 3Es, whether the news relates to the state of a country's economy, its educational system or the health of its population. As we will see in this chapter, many climatic events are results of our efforts to extract traditional sources of energy. Our methods of extraction impact the quality of air and water that form our environment. Air and water issues, in turn, are responsible for issues related to health and food scarcity.

Moreover, many seemingly unrelated events are closely interrelated. For instance, there is a correlation between the cases of armed conflicts and a climatic event. Syria has seen a cyclical cause and effect. In order to reduce dependence on food imports, the Syrian government encouraged wheat cultivation. This eventually led to soil degradation and droughts, which are among the known causes for Syria's civil war. Of course, there are other reasons too, but climate change is one of the main reasons cited for these conflicts in this region. While globally the rate of coincidence of a civil war and a climatic event is 9 per cent, this correlation goes up to 23 per cent for nations divided by ethnicity.[9] This stands to reason. When an already strained community not only loses its source of income from agriculture but also does not have enough to feed its families, food wars are inevitable.[10] Therefore, a civil war could actually have its roots in an environmental issue.

In addition to the problems related to energy and environment, there is another looming concern that needs our immediate attention—unemployment. Rapidly advancing technology has led to increased unemployment. It has also widened income, wealth and access disparity. Therefore, employment issues lie at the root of poverty, illiteracy and inept educational systems. If there was gainful and dignified employment for the marginalized groups across nations—and some issues related to caste, class and race discrimination can also be traced to pressures on income—we believe a lot of the present-day discord would not have become so intense.

In practical terms, therefore, almost every problem can be distilled down to relate to one of the 3Es. These factors are universal and universally critical. However, we believe that even as they are imposing problems, they present the greatest potential for reimagining human activity.

Energy—the ever-increasing demand and the skewed politics of supply

As we have known since times immemorial, our main source of energy is the sun. Many of the other forms of energy too can be traced to the energy provided by the sun. This is renewable energy. Wind and hydro-energies too are renewable forms of energy.

Some energy has been stored in the form of fossil fuels under the earth. These are non-renewable forms of energy such as coal and oil. This energy is condensed, has higher density and is thus storable. Since the work of creation and contraction of this energy has already been done by Mother Nature, all we do is dig it out, process, transport and use it. Until recently, using non-renewable energy in this manner has been a cheaper alternative to converting renewable energy into usable energy.

However, the use of non-renewable energy presents problems from environmental, economic and social perspectives, which we shall discuss at length soon. On the other hand though, even as we know the positives of using renewable sources of energy, the storage of such energy is expensive. Since the sun does not shine always, nor does the wind blow and rain fall at all times, we need to store the energy we source from them. So even though renewables are largely democratic—when available, they are accessible to everyone in the area—there is very little actual use of renewable sources of energy because of high storage costs. In India, only a little over 2 per cent of the energy we consume is through renewables, while an ominous 92 per cent is from fossil fuels. Despite optimistic global predictions, fossil fuels will still be satisfying about 82 per cent of India's energy demand in 2040. Currently, most of the renewable energy generated in India is used for cooking and other domestic purposes. Penetration of renewables in the transport sector, one of the biggest consumers of fuels, is negligible.[11, 12]

The truth is, if we were to continue 'as is', it presents a disturbing picture for the future because of the disastrous consequences of using fossil fuels. As we explore further in the next section, we are at the cusp of an environmental catastrophe. A large part of the onus lies in the hands of fossil-fuel usage. First and foremost, is the intense environmental damage of carbon dioxide and particulate emissions from burning coal and oil. Certainly, fossil fuels cannot be a sustainable source of energy.

Fossil-fuelled politics

The restrictions in the supply side don't end here. Over 6.4 billion people consume energy while there is only a handful of energy suppliers. A lot of the world's suffering can be attributed to the enormous inequality in people's access to energy. Most of the globe's oil requirement is supplied by only eight countries, while the coal requirement is met mainly by five countries. OPEC, Organization of the Petroleum Exporting Countries, is a consortium of countries that produce petroleum. OPEC caters to the interests of these countries in determining the quantities of oil that will be supplied and their price. There is no such agency that protects the billions of petroleum users.

The concentration of oil reserves in a few countries puts enormous financial strain on the consumers of importing countries. Even within countries, the producers and distributors of fossil fuel are few in number and the consumers disproportionately many. Therefore, there is continuous flow of income from a large number of consumers, mostly rural, to the small number of producers and distributors, who again belong mostly to the developed and rich countries. This inequality amongst citizens and nations is the source of many problems that seem unrelated.

Moreover, the data provided by the producers is far from transparent. It is restricted, and this is a cause for worry from a security and stability perspective too. Their control over supply has an impact on prices, skewing the imbalance even further. Oil prices vary according to production and reserves. Supply is controlled largely by OPEC, making prices volatile and dependent on the whims of the controlling nations. If there is a 10 per cent reduction in oil stock, it leads to a disproportionate increase in oil prices.

The international energy market is far from competitive in its current form. The inequality in access to energy resources leads, like no other force in the world, to inconsistent foreign relations. This, in turn, has major consequences on political stability.

Energy-related political instability isn't restricted just to the international level. It manifests starkly across sections of society within countries too. With a handful of notable exceptions such as Norway, oil-producing countries on almost every continent have seen political tension and strife as a direct or indirect impact of their oil industries. In other cases, overt political conflict is not apparent; nonetheless, dramatic inequality is imposed by those who have control of energy resources. As an example, the Venezuelan economic crisis is directly related to the drop in global oil prices which made oil exports unsustainable for Venezuela. The country depends heavily on its oil production and has the largest oil reserves in the world. In 2014, it had 298 billion barrels of proven oil reserves. Venezuelan oil revenue has been historically used to finance social programmes and food subsidies. However, when global oil prices fell, these social endeavours became financially unsustainable.[13] Valuable resources were diverted to fuel extraction instead of being used to create other infrastructure, further aggravating the crisis. Similarly, in the Middle East, the governments of some countries are in power only because of the support they have from valuable customers, such as the USA, which support the reigning political party to retain their fuel supplies.

The double whammy on energy demand

While it is obvious that energy consumption will increase in absolute terms as population increases, there are other factors that call for even more demand on energy. There has been a steep rise in energy consumption in per capita terms from 1974 to 2014. Over these forty years, China's per capita energy consumption has increased by over 350 per cent and India's by over 130 per cent.[14] This disproportionate increase in energy consumption in developing countries can be explained by economic development.

Consumption of energy reflects quality of life. How is an economy to grow if there is no energy to fuel its industry? While the cause-and-effect relationships are nuanced, the relationship between energy consumption and income across countries is obvious.[15] Income, arguably, correlates to other measures of well-being too. But even though we might not think of it in those terms in our day-to-day lives, energy is correlated to well-being.

Hidden in the growing demand numbers is the fact that the world's most populated countries are yet to reach their peak points of energy demand. As China, India and countries in Africa move from being 'developing' countries to developed ones, demand for energy will be more intense. Moreover, in contrast to developed nations, which have negative population growth, populations in China, India and Africa are rising. This means we are heading towards a disproportionate increase in demand on energy from both angles—population growth and economic progress.

Therefore, we have to be keenly aware that the environmental problems faced by the developed countries because of human activity might present themselves in developing countries too as they progress. As heartening as it will be for the people of the developing countries, it will also be a manifold burden on their environment as these countries have huge populations. Also, they are marching forward much more rapidly than the developing countries progressed. So the impact of their progress will be quicker and larger.

The environmental impact of the use of fossil fuels is unequivocally and gravely worrisome. Through fuel extraction what we are effectively doing is digging the earth to throw harmful byproducts into the air we breathe and the water we drink. The challenge then is to progress towards desirable outcomes while using energy that is not detrimental to the environment. Data from an MIT Technology Review points out that only zero-emission energy usage will help us redeem the damage caused by fuel extraction.[16]

Other than fossil-fuel extraction, many other related activities impact the environment too. This extracted fuel is used by us to further damage the environment. This leads to other problems that need a deeper look.

The environment—at full throttle towards air, water, species and mineral extinction

'Environment' is not a buzzword or a fad. The air we breathe, the water we drink, the soil that our food grows in . . . they are our basic needs. Clean air, safe water and healthy soil should not be luxuries we find in RO purifiers and organic food. We live in an ecosystem where we depend on worms for soil fertilization and trees for the oxygen we breathe. We die if our trees, birds and animals die.

Sure, there is a close connection between increase in energy requirement and its impact on the environment. But our concerns for the environment lie beyond the impact of demand for more energy.

We certainly need a change in our attitude towards the environment. However, to take positive action, we need to measure what we need to change. We think of the environment in terms of the elements—air, water, minerals, and species of flora and fauna. The impact of human activity on these aspects of the environment has led to the slow plague of our times—climate change.

Let us take a quick look at the current status of each of these aspects that forms and impacts our environment.

Abundant and misused air

We think of air as unlimited. However, if breathable air is depleting, we are heading towards air extinction. The stratospheric ozone layer in the earth's atmosphere protects us from the sun's ultraviolet rays. A reduction of ozone in this layer—what we commonly refer to as ozone layer depletion—lets these rays pass through to living beings on earth. This percolation is a known cause of skin cancer and extensive damage to marine and biological ecosystems. It is our activity on earth that releases chemical particles in the atmosphere that cause perforations or depletions in the ozone layer. Human activity took the depletion very close to unacceptable levels in the 1980s. But we stepped back in the late 1980s after a global agreement to retract from production activities that release ozone-depleting substances into the atmosphere.[17]

As the ozone layer depletes due to human activity, the quality of air deteriorates too. Air pollution is the largest risk factor for deaths in India. Air pollution-related deaths amounted to nearly 1.7 million in 2010, a figure that is 50 per cent higher than the second-placed factor.[18] High blood pressure, high blood sugar, smoking and the other usual suspects are far behind.

Public health experts estimate that the amount of pollution inhaled from cooking for just one hour on a biomass fire—common in rural India—is equivalent to burning 1000 cigarettes.[19] Urban areas are scarcely better off. One study concluded that fourteen of the twenty most polluted cities in the world are in India.[20] Conventional pollution from factories, power plants and vehicles releases microscopic particles that make for atmospheric aerosol loading. These particles in the air increase with inefficient burning of biomass and fossil fuels. This, in turn, increases the incidence of asthma and other lung diseases. India serves merely as a case study; the problem is universal.[21] Worldwide, air pollution took 4.2 million lives in 2016.[22, 23]

Water, water everywhere—neither good, nor enough to drink[24]

If the air around us is polluted, so is the water we drink or cook with. Not only is the quality of water deteriorating, but the sources of usable water are also depleting. By 2025, 1.8 billion people in the world will experience absolute water scarcity. Yes, our water is close to extinction too.[25] Of course, our usage is one of the main causes of scarcity of water. From dripping taps to inefficient use of water in farming and animal rearing, the indifference to water usage is appalling. For instance, it takes 7000 litres of water to bring a pound of beef to the table![26] What else other than our callousness can explain this not-so-rosy picture? Kenya is a huge exporter of roses to Europe, though parts of Kenya are some of the driest places in the world and Europe is a water-rich region. Every stem of rose requires about 90 litres of water from the time the plant is sowed and until the rose makes it to the Valentine's day markets of Europe.[27] Yes, a water-scarce area uses a disproportionate amount of water to get a rose to a water-rich area—to help us celebrate! To top it off, the entire ecosystem around the lake where these rose farms exist has gone bare, its soil quality depleted, and its flora and fauna gone.[28]

Along the way, we are also adding way too much phosphorus, nitrogen and other elements through crop systems in the form of pesticides and fertilizers. This is poisoning the earth. These chemicals then run off into waterbodies, harming aquatic ecosystems.

Like air pollution, water contamination too is a cause of disease and fatalities. Globally, at least 2 billion people use drinking water contaminated with faeces. Contaminated water transmits diseases such as cholera, dysentery, and typhoid.[29] This is only one aspect of our water woes.

What is environment friendly is also a very complex question. What we may think of as eco-friendly might deceivingly not be so. For instance, the jury is still out on the net effect of organic food being good for the environment. Organic doesn't necessarily mean environmentally good.[30]

Again, this is not a 'developing country' problem. Scarce or filthy water is an all-pervasive problem. Moreover, our oceans are accumulating garbage patches, some of them already the size of France. This debris has concentrations of plastic. If measured, this non-biodegradable plastic in waters all around the world is likely to outweigh the fish in our oceans by 2050.[31] Some of this could be on account of the fish dying from feeding on the plastic. Such is our ecosystem that an impact on non-human life—animals, marine life or vegetation—eventually impacts human life too.

No flora to smell, no fauna to fawn over?

It is even more worrisome that the current rate of species extinction is a thousand times higher than it would have been in the absence of human activity.[32] Flora, fauna and habitats are components of the ecosystem which provide to human systems. It cannot be overemphasized that any reduction in their quantity or quality impairs the larger ecosystem, including human life. If we follow our current, business-as-usual trajectory, one in six species is likely to go extinct in the not-too-distant future.[33]

Human activity not only leads to deoxygenation but also raises air and water temperatures. Warmer water holds less oxygen. This is one of the reasons behind the fourfold increase in zero-oxygen zones in our oceans since 1950.[34] It is a tenfold increase along the coasts. Marine life cannot survive in these areas, and many species will not be able to thrive. This, in turn, will directly and detrimentally impact the lives of hundreds of millions of people who depend on the sea for their livelihood.

Alas, the destruction of flora is even greater. Amongst the many related aspects, let us pick deforestation—the permanent destruction of forests to make land available for other uses. Between 1990 and 2015, forests were felled at the rate of one thousand football fields every hour! India alone has lost around 26 million acres (~11 million hectares) in just fourteen years, from 1999.[35] Degradation of forests leads to soil erosion, altered climate patterns, rivers changing paths, reduced biodiversity, less green cover for absorption of atmospheric carbon, and much more. This damage to forests and other aspects of nature could halve living standards for the world's poor.[36]

Mined out to the bottom of the pit

We are extracting minerals from the earth which are depleting fast too—mineral extinction goes beyond the exhaustion of coal and petroleum. For example, lithium— an element that is very important today in energy storage applications such as batteries—is extracted from rocks. But there is only a limited supply. We can narrate similar D-day stories for phosphorous, cobalt, and so on.

As you might have observed, none of the environmentally degrading human activities mentioned above acts in isolation. There are multiple vicious circles at play. For instance, aerosol loading creates a layer of smog that damages plant life by blocking sunlight. This in turn affects the water cycle, which affects crops, which affects soil quality, which leads to the use of fertilizers, which causes pollution, and on goes the loop.

Many such cycles exist all around us. From the Californian drought in 2016 to the 2017 hurricanes in Florida; from the 2010 floods in Pakistan to the current acute water shortage in South Africa—all are a result of some such series at play.

The bottom line is, the chemicals, compounds, plastics, nuclear waste, etc., that we have invented are alien to nature. However, they seep into soil and water. The fear is that one day these novel entities could even change the genetic code of different species of life, including humans.[37]

It all boils down to two words: Climate change

These complex interactions achieve monumental proportions in defining the environmental problem of our time—global warming.

To begin with, temperature impacts labour supply, labour productivity and crop yields. Every day of temperatures higher than 30°C in an average US county costs each resident $20 in uncarned income. In another case, a study of 1 billion tweets revealed that rising temperatures coincided with aggressive temperaments.[38]

While all the world suffers the ill effects of climate change, some countries will suffer more than others. A warmer world will impact warmer countries more than the cooler ones away from the Equator. Poorer and hotter countries in South America and Africa are likely to get even warmer, and thus even poorer. By 2050, the average income of 60 per cent of the world's poorest will be 70 per cent lower than it would be without the effects of climate change.[39]

We also have to realize that no climatic event is local. The global nature of our activities ensure that those in one part of the earth lead to repercussions on the other side. For example, Egypt relies heavily on food imports from China and Russia. A heat wave and the resultant drought in these countries in 2010 sent the prices of imported wheat soaring, making bread in Egypt very expensive. In a nation already rife with political unrest, rising prices of basic commodities only added fuel to the fire.[40]

The environmental challenges we have talked about are just a glimpse of the dire situation the world faces. There are many other global environmental issues, like solid waste and sewage in cities, which impact health and urban infrastructure. Most importantly, each problem interacts with others along complex biophysical, economic and social dimensions. And yet, there is hope.

It is not all 'gloom and doom'

We believe humans as a race are more responsible than irresponsible. Persistent demand for energy, the imminent danger of environmental hazards and our love for the planet have led to a passionate search by us for alternative sources of energy.

Many trends in energy consumption are reflections of desirable social outcomes too, even if the sources of energy aren't the most desirable yet. Some of the rise in India's electricity consumption follows a decrease in kerosene (lamp oil/paraffin) and polluting biomass-fuel consumption, suggesting a shift in the energy source for power. The effect this has on indoor air quality, and therefore on public health, is an excellent outcome.

Globally, about 500,000 solar panels were installed every day in 2015.[41] A record-shattering surge in green electricity saw renewables overtake coal as the world's largest source of installed power capacity. Since 2012, two-thirds of Britain's coal-fired power-generating capacity has been shuttered.[42] The trend away from coal as a source of electricity is structural, with coal-free days likely to become more common. Also, the costs of solar and onshore wind power have dropped to an extent that was 'unthinkable' only five years ago.

Disruptive scientific breakthroughs today will become the game-changing technologies of tomorrow. Scientific discoveries are occurring at an incredible pace.[43] Sure, the path from new science to commercially viable technology is a long one. But the innovations give us ample reason to be optimistic and eagerly await change.

Similarly, governments are taking a lead in establishing policies to bring about a cleaner and more equitable world. Chile has protected marine areas, and government agencies such as NASA have developed satellites that will measure the atmospheric ozone to ensure that we are headed in the right direction. Corporations such as Mobike have introduced business solutions to mitigate air pollution and climate change.[44]

All these developments aim to respond to global warming with proactive intervention rather than with the usual climate-change denial or political buck-passing.

As alluded to earlier, climate change might as well be the reason behind the employment issues in agriculture, fisheries and animal husbandry. Climate-change-induced disasters cause mass migration, which in turn also leads to employment problems. However, there are other contributors to unemployment too. We shall now direct ourselves to the third E, the third core reason at the root of many major problems of our world.

Employment, or rather, lack of employment

The world is beset by a deadly combination of declining incomes, increasing unemployment, and growing income and access inequality.

At the outset, we shall define what employment means to us. Employment is important not just as a source of income; it is much more than that. It is also a source of self-respect, purpose, security and stability. For this position to make sense, 'employment' must be somewhat redefined. It cannot simply mean the hiring of labour for a task. Considerations of dignity, competitiveness and stakeholdership are essential. A 360-degree view of the current employment situation is essential. This is why we define employment as 'a dignified manner of generating income'. Of course, employment includes self-employment. However, getting a government handout might not necessarily meet the receiver's sense of grace and honour. Therefore, sustenance that is based solely on such handouts does not mean employment by our definition.

Having defined employment as such, we hold that at the crux of changing employment situations lies technological change. Every technological development has seen a change in the manner in which people are employed. With every industry established, another less-advanced industry has been uprooted. With the upheaval has come unemployment and re-employment.

Counter-intuitive—children earn less than their parents

Concern over jobs is the primary challenge for people across the developed world. Surveys of American adults over the past few years show that employment has, almost without exception, been their top concern. In 2013, only a little over half of American thirty-year-olds earned more than their parents did. In these times of progress, who would want to imagine a next generation that earns less than the current one, or worse, a generation that will not be able to retire because the pensions are just not enough.[45, 46] In Britain too, wages are increasing at rates far lower than inflation.[47]

The pattern of employment in the developed countries is only a precursor of what we should expect in the developing and increasing populations of China, India and Africa.

Growing technology, fewer jobs

Declining incomes aside, lack of employment opportunities is a ubiquitous concern. And for good reason: unemployment has long been recognized as having major consequences, not only on economic security but also on the morale of individuals, families and communities, directly impacting their physical and mental health.

Unfortunately, relevant data on employment in India is unavailable, but we suspect the trend to ultimately follow the trajectory of the developed countries, only sooner rather than later.

We know that unemployment—especially unemployment among youth—is a leading concern in Europe too.[48] Even the jobs that were created only after the advent of computers are already seeing a decline. Total employment in American computer and electronic companies declined from under 2 million in 2001 to a little over 1 million in 2016.[49] The reason for this can be understood in terms of worker replacement by technology and a reduction in new avenues for jobs.

Historically, for every job that was taken away by technology, more were created by the growth triggered by the technology and the new industries it spawned. Additionally, people retrained, reskilled, refocused and found or created new jobs when displaced by machines. They moved, for instance, from agriculture to manufacturing to services. In the United States, agricultural labour fell from 74 per cent of total employment in 1800 to 2 per cent in 2000. But clerical, sales and service jobs increased from 5 per cent of total employment to 38 per cent around the same time period. However, while the working population in manufacturing rose from 14 per cent to 26 per cent during the 100 years from 1850 to 1950, it dropped back to 15 per cent in the fifty years following that.[50] Britain experienced a similar drop in manufacturing employment.

Sure, some manufacturing-related jobs are now categorized as non-manufacturing jobs, skewing the employment numbers. For example, product companies have handed over their supply-chain management logistics to courier companies. Therefore, instead of a product company's employees, courier service employees are making sure that the right part gets to the right assembly line. The courier company's employees will not be counted in the manufacturing job numbers, but the reduction in the product company's supply-management department is factored in as a drop in manufacturing jobs.[51]

But even after accounting for such reclassification, we find that there is a steep decline in the total number of jobs. This is largely owing to technological developments.

The irrefutable fact is that the worry about machines taking over is not completely unfounded. Despite rising productivity, employment falls, as technological substitutes for human labour become cheaper and more effective. Companies, after letting go of employees in a tough economy, found that they could restore and grow their productivity without those employees as a result of advanced technology.[52] Every manufacturer will appreciate increased production without an increase in salary/wages. In fact, organizations saw an increase in profits despite reduced sales because of reduced costs in saved labour hours.[53]

As cruel as it sounds, the truth is that robots, after all, don't quit their jobs, go on vacations or catch the flu. Moreover, the cost of robots has dropped from $100,000 apiece from when they were first introduced, to faster, smaller, easier-to-operate versions that cost only $25,000 each.[54] This advent of the robot has led to reduced creation of new types of jobs that humans can learn and move to. A 2016 report suggests that the technology impact on jobs will be far greater in the developing world than in the developed world.[55] The reason is the same—advanced robotics. Manufacturers of shoes and cars are moving production back to Germany, the UK and the US from China and India, thanks to advanced robotics, which does more complex jobs at much lower costs.

Newer avenues of employment are receding rapidly as information and communication technology (ICT) advances exponentially. The rate of advancement is unprecedented in the history of technological development. As ICT disrupts the economic landscape in myriad ways, people might not be able to refocus fast enough. This is likely to lead to a more problematic, pervasive type of displacement. Indeed, evidence suggests that such displacement is already happening, as machines become astonishingly competent and inexpensive at jobs that were, until recently, firmly within human territory.

Yet again, what is true for the developed countries is only biding its time before becoming true for the growing populations of China, India and Africa. In India, the working age population growth is already at about 16 million per year. However, only about 2 million jobs are being created annually. We can only shudder to think of the employment scenario when India will be in a position to automate jobs like the developed world.[56]

Technology is a boon and a bane and deserves a holistic consideration. We will have a detailed discussion on technology's impact on employment in a subsequent chapter.

The future is already here—it's just not evenly distributed[57]

This brings us to another worrisome aspect of employment—wealth, income and access disparity. This makes the reality even more stark. Progress, as we know it, in the last few decades has only widened economic disparity across the world. When compared with the nineteenth century, we are doing far better than we were, say, in

1820, when 94 per cent of humanity lived on less than $2 a day (in real $ terms).[58] This number was 10 per cent in 2015. However, even though the percentage of population below the poverty line has decreased, the rich have become even richer and the really poor have become even poorer, making the inequality larger than ever.

This is as true of the US as it is of India and the rest of the globe. In the US, the inflation-adjusted income of production workers is not very different from the 1970 levels.[59] Some areas have seen thirty years of wage stagnation.[60] This is bound to increase social tensions and frustration. Alas, this situation only threatens to get worse. New jobs, such as those created by Uber and Lyft, are allegedly not resulting in economic growth for their driver-partners.[61] This implies that the owners of these companies are the ones benefiting more than the other stakeholders.

According to Oxfam, the world's eight richest people have wealth equal to that of the world's poorest 50 per cent. Globally, within the next twenty years, 500 of the world's richest people are going to pass on wealth worth $2.4 trillion to their next generation. This is a sum larger than the GDP of India. In India itself, 73 per cent of the wealth generated in 2016 was received by the richest 1 per cent, while the poorest 50 per cent saw a rise of only 1 per cent in their wealth. In absolute terms, the new wealth of the richest 1 per cent translated to about ₹21 lakh crore (~$323 billion) in 2018. To put this in perspective, this amounts to the total central Indian government budget for 2016. This would have been fine, but other sordid statistics exist alongside—such as half the workers in the garment sector being paid less than the minimum wage.[62]

It isn't even that the middle class is growing remarkably well. In the period between 1980 and 2014, in terms of income, India's top 0.1 per cent grew at 550 times the growth rate of the bottom 50 per cent. The middle 40 per cent on the other hand, grew at a rate three times higher than the bottom half.[63]

Another growing fear is that this middle class too will be losing their jobs to automation.[64] This is a global phenomenon. There are growing avenues for super-specializations that make for high incomes. Low-paying, low-skill jobs too are moving from older industries to newer ones as the older ones get automated. However, the jobs in between are at the greatest risk.[65]

Sure, these income and wealth inequality numbers have come under criticism. The very source of these numbers has been questioned. For the developed countries such as the US, the numbers have been sourced from tax data. Similar methods have been used for generating the numbers for India too. However, tax data from India is hardly representative of the ground reality. For starters, tax compliance in India is 25 per cent, versus 80 per cent in the US.[66]

However, even if we take the numbers with a pinch of salt, will the truth be really very different? Isn't it likely that reality might be worse?

Other than income and wealth inequality, there exists inequality in terms of access to natural resources, education, health amenities and so on. These inequalities ultimately are part of a vicious cycle, and are both the cause and effect of income inequality.

Despite all these glaring inequalities, we believe the answer doesn't lie in blocking the growth of the top 1 per cent of the population. If the bottom-of-the-pyramid population were brought up the income curve, if their daily requirements were met, if access to basic amenities were made easier for them, the inequality wouldn't pinch them as hard.

Until then, though, the stark situation of inequality is disturbing, to say the least. Progress for nations has not necessarily translated to progress for their people.

Yet, there's more than a silver lining

While it is undeniable that some of the examples cited here are scary, we have good reason to be optimistic. Our progress takes us in directions beyond ordinary imagination. Many industries and products that didn't exist or were out of reach for the common man a few decades ago are arguably essential today—air travel, phones, laptops, smart devices, air conditioning, insurance and financing either didn't exist a few decades ago or weren't easily accessible. These new industries have created jobs anew in computing, electronics, customer service, technical servicing, etc. And many industries that always existed are growing in scope—agriculture, law, health and medicine, even as machines are doing some of the core jobs in these fields.

Today, while some of us feel threatened that machines may take over, we as technologists are confident that not many of us are going to completely enjoy 'doing nothing'. As mundane, repetitive activities will stop needing human engagement, humans will occupy themselves elsewhere in more meaningful ways. We did, after all, move to spreadsheets and accounting software. Shouldn't they have replaced accountants altogether? The accounting community is now engaged in roles such as troubleshooting, hand-holding, consulting and analysis. Also, consumer desires will change, and means to satisfy new desires will always be needed.

Our current and future achievements will help us make progress, but the history and current status of some social parameters tell us that the ride is likely to be bumpy.

Even as we are positive about a better world tomorrow, right now, our progress has certainly not been good for our earth or its people. This situation is likely to worsen if we as a race aren't proactive. Unfortunately, the grave concerns of the 3Es boil down to the following:

> We are guzzling expensive, exhaustible energy resources and precipitating enormous environmental crises in order to drive an economic engine that creates no jobs.

Evidently, things need to change. The decisiveness, creativity and responsibility with which we drive and embrace change will determine the legacy of our generation. Solutions that cater to the changing era cannot be reflex reactions but have to be controlled in nature. We have to do more than just kicking the can down the road. We have to rise above false reassurances that distract us from the magnitude, urgency and even the true nature of our problems.

Aiming high while staying rooted

The need of the hour is to look for solutions that create job-led advancement—advances that will create more jobs than destroy. Stop-gap solutions such as higher minimum wages or universal basic income will not suffice for humans who want to live with dignity and satisfaction. If technology-led, jobless growth in India, China and other developing economies continues, it will create huge social disharmony. Creating job-led growth, while at the same time maintaining competitiveness in a digitally disrupted world, will need innovative solutions.

By all appearances, we're in a golden age of innovation. Every month sees new advances in artificial intelligence (AI), gene therapy, robotics and software. Research and development as a share of the GDP is close to an all-time high. There are more scientists and engineers in the US than ever before. Capital is plentiful for innovative ideas, and some of the so-called hype for new technology is actually valid. Old-line companies and upstart entrepreneurs alike are making high-risk bets on cars, space travel and drones, and some policymakers are trying to tolerate more risk so that these bets succeed.

Sure, more-of-the-same solutions won't work. The first step will be to meaningfully understand the issues of environment, energy and employment within the wider context—the human and social constructs that they are embedded in. Once we accept that the problems are interconnected, we will appreciate that solutions cannot operate in isolation either. A systemic view of problems will lead to fundamental and holistic solutions.

A well-designed solution can address multiple aspects of a plethora of grave problems. What, if, for instance, certain technologies could be turned into opportunities for—rather than threats to—employment? What if such technologies also provided environmentally friendly, carbon-neutral energy that reduced air pollution and got rid of the need to cut down forests or mine coal? What if they allowed broad stakeholdership, providing greater opportunities for more people in the energy sector—currently a highly controlled, monolithic behemoth? Going further, what if such technologies questioned the basic assumptions of where energy should come from—to tap the potential of a new type of energy waiting to be discovered?

This is just one scenario. There are, we are sure, countless such possibilities. Existing structures and assumptions must be dismantled, with new ones taking their place. Environment, energy and employment—these are the parameters by which we will measure our success. We are constantly aware that technology is a powerful, dynamic tool at our disposal. At the same time, human and social well-being is the goal. While going forward, we will also need to include our brethren who have been left behind, economically and technologically. We will have to shoot for the stars and yet remain grounded.

The problems that we seek to address—namely those of energy, environment and employment—are very real for both of us, the authors of this book. Our drive begins with acknowledging the big challenges of our times and understanding the root causes. Solving these issues has been a matter of deep thought and great passion for us. These issues are not merely of academic interest to us. As technologists and scientists, we have been engaged in solutions to these problems. Our desire to build a better world will not allow us to regard these problems as peripheral or incidental. It is at the core of who we are.

Our company, KPIT Technologies, is engaged in finding innovative and cutting-edge solutions to the problems of energy and environment in the transportation sector. We work on clean, safe and connected transportation on a global scale. The work that we do is triggered by our passion to invent and implement technologies for a better world. This is our contribution to solving the issues of energy and environment. Even in our social work, the thrust has been to strive for creation of a better world through public participation. Janwani, the organization that we co-founded, has been working on urban solid waste management for the greater part of the last decade. It is also our commitment to a healthier earth, a better environment. Our learnings from Janwani has brought depth to the model we propose in this book. Our community initiatives prominently include improving science education in under-resourced schools and promoting technological entrepreneurship. This is with the intention of enabling the next generation to make themselves relevant in a world where many current skills will be redundant. In this manner we contribute to the third controlling concern, employment.

We do not measure our progress solely by the profits we make. We also measure ourselves by the yardstick of social goals. As innovators, we completely believe in the undeniable role that technology will play in the future. As entrepreneurs, we realize the importance of a solution's need to make economic sense for all involved. As businessmen, we know we need equal support from the other stakeholders—our policymakers and the people at large. Despite our best intentions, we will not be able to achieve much if we do not have an enabling environment.

In the coming chapters, we provide a framework to convert these challenges into opportunities. We need dynamic government policy, active public engagement, non-linear innovation and a fresh look at economic models—the STEP levers. These four levers will provide the ecosystem necessary for ASSURED transformative solutions.

THREE

ASSURED Total Innovation

The wheel. Farming. Vaccines. Mechanization. Wireless communication. Any successful solution that seeks to address the looming challenges of its times has survived to the present day only because it reached a certain scale and survived the test of time. Moreover, each of today's issues—energy, environment and employment—is vying for creative solutions urgently.

Many minds have applied themselves to finding solutions to each of the challenges that we face today and are likely to face tomorrow. But these solutions must assure success over a long period of time. Kodak dominated the photographic film market, and its revenues in the late nineties peaked at $16 billion. Its gross margins were an astounding 70 per cent! Yet in 2012 it declared bankruptcy, and 75 per cent of its employees lost their jobs. Another instance is that of Napster, the darling of the technology world around 1999–2001. It had a staggering, 80 million users who uploaded and shared billions of music files for free. Yet it had to be shut down in July 2001![1]

What is common among Kodak, Napster and so many other ventures that followed a similar path? They could not sustain their success because they did not follow the path of ASSURED innovation!

What is ASSURED? ASSURED is a transformational innovation that is:

Affordable
Scalable
Sustainable
Universal
Rapid
Excellent
Distinctive

While each of these attributes is important, they work better when put to use together. Combining these features with a change in the ecosystem's old-school mindset will lead us to what we like to call ASSURED Total Innovation. We must keep in mind that each of the attributes can vary with time. What is not affordable today, for instance, may become affordable tomorrow when competitors drop prices. Therefore, only when each of the ASSURED attributes is not only fully met but also constantly improving can we say that we have moved from leapfrogging to pole-vaulting.

Total Innovation, not just technological innovation

It was, of course, technological innovation that initially brought mobile phones to the market. A business model innovation expanded the market through customer analysis and online reach. Then technological innovation reduced the prices of handsets. The next thrust came from policy innovation, which created a competitive environment and opened doors to new technology with the aim of placing a mobile phone in every Indian's hands. Owing to this policy drive, when Jio made voice calls available at almost zero cost, this key business model innovation got millions of people on board.[2]

Similarly, India's policy innovation of making zero-balance accounting facilities available to the population with lowest incomes was combined with a push for a biometric identity system, Aadhaar. Aadhaar was adopted far and wide with the help of the prevalent technological innovations in the mobile-phone industry only because it included workflow and system delivery innovation that made linking one's Aadhaar identity with Know Your Customer (KYC) requirements a seamless and quick process.

We will come back to both these examples in greater detail later in the book. What we would like to emphasize here is that achieving all the individual elements of ASSURED also calls for a change in mindset internally and an enabling ecosystem. Only then will our solutions qualify as ASSURED Total Innovations. Such innovations might appear impossible to achieve, but need not necessarily be so. When we change an old-school mindset, it allows us to ask some challenging questions, questions that are in the spirit of achieving the impossible.

Can we make a high-quality Hepatitis-B vaccine, currently priced at $20 per dose, available at $20 for forty doses?

Can we make a high-quality artificial foot, currently priced at $10,000, at one-three hundredth the cost and not just one-third the cost?

Can we make high-speed 4G Internet available at ₹6 (~¢10) per GB, and make all voice calls free of cost—that too in a large and diverse country like India?

Can we invent a robust test for mosquito-borne dengue to detect the disease on day one, and that too at the cost of ₹130 (~$2) per test?

Amazingly, all this *has* been achieved in India, and some of these innovations will be discussed at length later in the book. This has been achieved by using not only technological innovation but also non-technological innovation. And most of these innovations meet the criteria of ASSURED Total Innovation listed above.

With this brief overview of what is required of a successful innovation, we are now ready to plunge into how the ASSURED requirements can be achieved and how their mix can be optimized.

Affordability needs no introduction

The cheaper a product or service, the more accessible and acceptable it will be to the people who need it. It is indeed as basic as that. Today, when selling prices drop, the added advantage is that we don't have to assume a drop in quality. In fact, as consumers we expect exponentially improved performances, equal in pace to dropping prices.

Even as we are witnessing this phenomenon in the world around us today, not all producers have internalized it. Industry experts and analysts are often guilty of underestimating or even dismissing the potential of ever-aggressive growth. From Microsoft to Kodak, many leading companies have suffered because they did not perceive the true growth potential of other innovations in their industries even though they themselves were a part of the innovation-led growth.

To underscore the mind-boggling pace of innovation, let us consider sensors. The cost of a sensor of a certain strength went down from approximately $150,000 in 2012 to one with much more superior capabilities, which was much smaller in size at $250 in 2016. That is a 600-times improvement just in terms of cost—without considering improvements in features and size. This happened at a time when industry experts in 2016 said that a $70,000 sensor wouldn't be possible until 2050. Yes, we must read that again.[3] Our disbelief in the potential of innovation is a sign that we have not internalized the possibility of exponential growth at multiple layers.

An innovation that is priced keeping the consumer in mind and not the producers' need for profit will succeed. New solutions will require innovators to do more with fewer resources—and for more people. Lowered costs are just one way to attain affordability. Other than revamping operating and direct product costs, organizations will need to shed the producer-to-consumer approach to innovation. While the organization can lay out a base innovation, the details will have to take shape with the help of its network of middlemen while not leaving out the front-line actor—the consumer. An empathetic approach towards the customer is more important today than ever before.

Here is an example of a company that attacked costs from multiple angles. Back in 2004, Bharti Airtel outsourced all its functions except six core ones. Additionally, instead of creating its own distribution channels, it piggybacked on the wide and deep networks of consumer product companies such as Godrej and Unilever. To penetrate rural India, Bharti Airtel teamed up with India's largest microfinance institution, SKS. The partnership enabled customers to get sachet-sized loans for their mobile instrument. The twenty-five instalments were as small as ₹85 (~$2) a month. Bharti Airtel also worked with a fertilizer manufacturer, IFFCO (Indian Farmers Fertiliser Cooperative Ltd), which sold co-branded subscriber cards through its retail outlets. Taking its attack on costs a step further, Bharti Airtel even collaborated with competitors to save capital. As it expanded into rural India, passive infrastructure, such as towers, air conditioning and generators, became large expenses, especially in sparsely populated areas. Since this wasn't a differentiating factor, the company merged its infrastructure with those of two other cellular service providers, Vodafone and Idea.

These unique disruptions at various points of the business model enabled Bharti Airtel to charge ₹0.75 (~¢1) per minute of talk time—against ¢2 in China and ¢8 in the US—making it the world's most affordable mobile telephone service. In 2009, the company had approximately 100 million subscribers. This Indian enterprise was one of the world's most profitable wireless carriers, with a 27 per cent return on capital employed.[4]

Scalability, the next logical step

Evidently, to achieve scale, affordability is inevitable. However, we know that no business will undertake innovation if it won't bring in the money. We believe that an organization that aims to cater to large sections of society will make money by keeping costs at the minimum. In the long run, with minimum costs, the top-line grows in terms of units sold. In turn, the bottom line will follow.

One would think that achieving a higher number of users or customers is as easy as having a cheaper version of a highly priced quality product. Just strip the product of its frills, get rid of the upscale features that have a high operating cost, and you are all set. If only it were as easy as that. An innovation that takes the consumer for granted cannot be called successful. It fails our test of excellence, as we shall soon see.

From an organizational point of view, scale can also be achieved by modifying organizational capabilities, which will lead to cost savings.[5] Admittedly, from an innovator's point of view it is a chicken-and-egg problem. A large number of customers is needed to achieve economies of scale. Scale economies are required to make the product accessible to a large user base. The network of users and distributors has to be aware of the product or service for it to gain momentum. But momentum is needed to create awareness about the product in the nexus of various players. This is when other ASSURED attributes can give a business the initial nudge required to break out of this cycle.

Other than affordability, scale can be achieved through universality or usability too. This merits a discussion on its own, one we will get to in just a bit.

Sustainability—a triple-edged sword

Just lasting long is not enough for an innovation. An innovation has to last long environmentally, economically and socially.

An innovation has to sustain a healthy world for us to live in. One of the primary requirements should be to not harm the environment in any way. In fact, wherever applicable, it should try to reverse the harm already caused. It is worth reiterating here that we die if the environment dies. Therefore, our first efforts should be guided towards making the planet sustain longer if we want our innovation to sustain on the planet.

Secondly, sustainable solutions have to be economically independent. After maybe an initial push from a venture capitalist or from government aid in the form of a grant, subsidy or procurement, the innovation should be able to wean itself away from the financial dependency. After all, only if a solution thrives in a free market economy can it be called truly sustainable.

The last and least intuitive but all-important criteria for sustainability are social relevance and social acceptance. The brilliant book by Calestous Juma, *Innovation and Its Enemies: Why People Resist New Technologies*, highlights the challenge of social acceptance of technologies. Many areas of exponential technological advances signal both hope and fear, leading to public controversy. For example, the rise of AI has stoked long-standing debates about the impact of technology on employment. Often, debates over new technologies are framed in the context of risks to moral values, human health and environmental safety. But behind these legitimate concerns often lie deeper, unacknowledged socio-economic considerations. Technological tensions are heightened by perceptions that the benefits of new technologies will accrue only to small sections of society while the risks will be more widely distributed. A true innovation will address these tensions.

This involves a nod from cultural norms, personal tastes and even tradition. When a solution from one culture is thrust upon another, it will not be accepted, or will face resistance, to say the least. To elaborate, consider the

example of a small village in India. In a drive to increase the
use of toilets, common toilets were built in the villages. It
was observed that women did not use these toilets, despite
their ease of access and availability of water. In fact, the inlet
and outlet pipes were often found broken. In conversation
with one of the authors of this book, Mashelkar, Neelima
Mishra, winner of the Magsaysay Award for Emergent
Leadership in 2011, spoke of her experience in a remote
village. Before sunrise, she observed, women went in groups
to the outskirts of their village to relieve themselves. This
was their time to socialize, away from family, away from
their responsibilities; it was their 'me-time', so to speak.
These women were sabotaging the pipes to reclaim their
time with their friends. This problem found a fix when
ceiling-free toilet booths set in a semi-circular row were
built; they had waist-high walls that enabled conversation.
Toilet usage converted to 100 per cent. This is just one
anecdotal instance of a culturally sustainable innovation
being accepted more easily than one requiring the breaking
of one too many habits all at once.

Universality: make it user-friendly

The example above points to a basic tenet that is often
ignored—knowing the user. Universality implies simple
and maintenance-free products and services. Consumer
tastes change continually. Aspirations for a better consumer
experience are constantly rising. Universality also includes
the ability to continuously meet these changing demands.
In addition, as alluded to earlier, scalability in the
innovation process entails consideration of not just the end
user's purchasing power, but also the user's capabilities
and mindset. This involves making the product or service

intuitive to use, making the consumer independent of you, and making your offering maintenance-free. This involves keeping the user's social, cultural, financial and educational status in mind, while still believing that a user will learn to use your product or service if it holds an inherent benefit for them.

These are—individually and in combination—all paths to universality.

This requires a fundamental shift from jugaad—the practice of quick-fix hacks—to systemic innovation. The former is a feature added by innovative consumers but systemic innovation would be the result of a producer-led understanding of consumer issues. Products that are user-friendly and maintenance-free are likely to fetch quicker and wider customer acceptance.

A case in point is the Nestle beverage dispenser. At first these dispensers were designed based on production feasibility. But their actual operation revealed hygiene and maintenance issues. Nestle redesigned the dispenser with a new front face that was easy to operate. Based on user experience, ease of servicing and cleaning, robustness and durability became central to the new design. This entailed having backlit buttons that didn't wear out, a flat surface that was easy to wipe clean, and a chrome finish that was pleasing to the eye. The new user-friendly product instantly clicked in the market, in no time becoming an omnipresent model in the commercial space.

Most of the successful models for scaling new products or services for the long tail reveal that it is a very non-linear play. A nexus of the lead innovator, network partners and end users works together to bring about a solution that works best for a specific population. Network partners cannot be seen as passive distributors, and end users themselves cannot be shelved into one broad category. They ought to be treated as mid-level and iterative sources of innovation. Usually, these innovations cannot be imagined by top-level management who are physically and socially distanced from the ground reality. When you approach the network of distributors and users as an innovation network and not just as a distribution network, you will have a universally acceptable product.

In fact, the huge lowest layer of population in terms of finances is wrought with dynamics that even the middle rung is slightly separated from. It is of the utmost importance to keep things simple, especially keeping inclusion in mind. This is when an innovator might realize that what they thought of as user-friendly is not truly, universally so.

From adding pictorial and video tutorials to keeping processes and documentation transparent—the easier a product is made for use by the typical bottom-of-the-pyramid consumer, the better the innovator's chances to win them over as a customer. It might help to start with an absolute, plain-vanilla version of the product or service and add features as modules/updates. This is not to be confused with diluting quality. This is done with the intention of coaching the end user step by step. This is exactly what WhatsApp did. Invariably, such an approach leads to a win-win situation for both producer and consumer. The producer gets the low-hanging fruit by making a product/service accessible to the target consumer.

The only way to learn these dynamics might be to have the grass-root customer use the product, interact with them, make changes to the product according to the feedback. And repeat. It is at this stage that the innovator ought to be equipped to make swift and smooth changes to suit the end user. For an innovator who wants their new product or service to be scalable in the truest sense of the word, this becomes a game of adaptation, with a lot of back and forth.

Rapidity—our challenges are immediate, there is no time to waste

Innovations are needed sooner rather than later, especially because of the challenges the world faces—energy, environment and employment—have already caused havoc. These challenges continue to accelerate with our behaviour and attitudes. We need our behaviour and attitudes to change. While demand-side change can be seen in small pockets with many individuals doing their bit, supply-side push in the right direction can truly speed up the innovation process to address our looming challenges.

Therefore, the biggest challenge is to be affordable, scalable, sustainable, universal—at a quick pace. Rapidly changing business environments need businesses to quickly and swiftly reach their customers.

Rapid innovation is also where we begin to see even more interplay amongst the ASSURED attributes. Speed demands a hold on consumer needs, which are a function of universality. The root of innovation lies in supply-led offerings that satisfy consumer needs—needs that they don't even know they have. We are not alluding to the social media platforms of our times. We are referring to dengue tests that deliver results in three minutes instead of three days[6] or non-invasive breast cancer tests that are less painful and more accurate.[7] Fortunately, these are not distant dreams but current innovations. Speed is not just about time-to-market, it is also about time-to-service.

The rapid pace of innovation also demands use of technology, which, in turn, is a function of scalability. Our forefathers couldn't have imagined that an invention made 10,000 miles away could be available for instantaneous use in the palm of their hand. Convergence of technologies has made unimaginable speed possible, as we have seen in the many examples so far. Yet another example of preparedness for speed of service is the Emergency Management and Research Institute in India. The institute wove together the latest telecommunication, computing, medical and transportation technologies to provide almost free emergency services in tribal, rural and urban areas. This fusion of technologies led to a solution that was implemented efficiently.[8]

Similarly, it is now common to see product development integrated with IT operations. A continuous delivery system leads to reduced lag in the production-feedback-correction loop of developing products and services. The top technology companies use these systems and update their algorithms practically continuously. Facebook releases millions of lines of code resulting in hundreds of changes every day—without downtime. Amazon has the capabilities to update its codes and servers every ten seconds. Most of these websites can roll back changes with a single command.[9] Therefore, technology can be used by mankind to recover quickly from failures and setbacks, thus saving valuable time in prognosis and treatment.

Also, in today's times, speed translates to keeping up to speed with the latest technologies because it is hard to reinvent yourself quickly if you haven't reinvented yourself at all.

Excellence. Affordable excellence

We are keenly aware that the world is full of solutions that are deemed successful but are accessible to only a few. They haven't needed scale to be beneficial to their handful of target consumers. Luxury products such as expensive accessories and high-end cars are a few cases in point. As a result, achieving affordability or universality was not even a consideration in their case. However, that, according to us, is not an ASSURED Total Innovation. We believe success that leaves the long tail behind is no success at all. We believe an innovation that can be used by or benefits only a privileged few cannot truly be called innovation.

We prefer what we call 'Gandhian innovation', because at the core of this type of innovation lie two of the Mahatma's tenets:

'I would prize every invention of science made for the benefit of all.'

and

'Earth provides enough to satisfy every man's need, but not every man's greed.'

This kind of inclusion requires not an improvement of 10 per cent, but one of ten times and more. Indeed, there are many who share our philosophy. India is home to dozens, perhaps hundreds, of such innovations.

To illustrate, we will cite the work done by some of the Anjani Mashelkar Inclusive Innovation Award winners. This is an award Mashelkar had instituted in his mother's name for innovations that will do good for the society at large and not just for a privileged few. The awardees believe in not just 'best practices', but 'next practices'—practices that replace the preferred organizational practices with those that will keep the organization ahead of its time, as much into the future as is possible. Most importantly, these innovations meet the tough criteria of ASSURED Total Innovation, representing 'affordable excellence', breaking the myth that affordability and excellence cannot go together.

In 2015, breast cancer replaced cervical cancer as the leading cause of cancer deaths among women in India. In India alone, almost 200 million women aged thirty-five to fifty-five do not undergo the necessary annual breast exams which could potentially save their lives. Late-stage detection is the main reason behind breast cancer deaths. The challenge was to ensure that women in every corner of India—in fact, the world—underwent breast cancer screening.

UE LifeSciences, led by Mihir Shah, developed a handheld device that is used for early detection of breast tumours. It is simple, accurate and affordable. It eliminates the need for painful mammography and potentially harmful radiation. Screenings are safe and private too. The team has also deployed an innovative pay-per-use model—instead of targeting direct sales—which can empower doctors in every corner of the country to start screening women at the earliest. The device is US FDA-cleared and CE-marked. It is operable by any community health worker. And it costs all of $1 per scan!

But UE LifeSciences is not only doing good, it is doing well too. In the last year or so, the device has received purchase orders totalling to approximately $2 million. The company has also entered into a strategic partnership with GE Healthcare for marketing and distribution of iBreastExam across twenty-five countries in Africa, South Asia and South East Asia. This benefits more than 500 million women.

This example is not a one-off success story. There are many such examples, each putting high technology to work for the poor. This is indeed what we call affordable excellence.

Distinctive; staying ahead of the curve

To move from leapfrogging to pole-vaulting, we surely have to move from incremental innovation to disruptive innovation. While it is understandable that a business cannot be disruptive all the time, it can always strive to be distinctive. The idea is to have your eyes set on where you need to be next so that you do not lose your hold on the market. You have to constantly strive to displace your own products before your competitors do the deed.

The truth of our times is that ideas are a dime a dozen. Copycats, even more so. In addition, a corollary to achieving both speed and scale is the capability to constantly innovate. At the crux of future innovation will lie adaptation. An organization that innovates once and considers the job done will lose the race even before it has begun. A business has to continuously interact with its environment and respond to changes. These changes could be industry-wide; they could be changes brought by competition, changes in consumer tastes and behaviours, and so on.

Constant and distinctive adaptation demands constant vigilance of the ecosystem. In order to get to market quickly, often companies do not design products that can adapt to future changes in the business environment. In other cases, organizations, in their attempt to keep costs low, often don't reinvent themselves. In either case, their products will not be capable of remaining in the fray for the long haul. They become stagnant, and thus irrelevant. To avoid such a situation, solutions will have to be one step ahead of industry trends, the competition and consumers. Enterprises will have to do this through innovations in each aspect of conducting business, maintaining a holistic approach throughout. This is what will lead to distinctiveness—both the cause and effect of ASSURED Total Innovation.

What, then, is entailed in staying attuned to the constantly changing environment?

Indeed, a study of that environment.

Innovations are as much about understanding and developing solutions for current needs as they are about creating new needs and markets. That is, innovations are both demand led and supply led. While an incumbent has to keep track of changing consumer needs, fresher minds are creating markets for products and services that were unheard of. Further, iterative adaptation and innovation has to be quick to stay relevant in the long run.

Sure, the speed of innovation depends on the industry. You cannot expect new medicines to be discovered, tested, legally accepted and reach the market as fast as you can expect an Android app to.[10] However, to stay relevant, a company, in the context of its industry, will have to invent at the quickest.

In many cases, even first movers have only limited advantage over competition. Seventy-two per cent of companies predict their industry will be affected by digital intelligence in the next three years.[11] One smart innovator has the potential to take you out of business. An instance of this phenomenon is what we are seeing in China. Xiaomi entered many product categories. It introduced a $13 activity tracker to push Fitbit out of the Chinese market. It has also invested in seventy-seven companies, four of which have a market capitalization of over $1 billion.[12] Chinese companies use speed to their advantage; costs are secondary. This approach to speed has led to top global universities and companies setting up research centres in China. In fact, China is likely to have the second largest number of patents filed globally, ahead of Japan.

Aspects that have been largely ignored so far, such as societal changes and policy innovations, need a detailed relook too. Businesses have to respond to changes in these externalities. After India opened up to foreign investment and technologies in 1991, companies such as Bharti Airtel altered the economics of fledgling industries, not by developing state-of-the-art technologies but by creating new business models. They set inexpensive price performance points and changed the way consumers could access their offerings. Some products and services needed new infrastructure for development and delivery. In response, these companies also built unique ecosystems.

ASSURED Total Innovation—an inevitable holistic outlook

As you must have observed, there is a fair amount of interlocking between the requirements for each of the elements of ASSURED. Fortunately, they work together and are rarely in conflict. In fact, a product that has achieved scale will most likely be sustainable. Similarly, a sustainable idea would have to adapt to the changing environment with speed. A solution is highly unlikely to be sustainable if it isn't continuously adapting to create distinctiveness.

Scale requires affordability and universality, which calls for user-friendliness.

Speed is important to solve today's brewing world problems and for a business to retain its competitive edge. Speed is also made possible because of the stage at which technology is today.

Sustainability is a composite of environmental, economic and social sustenance. Excellence and distinctiveness are prerequisites for our broader definition of sustainability.

Our experience has exposed an unfortunate fact. In terms of ASSURED innovation, often on the supply side, solutions manage the elements of A, U, R, E and D. However, the two S's render them unsuccessful. That is, the solutions fail because they could not achieve scale and sustainability. Many examples come to mind immediately. Let us consider two. One was a near miss. Another, a total failure.

Innovations walk on a tightrope

2017's Anjani Mashelkar Award winner, Navin Khanna, developed a three-in-one 'Dengue Day 1' test. Dengue is a neglected mosquito-borne viral disease, the incidence of which has increased more than thirtyfold in the past fifty years. The test results usually take two to three days to come through and are different for primary and secondary dengue. At the International Centre for Genetic Engineering and Biotechnology in India, Dr Navin Khanna's test affordably detects dengue within minutes on day one of the fever, even in resource-poor settings, while also differentiating between primary and secondary dengue. At a little over ₹170 (~$2.5) per test, it costs one-third to one-fourth of a conventional test. The test kit now has an 80 per cent market share and is exported to other countries too. However, the path to success wasn't an easy one.

Despite the high performance of the test, its acceptance was an uphill task. In 2013, many Indian cities witnessed a large number of dengue cases. Three companies—from the USA, Australia and South Korea—sold their yearly stock of dengue test kits within a few weeks and ran out of tests. Most of the end users wanted to wait for new consignments from these tried-and-tested countries rather than buy the new Indian kits. Extensive paperwork delayed imports from the USA and Australia. The South Korean company managed to ship a consignment, but the shipment landed up in Africa! Meanwhile, suspected dengue cases were creating mass panic. At this stage, the end users relented and tried the Indian kit—and then there was no looking back. All stakeholders were delighted with the easily available, high-performing and affordable dengue test kit. The imported kits had no takers when they finally arrived. In this case, serendipity and not a system played the biggest role.

Computer-Based Functional Literacy (CBFL), on the other hand, had no such luck. This is our heartbreaking complete failure. CBFL, an innovation by the iconic engineer Dr F.C. Kohli, identified 596 words in the English language that can be learnt as pictures. This is a substitute to learning to spell by rote. In forty-six hours of class, this program taught an illiterate person to recognize these words. This was enough to enable them to read a newspaper. We had actual examples of an illiterate woman questioning the promises made by a politician, or understanding what her daughter's marks in school meant. This did not require expensive computers. A knocked-down PC 386 was good enough, and the cost of this literacy measure was less than ₹100 (~$1.5) per person. Yet this innovation, which had the potential to make the entire country literate in five years, did not take off.

The national literacy mission rejected it because the methods used were unconventional.

This fall-through is the lack of support from the ecosystem. A friendly public procurement policy was missing, despite rural-specific demonstrations. Such social goods ought to have been encouraged through public procurement.

That ASSURED solutions will need out-of-the-box thought processes is an understatement. Moreover, since these solutions are likely to disturb the status quo, they will face resistance. To quote Niccolo Machiavelli from *The Prince*,

> There is nothing more difficult to take in hand, more perilous to conduct, or more uncertain in its success, than to take the lead in the introduction of a new order of things. For the reformer has enemies in all those who profit by the old order, and only lukewarm defenders in all those who would profit by the new order, this luke-warmness arising partly from fear of their adversaries . . . and partly from the incredulity of mankind, who do not truly believe in anything new until they have had actual experience of it.

This sentiment stands the test of time. There are certainly hurdles to ASSURED solutions.

Failure assured if ASSURED test fails

'Failure is the best teacher' is not just a maxim. To understand the efficacy of the ASSURED model, we have selected a few innovations that shook the imagination of the world. Each of the current successes, from Apple to Amazon, from Facebook to Google, from Samsung to Toyota, satisfies the requirements of the ASSURED framework. The common features among failures are common too—failure is assured in the long run if the innovation fails the ASSURED test at any point along its journey.

Out of the original 1955 Fortune 500 list, only seventy-one companies exist today. Analysis within the ASSURED framework shows that their successful run lasted as long as they passed the ASSURED test, but the moment they failed in any aspect of the ASSURED framework they failed as companies too. For instance, our initial example, Kodak, did not remain 'distinctive' and 'user-friendly' when the digital camera arrived. The same was the case with Polaroid, the leaders in instant photography. Borders, a leading international book retailer, failed to adapt to the digital and online books age, ignored consumer preferences, and was soon no longer 'distinctive' and 'user-friendly'.

We show the results of the ASSURED test for seven famous cases of businesses that eventually failed, despite some of them having tasted success for some time.

Napster, arguably one of the most innovative Internet programs created, allowed fans to upload and share music files for free. At its peak it had about 80 million users and was once the Internet's killer app. However, its system circumvented the music industry's business model and agitated artistes. Within a few years, Napster had to shut down for reasons of copyright infringement after being sued by Metallica and several major record labels. The record companies took the Napster founders to court for sharing their songs for free. As the lawsuits piled up, the company was forced to move to a subscription-based model to monetize its operations and pay back music owners. It failed in 2001 and was bought by Best Buy in 2011, to merge with Rhapsody, an online music store, thereafter.

ASSURED Test at the time of Business Failure

Solution	A (Affordability)	S (Scalability)	S (Sustainability)	U (Universal)	R (Rapid)	E (Excellence)	D (Distinctive)
Napster[13, 14, 15]	√	√	×	√	√	√	√
BlackBerry[16, 17, 18, 19]	√	√	√	×	×	√	√
PalmPilot[20, 21]	×	√	×	×	×	√	√
GM EV-1[22, 23, 24, 25]	√	×	×	×	×	√	√
Netscape[26, 27, 28, 29]	√	√	×	√	√	√	×
Motorola ROKR E1[30, 31, 32, 33, 34, 35]	√	×	×	×	×	×	√
Segway[36, 37, 38]	×	×	√	×	×	√	√

Napster failed the test of Sustainability from a societal perspective. Music creators did not want Napster to break IP laws that were long respected by society.

iTunes, with its vast catalogue of $1 songs, is often referred to as a more evolved and successful version of what Napster aimed for but could not achieve.

Next under scrutiny is the failure of BlackBerry. BlackBerry devices were top of the class and had successfully hooked email-obsessed Wall Streeters and other corporate users. They pioneered 'push email', and the QWERTY keyboard on their devices made it easier for users to fire off emails and instant messages. But the company, which was selling 50 million phones a year as recently as 2011, failed to anticipate the smartphone revolution, a revolution that would be led by consumers and not business customers. They failed to cash in on the emergence of the 'app economy' dominated by iOS and Android and the evolution of smartphones as full-fledged mobile entertainment devices rather than just communication devices. The iPhone had overwhelmed everything that had come before it. Also, Google's strategy of effectively giving away Android to mobile-phone manufacturers helped it flood the smartphone market with new android devices. At the product level, BlackBerry focused on full keyboards, but consumers had moved to touchscreens, which allowed for screen navigation and offered video viewing too. BlackBerry even kept their famous BBM (BlackBerry Messenger) locked down to their own hardware, while the cross-platform WhatsApp was growing across geographies. A historic blunder which cost them dear!

Eventually, when the BlackBerry 10 model made the transition to touchscreen and the Android platform, it was too late. Bear in mind, Blackberry had once met all the criteria in the ASSURED framework. They failed later because they did not offer customers better experience or user-friendliness, which their competitors provided. U and R from the ASSURED framework went sorely missing in the later stages of BlackBerry's products.

Similarly, we had Palm, a dominant player in the smartphone market along with Research-In-Motion's BlackBerry, and cell phone giant Nokia. However, Palm was unable to follow up on its success in the personal organizer business. The market was moving towards devices providing wireless voice and data along with a suite of multimedia applications. The industry was poised to serve a consumer market which demanded a full-fledged mobile entertainment device. Palm realized this only much later. While they started with a great combination of hardware and software, they failed to keep the hardware quality high and in line with consumer expectations. The limited carrier support only made things more difficult for them. They made a few bad business moves, like corporate restructuring, spinning off of the software division, only to merge it back again later, and opting for Microsoft's operating system. They were slow to react to fast-changing consumer needs and suffered many product delays.

In another industry, General Motor's EV-1 was one of the first cars that brought enthusiasm and excitement to the modern world of electric cars in America. In spite of being available for only six years in the market through direct leasing programmes, EV-1 had a relatively decent following during its time on the road. Under the lease model, GM held the right to revoke a lease whenever it deemed it necessary. The final cost to consumers ranged from $250 to $500 per month, depending on where they lived. Earlier EV-1 models drove about 70 to 90 miles on a full charge, which later increased to 110 miles. On a normal 110-volt outlet, the first-generation EV1 took about fifteen hours to charge. However, the speedy 220-volt MagneCharge chargers could fully charge the car in just three hours. These chargers were set up in public areas like malls and airports and also made available for installation in homes. So, technically the electric car was headed in the right direction. But six years after its launch, GM recalled all EV-1s and crushed almost all of them, citing high build costs and a small customer base as their reasons for the car's discontinuation.

An alternative view suggests a regulatory angle to the discontinuation. Development of the EV-1 was primarily driven by regulatory norms, which mandated that 10 per cent of all cars sold by car manufacturers had to be zero-emission vehicles by 2003. However, this mandate was revised, and car manufacturers were required to build electric cars only to the extent that there was a demand for them. It is believed that car manufacturers and oil associations were not in favour of electric vehicles (EVs) and hence pushed for relaxed norms. This impacted the EV-1's future. It is another matter that the enthusiasm created by the EV-1 and other EVs gave way to new entrants like Tesla, which later went on to make one of the world's bestselling, plug-in electric cars. Here, Scalability impacted Sustainability, which also later did not meet User-friendliness requirements with the required Rapidity.

Another case on our radar is that of Netscape, an open software that linked people and information over intranets and the Internet. They gave away their browser free of charge, allowing most of us our first peek through the Internet window. Being the first mover in the Internet browser market, they achieved tremendous growth and reaped rewards through demand-side positive feedback. The company was quick to expand its product line to include a full line of clients, servers, development tools and commercial applications. As the personal computer space exploded, so did the reach of Netscape. Its complementary, plug-in applications, combined with a host of multimedia applications, attracted more users. The rapidly growing market and the extent of profit potential invited the attention of competitors, who introduced a multitude of products to directly compete with Netscape's products.

Microsoft leveraged its dominance in the desktop operating system space. It integrated its browser, Internet Explorer (IE), into Windows 98. Microsoft's IE came pre-installed and free of cost, unlike Netscape. While Netscape's beta version was free for download over the Internet, it achieved scale primarily through retail and corporate sales. The personal computer manufacturers who were locked in to provide IE along with Microsoft's operating system didn't see value in providing a Netscape browser. Even developers started to tailor their websites to IE. Sure, Netscape later released its browser's source code and contributed to the Mozilla project, which led to the Firefox browser—an innovative browser which later triggered the decline of IE too. As cloud computing and mobile devices came into the fray, Google's Chrome too became a dominant force in the browser space. So a great start with a fully satisfied ASSURED framework slipped on being Distinctive and thus was not Sustainable.

Yet another example is that of Motorola's ROKR E1. Before Apple designed its famous iPhone, they partnered with one of the most successful phone-making companies at the time, Motorola, to make the ROKR E1. The idea was to create a fusion of two cool products of the time—Apple's iPod and Motorola's RAZR. The fusion experiment wasn't a pleasant one, though. ROKR E1's mediocre plastic design, poor camera and the limited music it offered, fell far short of RAZR's sleek design and iPod's elegance and promise of 1000 songs in your pocket. This was especially true because the new product cost more too. So, S, S, U, R and E were all missing from the ASSURED framework. And, less than eighteen months after Apple discontinued its partnership with Motorola, it launched the first-generation iPhone.

Last under scrutiny is the Segway PT, a two-wheeled, self-balancing, battery EV launched in 2001. A rider had to just step on it, and on-board computers, sensors and motors kept it upright. The technology was impressive. It satisfied commute issues while also being environmentally friendly. Yet it never really gained significant market acceptance despite being distinctive. The company sold less than 10,000 units in its first two years, and less than 24,000 in its first four years. Unfortunately, the product was expensive, with an initial price point of $5000. It was heavy and sometimes difficult to ride. A few high-profile accidents, including US President George W. Bush's fall from the Segway, invited bad press too. Even regulatory concerns were not addressed well. Many countries banned it on sidewalks and roads because it did not fit any existing vehicular category. Clearly, for the Segway, A, S, U, and R were missing from the ASSURED framework.

Roadblocks to innovation—we are our own worst enemies

Does this mean we avoid failure? On the contrary. The most common roadblock to transformation is an aversion to risk, an aversion to failure. Old-school players punish people who fail instead of rewarding those who take risks. Instead, we should be celebrating people who dare to try. It is understandable that failure costs and someone has to foot the bill. However, what most organizations don't realize is that failure doesn't have to be expensive. This automatically makes innovation less risky. The key then is to try many things and quickly let go of those that do not work.

One way to afford continuous innovation is to reduce upfront investment in new ideas, test a no-frills, viable product and make changes and additions according to the market response. Another way to go about it is to get customers and other partners involved in the innovation process.[39] Kenya's phone-based money transfer and micro-financing company, M-Pesa, would not have been successful had it not involved each person in the chain to continuously innovate and re-innovate usage, functionalities, price points and distribution methods.[40]

As we saw in the examples above, the other hurdle to ASSURED Total Innovation is lack of support from public policy. Bureaucracy is not always a friend of innovation either. There is not just governmental bureaucracy, but also corporate bureaucracy that will require, say, two forms and three permissions for your department to get a printer. Ironically, something that was introduced to enable efficient administration has, over time, become a leading cause of inefficiencies. Bureaucracy-induced hierarchical organizational structures give more importance to conformity than to the all-important out-of-the-box thinking that we deem necessary for ASSURED Total Innovation. How can one adapt to change with rapidity if there are layers of bureaucracy within one's own organization? It makes it worse that the merit of these bureaucrats is not measurable, because of which they are rarely held accountable.

Just as ASSURED solutions are more powerful when the individual elements come together, the businessman-politician-bureaucrat nexus becomes more powerful than its constituents. When the nexus comes into play, there is little room for creativity, let alone full-fledged innovation.

And yet, times are a-changing

However, people's, and indeed governments', attitude towards change is changing—ever so slightly. We hope that a concentrated effort by all stakeholders, including policymakers will, bit by bit, defeat the resistance to change. This hope is not just wishful thinking. By encouraging ecosystems, we have seen ASSURED solutions take root, blossom and bring benefit to all—in real life.

An exemplar in ASSURED Total Innovation has been successfully demonstrated by the Indian private sector. One of India's early successes was the mobile revolution. In the two decades from 1995 to 2014, about 910 million mobile phone subscribers were added—the numbers are incredible in themselves, but especially so if you consider that they are eighteen times the number of landline connections in 2006, the year in which landline subscriptions peaked at 50 million. The era of 'trunk calls' and phone booths had come to a definitive end. Thanks to liberalization, the private sector rose to the occasion and innovation flourished in devices, processes and business models. But despite these impressive achievements, the benefits of the digital revolution were not shared by all, thus creating a 'digital divide'. In spite of having a phone and a telecom connection, many could not afford to actually make calls. Indian jugaad came to the rescue, and people began using 'missed calls' to communicate. Many a parent, spouse and loved one signalled that they had arrived at their destination by making a 'missed call' to their anxious relatives and friends. Restaurants that catered to students started 'missed call ordering'. In fact, an entire marketing field called Missed Call Marketing or MCM was born. All because calls were expensive.

Today the situation has changed drastically. Competition in the Indian telecom sector reached fever pitch in 2016 with the entry of Reliance Jio Infocomm Ltd, or Jio. Today, millions of Indians enjoy the benefits of free calling and extremely affordable—¢1 per GB!—high-speed 4G Internet. And none of this at the cost of quality. Communication behaviours are changing across India as we speak, with the focus shifting from exchanging information to expressing emotion. One incredible example is that of speech and hearing-impaired people using video calls to communicate with each other in sign language. Earlier they were confined to using SMS and other texting apps.

In 2000, there were about 5 million mobile phones. Come 2016, and we had over 1 billion![41] How did this market grow 200 times in a mere seventeen years?

There was policy innovation. From the New Industrial Policy in 1991 that delicensed the telecom industry to the adoption of pro-competition policies in 1999, the government set the way.[42] It further pushed the envelope with a bold decision to have voice-enabled Internet that did not rely on laying more copper lines or landlines.

However, that push would not have been enough. At $250, there would have been few takers for mobile instruments. Nokia and Ericsson brought the price point down to $25. These international companies saw value in the long tail market. This was their attempt to achieve scale by dropping prices.

However, the industry was still far away from the ground reality. Even if phones were given away for free, it wouldn't hit scale if the call rates stayed at ¢10 per minute. With 70 per cent of the Indian population earning incomes of $2 per day, a twenty-minute call would eat away a day's earnings.

Technological innovation came through too, with the first countrywide deployment of VoLTE or voice over LTE. This allowed Jio to offer free voice calls to any network across the country. Jio also fast-tracked Aadhaar-based eKYC across thousands of stores. This allowed SIM activation in under five minutes, which made things easy for both SIM card providers and users. Before Jio, the activation process usually took hours if not days and was expensive for the companies too.

Jio made the mobile instrument practically free of cost. The Jio instrument is returnable against a three-year, $25 refundable deposit. 4G data is offered at under $3 per year. Jio also offers smaller-denomination sachets that suit the smallest pockets. The company holds the world record for reaching 50 million customers in just eighty-three days! In just six months, data consumption in India went up six times.

Behind the success of Jio lie many major product, business model, process and service innovations which fulfil all the elements of ASSURED innovation. More importantly, Jio has also moved India from 'missed call' to 'video call', a shift from jugaad to systematic innovation. And all of this while being a profitable venture. The scepticism that free users wouldn't convert to paid users has been laid to rest. In March 2017, Jio crossed 100 million paying users. This is the largest migration from free to paid services in history. A year later, the number of paid subscribers had almost doubled.[43]

It is important to point out that just technological innovation would most likely fail if it did not go with a reworked business model. Also, in Jio's case, just technological innovation would not have worked were it not for policy innovation in the form of Aadhaar. The success of Aadhaar itself is a case worth exploring, which we do in a subsequent chapter.

Now one might say a company like Reliance has deep pockets and Aadhaar has government backing. What about small businesses? What about start-ups? We reckon they too can aspire to achieve similar success. The success stories for the Anjani Mashelkar Inclusive Innovation Awardees mentioned above are such examples.

Towards a new world

Many of these game-changing, ASSURED Total Innovations have some tenets in common—conversion of non-consumers to consumers; rethinking—not just remodelling—of offerings; innovation across products, processes and business models; and the placing of 'better' before 'cheaper'. The innovator's perspective should shift to see suppliers as partners, employees as innovators and customers as people.

On the consumer front, it is important to foster empathy and explore co-creation, and to attack problems that MUST be solved, and not just those that CAN be solved. What can be done internally? Setting 'stretch goals' that sound impossible, challenging the fundamentals, putting the best minds to work, learning from unrelated domains and interacting with top-notch innovators. Making high technology work for the poor is important, but even more important is believing that they can adapt to it—and they always do. They are demanding and exacting about what they want from a product or service.

The research, design and development teams must change their mindsets. Besides aiming at technologically sophisticated, performance-rich products, they must move towards frugal, functional but high-quality products. Rather than removing features to reduce costs, they must reinvent the products from the ground up. Rather than holding a 'technology-push, product-out' approach, they must move to a 'customer-centric, market-based' approach. Rather than using products from the developed world to transform the existing developing markets, they must build new global growth platforms based on emerging market needs.

Business must also try to straddle the entire economic pyramid by not just aiming for premium-price, high-margin products but also going for affordable-price, high-volume products. Finally, it is time to give up on the current market's old money mindset, with its participants continuously fighting for an increasing share of a constant-sized pie. Instead, they should adopt new markets and a new money mindset, which will help them get a share of the resultant bigger-sized pie.

Fundamentally, this can come about when they believe in the idea that happiness, health, prosperity and peace are basic human rights; that people, regardless of caste, creed, gender, nationality, etc., are people first; that innovation is not just for those who can afford it but for those who need it most.

It is glaringly obvious that the tide of exponential technology, where performance is rising exponentially and costs are falling exponentially, will make many things previously considered impossible not only possible, but also possible in entirely unbelievable ways and at unimagined timelines, making the goal of achieving ASSURED innovation easier.

ASSURED innovation can greatly help any country in achieving multiple objectives. First, social harmony. It will help in creating access equality even if there is income inequality. Second, affordability. It will lead to scale, thus bringing equity to any population. Third, excellence. On the one hand, excellence will meet the rising aspirations of a local populace for high-quality goods and services. On the other hand, excellence will open up opportunities for competitive exports to global markets.

ASSURED Total Innovation is the way by which the private sector can achieve the noble goal of 'doing well by doing good'. ASSURED Total Innovation can be a three-word National Innovation Policy statement for countries across the world. ASSURED Total Innovation can dismantle inequalities, thereby restoring social harmony, which is the need of the hour.

This, however, is not and cannot be a stand-alone model. ASSURED Total Innovation is a tool for transformation. In itself, however, it is not sufficient to create transformation; especially transformation that the imposing problems of the 3Es—energy, environment and employment—call for. The magnitude and nature of transformation will require support from the STEP levers in the ecosystem, namely Technology, Public Policy, Social Engagement and Economic Model. Innovation can be thought of as a force multiplier, but it cannot operate unless the four levers are in operation too. The path from innovation to transformation has to be created and maintained by the four STEP levers.

FOUR

The Four Levers: In STEP with Each Other

Our study of the essential ingredients needed for tomorrow's successful transformations has highlighted the need for an enabling ecosystem. That the problems we face as humanity are serious and urgent is an understatement. They call for transformational solutions, solutions that require coordinated and well-thought-out strategies. Part of their complexity is intensified by the challenges posed by environment, energy and employment issues. These issues exist, mutate and exert their impact on our physical worlds, influence our government policies, impose on our social structures and push our economic constraints. They are omnipresent and intertwined. Simplistic, near-sighted solutions falter in the face of this Pandora's box. Seemingly 'workable' solutions fall apart when relationships and dependencies unravel in the form of unexpected repercussions.

In our experience, effective solutions must be multi-faceted. To ensure holistic solutions, we must assess the role of four vital facets of every solution, what we like to call the enabling STEPs: Technology, Public Policy, Social

Engagement and Economic Model. The extent to which each facet is used may differ in importance for different situations. However, their enabling support is necessary for transformations to be successful. If neglected, each of these aspects can lead to setbacks or failure. And if developed smartly, each can provide significant leverage for the implementation of long-lasting solutions.

In the past, new technology, empowering policy, active social engagement and fair economic models have been used as levers to achieve desirable outcomes in diverse fields. This confluence can be seen in various examples, such as the White Revolution and Aadhaar in India, which will be discussed at great length in subsequent chapters. Unsurprisingly, the results are most spectacular when solutions employ the synergies presented by all four levers.

Technology: Nothing is impossible

Every few decades over the last 200 years or so, the human mind has invented and reinvented the tools at its disposal to make life less cumbersome and more efficient. The resulting innovations have surpassed current imagination. From electronics to genetics, from transportation to communication, new technologies have sought to solve imposing problems. We excitedly anticipate the wave of disruption that newer technologies such as blockchain, AI and 3D printing are bound to bring along. In the next chapter we will see how technology is currently being used to recover from the damage that our activities have caused to the environment, to energy generation and consumption. We will also see the undesirable impact technology has had on both employment and income equality.

Public Policy: A delicate balancing act

It is our conviction that by and large, when human beings are left to themselves, they would pursue their own good. And generally, societal good would result when all individuals pursue their own good. This is the fulcrum of the free market economy. But unfortunately, this is not always true. Society therefore has to act in some areas, hopefully only peripheral, where some activities have to be promoted and some others discouraged. To illustrate this, if one were to allow normal commercial activities, some people are likely to garner most of the income and wealth, leaving a large number of people with nothing, not even sustenance levels of income. Such a situation is quite disastrous for society as a whole, including for the fortunate few. To avoid such situations, society has been stepping in through public policy. Solutions to the 3E problems will call for the correct implementation of public policy. The ingredients of a good policy and appropriate intervention will be considered in great depth in the chapter on public policy.

Social Engagement: The power of people

Public policy is often influenced by people or by groups with vested interests. The resistance to gun control due to the influence of the National Rifle Association in the USA is one such example. In many instances, policymakers have limited motivation to initiate change. However, a change may be required for social good. This change, then, has to be brought about through vocal and vehement social engagement by the people sensitive to the need for change. It is indeed the 'Smoking Kills' movement that led to both warnings and high tariffs on tobacco products across the world. Similarly, the price support and loan waivers offered to farmers in India are also often a result of marches led by or for the farmers. When we talk about this third pillar that can make socially necessary solutions successful, we will study numerous movements that worked, to understand what made them successful.

Economic Model: Doing well by doing good

Lastly, in a society that is based on economics, no activity—technological development, policymaking or social engagement—would be of much value if it isn't advantageous to everyone involved. Only when a solution adds economic value to each stakeholder's life will it be considered worth pursuing. Our model includes the planet as a stakeholder, and minimizing damage to it is its stake, a stake that we as a race are responsible for. We will look at the traditional understanding of economic models and the need for redefining progress and growth in our chapter on 'Economic Model'.

In the following four chapters, we show what each lever means to us, how it has worked in the past and where it has not been explored to the greatest extent. We shall then explore the use of each of these levers to solve some very imposing problems. We will also look at solutions that have worked or failed as a result of support or lack of support from one or more of the STEP levers.

We will then see the interplay of these levers through examples of successful solutions. These are applications of the STEP framework in an integrated manner. Thereafter, in the subsequent two chapters, we pick up impactful and critical problems to assess how they can be addressed by the application of all four levers together. Two of these problems are solid waste management and mobility—areas that we have worked in ourselves. This assessment culminates in our strong conviction about the need to create an atmosphere that grooms and fosters pole-vaulting leaders.

All this builds up towards our belief that the world tomorrow is one of immense possibilities. We are with the optimists of the world who think that if we can imagine a world with clean air, healthy food and well-managed cities, we will have it. Our progress is only limited by our imagination and the strength of our resolve to convert our imagination into reality.

FIVE

Lever 1 of 4
Technology—Nothing Is Impossible

Every day, Savithri from Banhatti, India, can see and talk to her son who is stationed at a remote army border post thousands of kilometres away.

In a local vegetable market, deep in Nigeria, Olabisi gets a daily loan on her phone to buy her produce for the day.

Uri suffers from chest pain in his apartment in Haifa, Israel. Within minutes he receives a doctor's advice without leaving his home.

Could any of this have been possible even a decade ago? Is it so difficult, then, to imagine a future, not too far away, when we will experience the following in real life?

Ganesh's commute time from Pune to Mumbai is not a weekly four hours but a daily eight minutes. Now he can actually be with his family every day instead of just once a week!

You and I will surf the Web not through a computer or a mobile device but just by the power of our thoughts through an implanted device.

An AI machine will be a corporate board member with voting rights because the solutions they provide are far beyond human imagination.

The ailing man in Israel can get a 3D organ printed in hours for a transplant, if needed, instead of having to wait months for a matching organ, as he has to today.

Ninety per cent of harmful emissions from animal breeding will vanish as 'meatless' meat becomes the preferred choice, with synthetically engineered meat tasting, smelling and feeling like animal meat.

These are just a few of the marvels of technological innovations, owing to which millions of people will lead healthier, longer and safer lives. None of these advancements would have been even imaginable a few decades ago, and some of them have been made possible only in the last few years.

It is an understatement to say that each human being's life today is touched by technology in some form or the other. We are engulfed and consumed by technology in the truest sense. In fact, humanity's progress can be directly related to the progress of technology. Changes in all dimensions of human life can be mapped directly or indirectly to changes in technology. From the invention of the wheel to the dramatic changes in the way we travel and communicate, to the agricultural and industrial revolutions, technology has played an intrinsic role in shaping our lives.

Just look around you, and you will find innumerable examples of development that were unimaginable some time ago. Things that dominate our life today did not exist fifteen years ago! The iPhone, WhatsApp, Facebook, Twitter, 4G, Android, Kindle, Uber . . . and the list goes on. In fact, one of us, Mashelkar, while predicting the potential landscape for Technology 2050, added a cautionary note saying how, throughout the last century, attempts to predict the future technologies have failed.[1] We will elaborate on this warning in a later chapter.

One thing is clear, though: today's common man lives a better life than the kings of yore. Even as recently as in the 1960s, globally, people—kings and the rich included—had an average lifespan of fifty years. Just five to six decades later, it is almost seventy-two.[2] In India itself, this number has gone up from forty-one to sixty-eight during the same period. A large part of the increase in longevity is attributed to lowered infant mortality. For example, just measles vaccination has saved over 20 million lives globally since 2000.[3] In India, an annual decline of almost 6 per cent in child mortality after 2005 suggests that the country has been able to prevent 1 million more child deaths between 2005–15 than we would have, if we were to follow the trajectory until 2005.[4]

Older people too are living longer and healthier. WHO has recently started measuring Healthy Life Expectancy (HALE), a measure of years of life spent in good health. Indeed, HALE is increasing all over the world, and is expected to continue to increase.[5] Technological developments such as disease treatment, adequate food supply and hygienic plumbing are a few of the reasons we have an increasing number of hale and hearty eighty-year-olds, and, indeed, fifty is when many people today begin enjoying life!

Not just health, technology also has touched and transformed all aspects of life. You may imagine the palaces of olden times as mesmerizingly grand, but they carried filth due to the lack of proper drainage! Technological progress has become a lot more inclusive too. Consider transportation. In the 1930s, going from Bombay to London was possible only by ship. That too was a month-long trip, which only the select elite could afford. Let alone the common man, even the most resourceful of the richest must have had to think twice before booking a trip across the Indian Ocean. Today, the nine-hour flight from Mumbai to London is affordable to a much broader population of Indians. In India alone, domestic air passengers have gone up to 139 million in 2014–15, from 29 million in 2002–03.[6]

These numbers are astounding when compared with statistics from even older times. Two hundred years ago, around the time of the industrial revolution, 94 per cent of the world's population lived in extreme poverty, and less than 20 per cent was literate. Today, less than 10 per cent of the global population lives in extreme poverty, and over 80 per cent is literate.[7] A lot of this change is attributable to technological advancements.

Electricity, credit cards and even a pill for headache were luxuries a few decades ago. Today they are necessities. And today's conveniences, such as online shopping or online education, had not even been dreamed about, let alone been thought of as luxuries.

What's more, some advancements that sounded futuristic even a couple of years ago are already here. Paris, Las Vegas, Boston and Chandler (Arizona) have driverless vehicles on their roads.[8] Holograms are no more just for *Star Wars* characters. Microsoft's HoloLens is in action and open for developers to build applications on. It isn't far-fetched to say that these technologies will be commonplace soon. After all, a landline telephone that was a luxury just fifty years ago has given way to the ubiquitous mobile phone. In the last decade the mobile phone has become our postman, our bank, our entertainment portal and our shopping mall.

Technology is accelerating at an accelerating pace

If you look closely at the examples mentioned so far, you will observe that their impact is twofold. The increasing pace of innovations themselves and the democratization of innovations. Not only are we engaged in more innovation, but the innovations are also becoming accessible to more and more people. This vertical and horizontal spread has been possible only because of technology.

In addition to an increase in the number of innovations, the cycles of innovation have an exponential multiplier effect too. Not only does a small change in knowledge have a butterfly effect on its ecosystem and beyond; but the speed with which the change comes about is exponentially faster with every iteration.

This can be seen in the advancements in communication where the increase in Internet and processor speeds and the capabilities of mobile technology are leading to mind-boggling numbers. In 1943, Thomas Watson, then president of IBM, had made the following prediction: 'I think there is a world market for maybe five computers.'

Today, 300 million mobile phones sold around the world have more power than an IBM machine sold in 1943. Moreover, it is expected that this growth in communication technology will continue uninhibited. Masayoshi Son, CEO of SoftBank Robotics, predicts AI in all smart devices, taking their intelligence way above human intelligence in just thirty years' time. A single chip, he contends, will have an IQ of 10,000 by then.[9]

It is heartening to note that the benefits of this non-linear growth are not restricted to the handful who can afford the new technologies. Technology is truly being democratized. A Masai warrior in the deep savannahs has better mobile connection today than the Oval Office in the White House did twenty-five ago.[10] It is estimated that by 2020, 80 per cent of adults all over the world will have an Internet-connected smartphone. This reach pushes developers to create products and services that work for people and become more affordable with every update; they become progressively cheaper despite having additional features and capabilities. When rapidly declining costs are added to increasing productivity, we see an accelerated pace of democratization through affordability. The table here demonstrates the combination of an increase in features in Internet-access technology and a decrease in costs.[11]

Technology	Speed	Year introduced	Internet transit prices when the technology was introduced	Basic capabilities
1G	Max: 2.4 kpbs	1980s		Basic wireless technology. Analogue signals. Only calls with frequent call drops
2G	Max: 64 kbps	Around 1992	$1200 per mbps	Text, picture and MMS messages
3G	144 kbps to 2 mbps	Around 2003	$9 per mbps	Video messages. Video conferencing. Large emails. Gaming
4G	100 mbps to 1 gbps	Around 2012–13	$0.63 per mbps	All of the above, at much higher speeds and more reliability

Another way to look at this faster-paced democratization of technology in the last 100-plus years is by considering how long it took for a new technology to reach critical mass. Beginning with the spindle, which was the first depiction of the industrial revolution and completely changed the textile industry, and leading up to technology used in mobiles, it has taken newer technologies less and less time to reach a sizeable demand, say 50 million users.[12]

Year of invention	Technology	Time taken to reach 50 million users
1764 (Spinning jenny)	Spindle	119 years
1876	Telephone	75 years
1895	Radio	38 years
1927	Television	13 years
1991	Internet	4 years
2004	Facebook	3.5 years
2016	Reliance Jio	83 days

When you consider the last two tables, you can only marvel at the pace at which technology is improving and how it is taking larger and larger portions of the population along.

This is really no time to look in the rear-view mirror, for the future is closer than it seems.

Today human beings are at the cusp of shedding their conservative approach to technology and looking forward to the exciting disruptions that technology is truly capable of. Life in the future will be more intelligent, more connected, more economical and more enjoyable.

We have identified a few technologies that will be the building blocks to making such a life possible. Each stands out for the innovation it is undergoing and the potential applications it has. Each is undoubtedly important. However, none is as powerful by itself as when combined with other technologies. The applications of the combined technologies range from weather prediction to efficiency of health instruments and improvement of agricultural produce.

Imagine a world where your loved one is geographically thousands of miles away, but an experience of sitting right next to them was made possible. A convergence of technologies, such as augmented reality, sensors, computing power and software technology, has the potential to give you the experience of your loved one's sight, smell and even touch. While it will be no substitute for actually being with the person, it will certainly be the next best thing—without the hours of travel or the other impracticalities.

Unimagined technologies making unthinkable progress!

While many current technologies are building blocks of an unimaginable future, such as 3D printing, blockchain and quantum computing, we have picked a few to see their immediate impact on our day-to-day lives. This impact magnifies manifold as the technologies merge to form undreamt-of combinations.

We are now used to devices like smart watches that measure our walking speed, sense fluid levels in our cars and detect faces on our mobile phones. They use sensors. As mentioned in our chapter on ASSURED Total Innovation, not only are sensors becoming cheaper, but with every iteration of improvement they are also becoming much smarter. This is why one finds sensors in almost everything used in day-to-day urban life. Sensors are making marked improvements in healthcare. It is sensors that maintain heart rates in pacemakers, operate in handheld ECGs and home blood-sugar machines. Now, by getting connected to the Web and cloud-based services, they are relaying real-time data too.[13]

Then there is the technology that breaks down, analyses and manages material at the subatomic level—nanotechnology. At subatomic levels, materials behave differently. Nanotechnology makes use of this behaviour to make, for example, extremely light material that is a hundred times as strong as steel. Areas such as transportation use nanotechnology to make cars and aircraft that consume fuel more efficiently because they are lighter in weight. Similarly, early diagnosis of illnesses using nanosensors has led to timely treatment. Carbon nanotubes in bulletproof vests make them easier to carry and more resistant to impact.

The much-feared word, 'robotics', can actually leave all jobs that are dull, dirty and dangerous to machines. Robots are used to take away monotonous chores from our lives, the filth off our streets and perform jobs that can be fatal. Thus far, robots were not intelligent enough to do non-trivial jobs. But today a robot can be programmed to learn from a few repetitions of any human activity. They are cheaper, easier to program and, most importantly, are capable of interaction. The future of robotics is not 'man vs machine', it is 'man with machine'. Already, robotics is making surgeries less invasive. It has led to inconceivable disruption in manufacturing. One negative fallout, though, has been its impact on employment, which we will address later in this chapter.

Developments in the field of genetics have made us understand ourselves better. Advances in computing, analytics and imaging units of DNA have improved our understanding of the genetic structure of plants, animals and human beings. This insight will not only lead to improved agriculture and animal farming, but also to discovery of treatments for diseases such as cancer. Further advances will enable us to change genetic code. Owing to this technology, medical treatment can be made more specific to your particular DNA structure. As with other technologies, genome sequencing is becoming cheaper too. Just fifteen years ago, it cost $3 billion to sequence a human genome.[14] Today it takes about $1000, and the cost continues to fall.

While many of these examples relate to our physical health, technology can also be used to sensitize us to ourselves and to the people around us. A virtual reality film, *Clouds Over Sidra*, places you inside a refugee camp in war-ridden Syria.[15] You can imagine the impact on yourself of traumatized Syrian children responding to your gaze. The hope, of course, is to generate empathy in the viewer. In another such experiment, Stanford University's Virtual Human Interaction Lab conducts experiments to check if seeing an older version of yourself prompts you to save for retirement.[16] Yet another experiment has you see the world through a colour-blind person's eyes.

Augmented reality will take all this a step further. It will use the available digital data to create 3D images. Sitting at home, consumers will be able to experience products in warehouses, as if the products were in their hands. Interior designers use the technology to walk their clients through completed floor plans of their new homes, and archaeologists use it to reimagine the world of thousands of years ago.[17]

As we mentioned earlier, these are only a few technologies. Many technologies, such as wearables and implantable devices, 3D printing and blockchain, Internet of things and big data analysis, smart homes and smart cities, are all in their nascent stages but are already shaking up the worlds of technology and economics. Their ultimate impact cannot even be imagined from where we stand now.

And when they come together . . .

Applications of each of these strands of technology pale in comparison when compared with what they can do when they come together. When products and services combine these technologies, completely new solutions are made possible.

Put together sensors with advanced computing power and AI, and you have driverless cars. This combination has also been used to monitor conditions such as diabetes and blood pressure. Add to this mix the already ripe technology of telecommunications, and you have remote health monitoring.

Telecommunications and computing power have already been combined to bring us inclusive education in the form of online courses. They also join forces to make micro-banking and micro-financing platforms accessible to the poorer sections of society. These are the same technologies that have brought us aggregator business models such as Airbnb, Amazon, Uber and Netflix. To pick one example, Uber started as a simple idea—to enable people to request a ride from their phone. Uber has now grown into a global logistics player, transforming an entire industry in the process. Its network relies on peer-to-peer coordination between drivers and passengers, enabled by sophisticated software and a clever reputation system. It is one of the largest point-to-point transportation networks built around an incredible aggregation model, where it owns no vehicles, employs no drivers and pays no vehicle maintenance costs.

Merging nanoscience with robotics and AI has produced efficient automated factories. Similarly, genetics and computing power can accurately detect disease. At the same time, this combination can also be used to create new plant forms.

It is almost as if each thread of technology is an ingredient that we use to create a recipe—the taste, aroma and presentation fusing to create a wholesome dish to suit our palate.

Fresh themes, refreshing positive impact patterns

When this overview of upcoming technologies is studied in further detail, some patterns emerge. Some of these trends are encouraging, and some have to be taken with a grain of salt. However, there are two other patterns—unemployment and the resultant inequality—that have to be handled with great care.

Shared economy: Newer corporate giants have business models that need no assets as they bring underutilized assets into the economy. Airbnb has shrunk the need to build hotels because you and I can put up our spare rooms for rent. Therefore, without building a single new room, more vacation needs are being met. Uber has made commuting easier and at the same time has reduced the need for individuals to own vehicles, reducing the number of cars manufactured. Amazon and Alibaba are marketplaces that have the potential to seriously reduce the need for shopping malls. This concept of shared ownership of assets has extended to as far as the renting out of clothes and shoes needed for special occasions![18] A reduction in the need for capital assets such as cars and buildings will translate to relatively less mining and energy use.

Narrow-casting: How much of your daily newspaper do you read? Not every person who is interested in football will savour news about the latest film release. What if a newspaper was put together with topics of only your interests? Our Twitter timelines and subscriptions to blogs and podcasts have become our personalized newspapers, at the cost of a print newspaper, or even lower. As opposed to broadcasting, where the same piece of information reaches all users, businesses can now customize and package information for every single user. We see this broadly in Facebook advertisements.

Narrow-casting is not just about customization. It also results in use of least resources for maximum impact or, at the very least, causes least harm. This customization is being done at little to no cost, economically and environmentally. Farming has moved from 100 per cent dependence on rainwater to irrigation to drip irrigation—minimizing the use of water to reach the specific part of the plant that needs it. Similarly, medication that impacts only the affected part of the body rather than the entire body is a possibility. This has huge implications for the use of antibiotics and steroids.

Platform-based solutions and aggregation: In economies that technology has not impacted, we observe small mom-and-pop corner stores running their businesses year after year. However, digitized economies are seeing many of these shops closing down or being assimilated by the Amazons and Alibabas of the world, on whose platforms the shop promoters now sell their products. Restaurants that otherwise wouldn't have considered home delivery are on Swiggy and Grubhub. This is the power of platform-based solutions. It has led to reduced prices and wastage. Unfortunately, it also has the potential to put a lot of people out of jobs.

Atomization of enterprises: Until recently, many professionals such as singers, actors or software professionals—had to work in large corporations or in large groups. Technology is now making it possible for such corporates to be 'atomized' because more and more individuals are becoming freelancers, and corporates are outsourcing functions such as writing, coding and visualization to freelancers. Individual professionals can now choose when they will work, how much time they will spend working, the field in which they will work and who they will work for. Individuals can now decide their own priorities depending on their need for income and need for free time. This is opening up a completely new world to professionals and in the process making enterprises leaner and more focused.

Volunteerism: Technology has pushed Encyclopaedia Britannica out of business because it enabled Wikipedia to come up at zero cost. From expert opinion available through blogs, a lot of today's knowledge is available at no cost to the user. We expect this trend to continue, where passion is as much a driver as the revenue model, where people willingly contribute and donate so that such resources can stay free. All this has been possible as a result of low-cost technology.

Ripple effect on various industries: Symbiotic ecosystems will be global. A change in one industry will have far-reaching impact on other industries and, therefore, other countries.

A look at the advent of autonomous cars gives us deep insight into the far-reaching impact of change in one technology leading to changes beyond its own ecosystem. Car-crash-related injuries are responsible for 1.25 million deaths ever year, worldwide.[19] Self-driving cars are already safer than human-driven vehicles.[20] The technology is going to become only better, thus safer. Cars on the road will communicate with each other to avoid accidents and traffic jams.

Riders will now have free time during their commute to work or to socialize. The other positive aspect is that when the technology and its use have matured, self-driving cars will be in continuous use for 95 per cent of the day, reducing both the number of cars and the need for parking space, which, in major cities, accounts for 20 to 30 per cent of public space.[21]

Given this scenario, the impact of driverless cars on ancillary industries and professions such as automobile and life insurance, auto-repair, auto dealership, auto-parts, taxi services, public transport, and professional driving and delivery services, is not surprising.[22] However, the disruptive impact on industries such as real estate, media and entertainment, health, airlines, fast food and urban planning might take us by surprise.

Currently, residential property, brick and mortar stores, parking lots and gas stations are located in close proximity to each other to make it convenient for the customer. As soon as self-driving is taken out of the equation, the need for this proximity can be done away with too. This will affect the price of real estate—urban, suburban, rural and commercial.

Taking this further, what are we going to do if we won't be driving our own cars? A completely new arena will open up for media and entertainment. This, in turn, will call for better Internet services and improved cybersecurity. The internal design of vehicles will have to innovatively accommodate meetings and leisure activities. Driverless vehicles will require a complete re-imagination of traffic enforcement too. Therefore, a change in the automobile industry will need changes in industries beyond its own sphere of direct impact.

This is just one example. Not only are there many such examples, they will only grow in number in the coming years. And none of this is futuristic. As we speak, MIT's Technology Review highlights 3D metal printing, easily available cloud-based AI, real-time translators, stronger online privacy and genetic prediction of serious medical conditions as some of the currently available technologies.

Smart city projects, such as the one in Toronto, will lead to more affordable and liveable cities in the next couple of years. Another couple of years and we are likely to see zero-carbon natural gas, which has no harmful emissions. By the end of another decade we will have materials that generate and distribute energy even more efficiently through the use of quantum computing, because it helps understand the details of molecules better.[23]

This interplay of technologies and themes will make for a far better world—a world of more with less.

Firstly, and most obviously, technology is reducing the cost of living. A rental car costs less than owning one, a home share less than a hotel, and the smartphone in our hand cuts down the investments required in a camera, a dictating machine, a computer, books, and much, much more.

It will be a world of better transportation with fewer cars, thanks to ride-sharing and the like. A lifestyle that has more vacation rooms with fewer hotels owing to room sharing. A more efficient supply of goods with fewer malls and shops due to e-commerce. This world will have better food—grain, vegetables, fruit and meat—that will have a less harmful impact on environment because of synthetic meats, foodgrains that consume water more efficiently, etc. New biological innovations and healthcare technologies will lead to better health for all with less need for medication. More goods will be produced using less raw material and less transportation than before as technologies like 3D printing and AI mature. Cleaner air will go hand in hand with prosperity. We will have more leisure time and a better quality of life, at a lower cost of living. This list of benefits to mankind from technological progress is endless.

All of this put together, in turn, will reduce our demand on energy having a powerfully positive impact on our environment. However, it is not necessarily so for the third E, Employment. It is time now to consider the much-talked-about ill effects of technology—unemployment and income inequality.

Tread carefully, for technology's impact threatens employment

It is clear that technology has an impact, a very positive impact, on energy as well as environment. Or, at least, our efforts are guided towards creating a positive impact in these areas. But technology can have a disastrous impact on employment, if not managed well. If done right though, it has potential to bring heaven on earth. Through appropriate use of technology, we can get rid of all those jobs which are dangerous, dirty or akin to drudgery. However, there is the dangling sword of unemployment and increased income and access disparity that society needs to deal with.

We now study the impact of technology on employment by following four broad themes—fewer jobs, redistribution of jobs, growing inequality and freedom to be creative. Each of these aspects has positive and negative indicators, because while new technology takes away some jobs, it creates new ones too.

Well-known MIT academicians Brynjolfsson and McAfee created an interesting graph showing two lines, one representing productivity and the other total employment in the United States. For years after World War II, the two lines closely tracked each other, with increases in jobs corresponding to increases in productivity. In the early years of the new millennium, starting in the year 2000, the lines began to diverge. Productivity continued to rise robustly but employment suddenly started to drop. By 2011, a significant gap appeared between the two lines, showing growth in the economy but no growth in jobs! Brynjolfsson and McAfee call it the 'great decoupling'. According to them, technology was behind both the healthy growth in productivity and the weak growth in jobs.[24]

Fewer jobs

Technological advancements have been filling in for humans in various jobs even before the industrial revolution. They had been opposed even at that time. (Queen Elizabeth I refused a patent to a knitting machine for fear of rise in unemployment![25]) Technologies can be put into three categories as far as their implications for employment are concerned. First come the technologies that automate physical tasks carried out by professionals such as typists, bank tellers and switchboard operators. From 1991 to 2001, the number of secretaries declined by about 35 per cent.[26] Then come the technologies that do the customer service tasks; some examples being tasks such as self-help kiosks and grocery-store scanners. Between 2000 and 2012, computers have taken over $2 trillion worth of work earlier performed by programmers, librarians and engineers.[27] Last come the technologies such as cognitive computing and AI, which perform intellectual tasks that are beyond human capacity.

These technologies, however, have also increased productivity and reduced expenses, making more products and services available to people at lower costs. The resultant increase in consumer savings and spending has led to more opportunities for employment in the consumer goods market. This is one example of automation-led, productivity-led, economic-growth-led job growth! The only glitch in this system is that it takes society, and therefore the economy, some time to adjust to the increased levels of productivity.

Having said that, the trends of the 2000s, however, are a cause for concern. When Kodak and similar companies were in their prime in the 1980s, tens of thousands of machine operators, warehouse workers, clerical assistants and the like could count on steady work and good benefits that are rare today. These days, companies like Apple outsource warehousing, clerical and cleaning jobs. Today, 23,400 Apple employees take home six-digit salaries. Just three decades ago, 60,000 Kodak employees in Rochester had average pay-cum-benefits worth $79,000 in today's dollar terms.[28]

At the end of 2015, Google's Alphabet Inc. and Facebook Inc. recorded a total market value double that of Microsoft Corp. However, together they employed only 74,505, a third fewer than Microsoft Corp.[29] Instagram had only thirteen employees when it was acquired for $1 billion in 2012. The corresponding numbers for WhatsApp when it was taken over in 2014 were fifty-five and $19 billion.

The five largest US-based technology companies of 2016—Apple, Alphabet, Microsoft, Facebook and Oracle Corp—are worth a total of $1.8 trillion, 80 per cent more than the five largest technology companies of 2000. However, they employ 22 per cent fewer workers than Cisco Systems Inc., Intel, IBM, Oracle and Microsoft, the big five from 2000.

Sure, there has been some trigger effect that created new industries and thus new employment. Social media marketing and app creation have made new jobs available. Facebook has 8000 employees but has created 1.1 million jobs in the US, adding almost $100 billion to the nation's economy.[30]

These numbers give context to the disillusionment of the American middle class with technological developments and the state of the economy. All the benefits of the rise of these technology companies have been accrued by a handful of people. People who lost jobs in computer and electronics manufacturing were employed by warehouses and transportation companies at less than half the pay of a person in high-tech manufacturing. So, while Silicon Valley has relatively prospered, the deeper pockets of America have either stagnated or deflated economically. The frustration of a generation that earns less than its parents and grandparents is seeping into the country's politics.

The story isn't any better in other industries either. Interestingly, one would think a rise in oil prices after their fall would bring cheer to the oil industry. When oil prices fell by 70 per cent, 30 per cent of jobs in the industry were lost from its peak in 2014.[31] As prices rose again, some people got their jobs back. But the re-employment was nowhere close to the 30 per cent loss of jobs because in the interim a lot of the industry went through automation. So, while the industry is seeing rising profits induced by lowered costs, the jobs haven't all come back.

Some of the drop in employment in other industries might be due to migration of jobs to developing countries, but the real killer has been automation.[32] Study after study has proved that the loss of jobs in the US can be attributed to automation-induced increased productivity rather than migration of jobs to countries such as China.

Ironically, China itself is moving from humans to machines. The country hired the most number of robots in 2016.[33] More than 75 per cent of the country's jobs are at risk because of automation.[34] Even though the timing and magnitude of this move are not currently predictable, we guess it will be soon, and gigantic. The country's drive to increase productivity per worker implies a shift to automation, and thus fewer jobs.[35]

Back home in India, the technology-led unemployment numbers aren't as bad. However, it is safe to assume that India will follow China, give or take a few percentage points, especially once robotics becomes mainstream here. One of us, Mashelkar, has written extensively on the impact of new technologies on employment in India.[36] Among many other trends is that of jobs even in the Indian Information Technology and BPO (Business Process Outsourcing) sectors not being secure any longer. Traditionally, these industries were competitive for the employer because of lower labour costs. Advances in user interfaces, such as speech and gesture recognition technology, are giving computers the ability to respond directly to human commands and requests. Google Now and Apple's Siri use natural user interfaces to recognize spoken words, interpret their meaning and respond appropriately. It is only a natural progression that these technologies would replace traditional call centre employees and manual agents. After all, it leads to higher efficiency and lower costs of operation. AI is getting ever closer to doing these service jobs with much more efficiency, and at even lower costs. On many online portals, a chat bot has taken over the standard questions a customer service representative would otherwise answer. While training the first computer is expensive, subsequent iterations are progressively cheaper.[37] In the not-so-distant future, AI is likely to be provided as a metered service, like electricity.

3D printing is establishing itself as a credible, scalable way to manufacture goods. This will have a huge impact on manufacturing jobs, threatening the livelihood of machinists, welders and maintenance technicians.

Machines are even taking over the job of their own makers. Computers are becoming more intelligent at breakneck speed, threatening the jobs of programmers, database managers and other computer professionals, except perhaps, those at the forefront of AI. For now.

Machines are not just taking over repetitive jobs in factories. Soon, occupations that we didn't ever imagine becoming obsolete will no longer be available as job opportunities for humans. An activity like care-giving is now outsourced to machines. Japan already has robots that care for the country's ageing population.[38]

Machines can replace millions of bureaucrats. Government clerks who do predictable, rule-based, often mechanical work can potentially be replaced by machines. In a recent collaboration with Deloitte UK, Professors Osborne and Frey estimated that about a quarter of the UK's public-sector workers are employed in administrative and operative roles which have a high probability of being automated. In the UK, they estimated, some 861,000 jobs could be eliminated by 2030, creating 17 billion pounds ($21.4 billion) in savings for the taxpayer. While some of those who lose jobs could include underground train operators, they will mainly be local government paper-pushers.[39] The public sector is one of the biggest potential arenas for automation—one which is arguably desirable. When automation saves taxpayer money, it is less likely to face opposition. Interestingly, we see little traction here because of an absence of political will, which does not come as a surprise at all.

However, there is a flip side. Technology increases connectivity and therefore an ability to reach a larger set of customers without having to make large investments in marketing or physical infrastructure. Technology reduces transaction costs and increases the ability to transact over longer distances and a larger customer base. Technology makes it possible to collect data regarding the behaviours of sellers as well as buyers, about the quality of the products sold and about buyers' 'trustability'. This information makes credit more easily available. All these aspects can help bring organizations from the informal sector to the formal sector of the economy. These transformations have the potential to create much greater employment as can be seen in China. But the extent of job creation will be different in different sectors.

Redistribution of jobs

Interestingly, in the forty-five years since the invention of ATMs, the number of bank tellers employed in the US has doubled.[40] We no longer keep our accounts in actual books, yet this has not led to a decrease in demand for accountants. In fact, in the US, the number of advertised accountancy and finance job vacancies went up by 21 per cent in 2017 because of a higher demand from small and medium enterprises and start-ups. This was almost double the previous year's growth in demand, at 11 per cent.[41]

While not related, with an increase in ATMs also came an increase in the number of bank branches, which led to an increase in the number of bank tellers. But these tellers didn't dispense money any more. They became relationship managers for the banks' customers. Taking mechanical jobs out of the equation brings more economic value to softer skills. In addition, humans innovate further. We are always going to want more, do more, and therefore create more jobs.

Growing inequality

However, new technology does not always translate to greater well-being. It all depends on how we use the new technology. The employment problem relates as much to quality as it does to quantity. New-age businesses such as Facebook, Uber and Airbnb undermine the very promise of capitalism that as technology advances the wider economy will benefit everyone.[42]

Also, the new jobs created are not necessarily good jobs—jobs that people want to do. And people cannot do the jobs they want to do because they are not qualified for them, as they involve new technology. High-education, high-wage jobs such as those in medicine, engineering and marketing are on the rise. Similarly, growing consumerism is aiding employment growth in many low-skill, low-education jobs such as food service, cleaning, home delivery, etc. However, jobs are reducing in middle-education, middle-wage jobs, like manufacturing, operations, clerical work and sales.

These jobs in the middle layer are most easily automatable, almost wiping this layer out. Where do these people go? They don't have the skills required for the higher-level jobs. And the lower-level jobs neither pay enough nor accord them the dignity of their earlier jobs. Does that mean they will stay out of work forever? Unlikely. What will they do, then?

History tells us that we don't really know the answer to this question. But just because we don't know the answer doesn't mean there is no answer. We did not know fifty years ago that there would be fields such as bioengineering and app development. We did not know that fitness and nutrition would be an industry, a necessary one at that.

Could we have imagined that animal grooming would be a full-fledged job and animal psychologists full-fledged professionals? What's more, these jobs serve the doer's passion, bringing them immense satisfaction too.

Falling costs of advanced robots coupled with rising costs of labour in emerging economies will start levelling the field for both developed and developing economies. The legitimate question is: What's the difference in costs between cars manufactured by robots in Detroit and those manufactured by robots in India or Vietnam? There will be close to no difference because disruptive technologies, such as 3D printing, will see companies bring manufacturing back to their home countries. After thirty years of production in China, Adidas moved its production to Germany in 2016. This is not owing to rising labour costs in China but due to the substantial advances in affordable automation and robotics.

A question that we have to answer then is, how inclusive is our development? BMW Brilliance's world-class Shenyang car factory in China was commissioned at breathtaking speed, in just eighteen months, from land levelling to two-shift production. With 85 per cent automation in the body shop using 675 robots, there are hardly any workers on the shop floor. Apart from producing the premium BMW cars, this car factory has productionized, ground-up, the first zero-emission electric car, the Zinoro.[43] Where does that leave human beings?

India is exploring massive technology-led inclusion through its JAM endeavour, referred to in greater detail in another chapter of this book. The idea is to bring the underserved majority into the banking system. What is true for financial inclusion will become true for inclusion in education, health services and other fields too. This will have huge implications for creation as well as destruction of jobs.

Freedom to be creative?

Another argument in favour of growing automation from an employment point of view is that humans will be left with jobs that they really want to do and jobs that will bring emotional satisfaction. These jobs will require creativity, problem-solving skills and expertise at intelligent interpretation of a situation. But even as we conceptualize a new world with such jobs, these jobs too are already being done by machines.

Mastery in radiology, for instance, requires several years of hard work and experience. But now, systems such as the ones made by BD FocalPoint can interpret medical images and look for abnormalities such as tumours with greater speed and accuracy than a human can.

Machines bring instant access to information and substantial enhancement in the quality and pace of decision-making. This will lead to an improvement in our own performance.

Deep Blue, a supercomputer, beating Garry Kasparov the ace chess player isn't surprising because Deep Blue was programmed to win the game. But AlphaGo was not preprogrammed this way. It learned using a general-purpose algorithm that allowed it to interpret the game's patterns. When beating Fan Hui, an ace Go coach and champion, it had trained on 100,000 existing games, then played about 30 million games against itself to develop new strategies.[44]

Scott Finch programmed his Macintosh computer to write three-quarters of the prose for a potboiler titled

Just This Once. Vince Di Bari, former vice president of the local Los Angeles chapter of the American Federation of Musicians, estimates that recording jobs for human musicians have dropped by at least 35 per cent because of synthesizers. Google's new AI group, Magenta, is set up with the intention of finding out if AI can train a machine to create original music, art or video.

Similar techniques will be applied in other AI domains which need complex pattern recognition and decision-making based on long-term planning—only to benefit humankind, but also leaving humans with fewer jobs to do.

Having said all that we have above, as scientists and technologists, we have enormous faith in technology and its potential to transform human life. We recognize that unemployment is a dangling sword over our heads that needs to be put back in its scabbard.

Technology-led jobless growth is increasingly a topic of intense discussion around the world, and in both developing and developed economies. The good news and the bad news is that technologies are getting obsolete at an increasingly accelerated pace. Therefore, we need more people who will create new technology.

People are also required to maintain emerging technologies, be it the Internet of things, advanced robotics, automation of knowledge work or 3D printing. People are also required to assist other people in using new technology. Finally, new technology requires new labour forms. For instance, technicians will be needed to repair a billion mobile phones in India. There will always be a great demand for experts to design, test, implement and refine smart automated information systems. All this translates to more jobs in the future. What changes, though, is the nature of jobs.

After all, technology can deal with logic very well. But logic is only one capability of the human mind. Inspiration, creativity and intuition, interpretation, storytelling and communication are all things that humans can do so well that it will be hopefully difficult for computers to accomplish. We do realize that the operative word there is 'hopefully'!

Going forward, the proportion of the population engaged in traditional full-time employment in order to keep humanity fed, supplied, healthy and safe will inevitably decrease. However, we believe that this will lead to a humane restructuring of the general social contract around the type and number of jobs. This also means that making the world a better place is in our hands and not under the control of a machine.

The need of the hour is an adaptable workforce rather than one which would be lost if its current jobs were taken away. The current working force and the next generations will have to look at having three careers in their lifetime. Therefore, over and above domain expertise, they have to hone life skills that will make them receptive to learning as a lifelong process and adapt to changing trends.

Constant retraining is the new way to be. Acquiring skills and keeping them updated will be our biggest challenge. Today's education systems cannot cope with the pace of change. A human being's capacity to learn new things is limited. If technology displaces jobs faster than humans can learn new skills, the changeover period will be long and damaging. This is the stark reality of our times. Acknowledging and being aware of the issues around the relationship between technology and unemployment is the first step towards thinking about and creating job-led technologies instead of technology-led innovations.

And, yet, technology can take us only so far

With this understanding of the impact of technology, we have to brace ourselves for the fact that technology alone cannot change anything, be it in agriculture, health, transportation or any other industry, especially when positioned against the three imposing problems of energy, environment and employment.

Sure, as we will see in the coming chapters, technological changes will strongly and inevitably influence the other levers. For instance, clean technology will drive clean policy and will add force to clean social movements. As technology gets cheaper, it will also make the economic model viable for all concerned. However, the side effects of technology will need to be handled through other mechanisms and will need support from the other STEP levers too.

Even otherwise, we could be taking two steps forward and going one step backward if we relied solely on technology. A case in point from today's world is US President Donald Trump's stance on emissions, which could mean cars continue to stay as pollution makers rather than becoming pollution savers. The challenge is to use the technology lever effectively in conjunction with the other levers—social engagement, economic model and policymaking. To ensure that technology enriches life while addressing the challenges presented by energy, environment and employment, we need effective public policy and we need to recognize the impact of social engagement. We also need an economic model that balances the needs of all stakeholders.

At other times, there could be a tug of war between the levers, and we will need to strike a balance. For instance, the wide application of blockchain technology is at the intersection of the policy and technology levers as governments seek to bring in regulations to monitor its usage. This would be true of any major transformational endeavour. Another example of this tug of war is social opposition to genetically modified foods. Many other examples have been cited in the chapter on ASSURED Total Innovation. The interplay between the four STEP levers has to be negotiated to bring about solutions that are for the general good of humanity.

Keeping these converging and diverging forces in mind, let's take a look at the role of the next enabling lever—policy.

SIX

Lever 2 of 4
Public Policy—A Delicate Balancing Act

In almost every society, the government is probably the strongest authority. Its very function is to influence what its citizens can and cannot do. The government also has powers to create positive and negative incentives to persuade or dissuade citizens from specific activities or behaviours. Along with statutory powers, the government has enormous resources under its control and can use them to pursue its objectives.

The might and authority of the government is also sometimes accentuated by the desire of the politicians to act rather too quickly. Decision-makers are known to promulgate bold policies. This demonstrates their authority and is also a show of so-called responsiveness. Sometimes, this potential to display power motivates policymakers to hastily push new policies through. So, while policies can be highly useful—in fact, appropriate ones are a prerequisite for major transformation—they can also be a rather dangerous weapon.

It is therefore imperative to discuss the nuances of policymaking. Our thoughts on public policy have been influenced enormously by Dr Vijay Kelkar's thought leadership in this area,[1] which lead us to some pertinent questions. When are policies necessary? When should the government intervene and when should it not? When should intervention start and when should it end? How do you assess the effectiveness of policies?

These questions are important because policies touch your life on a day-to-day basis. It is the common man on the ground who gets affected by the decisions made at the top.

A few years after the great recession of 1929, the US saw a drop in production by one-third, and 25 per cent of its population was unemployed.[2] Of the employed, another third earned lower wages than earlier or were working only part-time. Dire measures were needed for the economy to recover from this deep depression. After President Franklin Roosevelt took office, he gradually introduced several fiscal and monetary reforms, and many welfare schemes and measures to create livelihood, collectively known as the New Deal. Not immediately, but eventually, the nation bounced back as a result of these policy endeavours.

Roosevelt's dynamic reforms covered a gamut of areas. Amongst the many initiatives were the Tennessee Valley Authority Act that built dams to control floods and generate inexpensive hydroelectric power. The Emergency Banking Act reorganized banks and closed insolvent ones. When all this did not achieve the desired results fast enough, the reforms became even more aggressive. The Works Progress Administration in 1935, for instance, created employment in the public goods sector. This programme did not allow competition from the private sector. Therefore, several public goods received attention—new roads, schools and parks were built with the aim of creating jobs. This led to state-of-the-art infrastructure in the country. Social security, unemployment insurance and federal agricultural subsidies are policy tools from the New Deal that exist up to the present day.[3] Some may question the current impact of some of these measures, but undoubtedly they brought relief at the time.

On the other hand, the Great Leap Forward of the late 1950s, an economic and social campaign by the Communist Party of China, proved quite disastrous. Among the many drastic measures undertaken was a government push towards industrialization. In an attempt to aggressively industrialize an otherwise agrarian population, Chairman Mao Zedong introduced policies that prohibited private farming and forced private industrialization. It is believed that each community was required to build a furnace to produce steel out of scrap material.

This push led to an employment shift from agriculture to manufacturing, and thus the urban population swelled. This shift also meant that bumper crops were untended and left to rot. Under pressure to announce unprecedented growth, state officials claimed exaggerated numbers for agricultural production, numbers that included the rotting crops. These numbers were used by the central government to make export decisions leading to an export of grain that was not really in surplus. The poor peasants starved even though there had originally been a bumper crop. Mao's measures are believed to have led to the Great Chinese Famine, which saw the death of over 50 million Chinese citizens. Fifty million human beings![4]

These two examples illustrate the power of government intervention and the profound, long-lasting impact it can have. When done right, policies have nursed broken economies back to life, and when they have failed they have wreaked havoc in all directions. The challenge is to use policy tools effectively at the local, state and national levels for positive change. Unfortunately, good intentions are not enough. Good policies are required, because inadequate, thoughtless policies are likely to backfire. The impact of policy is much like that of nature. One small tweak in one corner of an ecosystem can have an unexpected, cascading effect through the environment. This effect is not always beneficial to society at large.

Appreciating the impact policies can have—both positive and negative—we are now ready to consider the ideal process that brings about useful policies. We shall first consider the conditions that should exist for authorities to weigh in with policies.

So, when should policy intervene?

If we were to go to the very source of policymaking we would come to the basic theory of free economy. Policy intervention can be avoided if free economy always functioned as it is supposed to. Free market theory assumes that every consumer who spends money on a product receives some benefit from that product. The expenditure that all consumers make to purchase products indicates the total benefit from that product as perceived by society as a whole. If all producers directed their energies to generate products that consumers wanted, maximum social benefit is bound to occur. Producers would, logically, make products that brought them profits. In effect, the market is the perfect place for consumers and producers to interact in a way that maximizes benefits for all.

In all earnestness, we believe that, by and large, pursuit of self-interest results in the maximization of societal interests. A fundamental belief about private enterprise is that every rupee spent by an individual is a vote for a 'good', and that a summation of those votes would equal the societal good. This is in line with another free economy concept—the law of competition, which envisages the death of inefficient players. When a business is leading itself up to bankruptcy, for instance, the underlying implication is that it doesn't have enough votes. Letting such players die a natural death is part of the process of maximizing benefit to consumers and also maximizing the use of public resources.

This is a much better solution than planned economies with unwarranted government intervention. This argument generally holds good, and at least until recently, by and large, the capitalist or free enterprise society delivered better results than socialist or planned economies, where capital allocation is decided by an appointed central planner.

Unfortunately, while the system works in many cases, in many others it does not. This is when we need policy to guide things in a desirable direction. Healthcare for the poor or an appropriate education system for those who cannot afford it are instances of societal good which might not have many takers in the private industry. These can be areas where policy can intervene to make adequate provisions to bring about societal good.

However, these interventions cannot be so significant that they take over the core role of private enterprise. Most importantly, they should be withdrawn when market forces begin to take care of the inequities that the intervention set out to address. Intervention ought to be very selective, and only to the extent to which it can guide market players towards greater social benefit for the entire community.

Keeping the above ground rules in mind—that of minimum intervention and withdrawal of intervention when its job is done—we need policies when markets fail to deliver an efficient outcome. This could be because one stakeholder has more power than another; or because the business practice is not good for society at large even though no single stakeholder suffers directly. Sometimes policy intervention helps reduce inequities in the market. These are situations in which the state needs to step in, and we will take them up in turn in a bit.

Together, these situations boil down to two broad reasons for policy intervention—to address market failures such that there is an increase in growth and efficiency, and to encourage or discourage certain goods or services on grounds of ethics and morality.

When does the market fail?

Since market failure is the fundamental justification for macroeconomic policies, it brings us to the question: When does free market economy fail us? We reiterate that market failure is not just when a free market economy doesn't operate as expected; the market has also failed when economic forces do not lead to overall societal good.

To understand the nature of market failures, we can break them down into four major types. While we will take up each of these failures in better detail, let us start with a snapshot. The first of these failures are externalities when none of the direct stakeholders is significantly and individually affected by an activity.

However, the activity impacts society at large because a common property is being damaged. The next type of failure is caused by asymmetric information among different stakeholders; for instance, a consumer cannot make an informed decision because of lack of access to the required information. The third type of failure results when the market power of one or more stakeholders leads to inequity. This needs to be checked at both ends—by controlling concentration of power and by enabling those with less power. The last type of failure is when the free market doesn't take care of public goods because producers might not be interested in them or the products or services are such that the state ought to provide for them.

There are also situations in which consumption of certain goods or a particular behaviour is to be encouraged, while other goods or behaviour is to be discouraged. Let us consider each of these market failures individually.

Can we pollute the air you breathe? It's yours and ours.

Policies are needed to curb business practices that cause damage to the commons. This doesn't come to the fore because damage to common property doesn't hurt anyone immediately. Commons are parts of our environment that are not owned by any individual but are essential for everyone living in the society the commons serve. Clean air is such a common. It is freely available to all. We all use it as our right. Does that mean businesses can pursue practices that deteriorate air quality? Should damage to the air we breathe carry on uninhibited? Since nobody owns clean air, state policy can ensure that those who destroy this common property are made to pay for it.

The Montreal Protocol, a global agreement between participating countries, was instrumental in controlling ozone layer depletion. As mentioned in an earlier chapter, depletion of the ozone layer has led to harmful rays passing through, causing damage to humans, crops, natural vegetation, animal and marine life. The Montreal Protocol in 1987 has led to a 10 per cent reduction in ozone-depleting particles from their peak levels.[5] The latest reports suggest that despite the Montreal Protocol, the ozone hole over Antarctica is nearly as large as it was in 1978. However, without the protocol it would have been 40 per cent larger. Also, were it not for the protocol, the ozone layer over Europe and North America would have been 10 per cent thinner and we would have had 2 million more cases of skin cancer by 2030.[6] It is estimated that by 2032, the current measures will bring the ozone layer back to 1980 levels.[7] And yet, this protocol needs to be updated constantly because new chemicals are being produced by our industries.

Exploiting ignorance

Market failure also results when the consumer does not have the expertise or know-how about a product. The law of economics assumes that there is perfect information symmetry in the marketplace. However, in real life, not all sections of consumers have access to information that is necessary for them to make prudent decisions. This asymmetry in knowledge leads to poor choices and damaging consequences. This is why we have strict policies for insurance agents or investment brokers, as the consumer might be unaware of the practical details about how different schemes work. Similarly, doctors and lawyers have strong ethical codes they need to abide by. Packaging labels on products are legal requirements because the standards approved by the government indicate the quality of goods to the consumer. That goes for food products too; their manufacturers are legally required to describe the ingredients and indicate if the contents are vegetarian or non-vegetarian, etc. These disclosures might have been skipped in a true free market.

Balancing the power equation

Free market economies often lead to monopolistic corporate behaviour. This indicates lack of competition, which is unhealthy for the economy. Thus, regulations to curb monopolistic tendencies are brought in to encourage new firms into a market. Antitrust laws promote fair competition to benefit consumers. A collection of these legal acts inhibits cartel formation and prevents other collusive practices. They restrict mergers and acquisitions of companies that can substantially lessen competition.

At the other end of the power spectrum, policies are necessary to reduce income inequality as well as access inequality. Some economic policies seek to distribute the outcomes of a development equally amongst all sections of society. Competitive behaviour, which is at the core of free economy, has the potential to leave large parts of society behind. Such large disparities are not good for cohesion in society. Lack of cohesion can result in destruction of peace, which degrades the well-being of the society.

Avoiding such a situation is in itself an important reason for laying down appropriate economic policies. To coexist in harmony, we need to sacrifice some of our freedoms including the freedom to prosper, unreined, through competitive behaviour. Every society has to find its own equilibrium. Across the globe, this balance is brought about through taxation, subsidies and welfare systems. These measures are imposed with the intent of tackling unequal wealth distribution and limited access to services for some sections of society.

Every country that has progressive taxation and subsidies for certain sections of the society is trying to reduce income inequality through policy intervention. On the other hand, free state education, policies that use state resources to provide training, and reservations for minorities are means to reduce access inequalities. The state also invests in education, training and capacity building. This is a matter of particular import in today's times, when constant retraining is the only way to job-led growth.

This access and income equality can be extended to businesses too. Policies are needed to support new businesses that cannot operate without economies of scale. The cost of making a product goes down as the volumes produced increase. The reduced cost leads to lower prices for the consumer, which makes the products accessible to a larger population. When a product leads to social good, it is important for the government to give demand a nudge. This would bridge the gap between the current scale of production and the desired scale that enables lowered prices. This could also be done by the government when it procures the products for its own use.

Public procurement could be key to achieving scale and prevent many a good innovation from failing. When the government buys products in bulk, it is a demand-side innovation. Owing to their huge purchasing power, governments have the power to create demand for an innovation. Acting as a lead user, the government, through policies, also signals its belief in an innovation, thus influencing the demand for it.

India's Unnat Jyoti by Affordable LEDs for All (UJALA, meaning 'light' in Hindi) is a case in point.[8] While UJALA is a market-driven initiative, strong support from government initiatives has made it self-sustaining. This has led to dramatic savings in energy consumption while reducing carbon emissions. More importantly, it has also brought in large-scale investment in the manufacturing of LED bulbs, generating employment that leads to other macro benefits.

From 2012 to 2016, this bulk procurement has led to a 75 per cent drop in the retail market price for LED bulbs that were sold outside the UJALA scheme. This is one of the fastest LED price reductions in the world. This has made LEDs more acceptable and available in the Indian market. The government has clearly helped by creating large-scale demand for LED bulbs, which has gone up fifty times from 2014 to 2017. By 2019, UJALA aims to replace 770 million high-energy-consuming lamps with efficient ones. Remarkably, this has been done without any government subsidies; the initial procurement was good enough.

This success is tremendously encouraging for other initiatives, because the model is replicable for other equipment such as water pumps. It has also led to healthy competition amongst Indian state governments to form energy-efficiency programmes.

While such procurement is an extraordinarily effective tool to reach scale with speed, it is challenging. The state cannot support demand for a product or service forever. We reiterate, it is important to judiciously wean out support once a certain scale is achieved. This is to get the product to economically sustain itself.

In other cases, efficient solutions are slowed down because of unavailability of large-scale funding or inaccessibility of funds due to high interest rates. The state could become a financier to meet the present costs of such projects in lieu of future benefits.

Providing and protecting

The last type of market failure is when producers are not interested in a product or service that is important for the society. This includes provision of infrastructure such as roads, railway tracks and city amenities like street lighting. The government, therefore, takes over the job of providing these public goods.

Likewise, national security is a public good too. States need to build key resources within their own boundaries so that they are not held to ransom by other countries. They might have to restrict business in the course. Every nation has policies related to food security that ensure quantity and quality of food production, processing, distribution and storage. From price security to state procurement, governments take care of these aspects to secure food for their country's population.

Similarly, economic nationalism requires nations to protect their own producers and monitor the consumption of natural resources, from energy to rare earth metals. Data usage and privacy laws also fall in this category, with nations regulating them to protect the interests of their citizens. The development of key technologies is another such arena. Even here, the interventions should be time-bound. This is a clear trade-off between economic nationalism and gains of international trade were such laws not put in place.

Apart from addressing these four types of market failures, policies are also used to deal with the ethical or moral implications of products or the way in which they are made. Policies to encourage merit goods and discourage demerit goods fall under this category.

When consumption of certain types of goods is to be discouraged, it is done through information campaigns and policy interventions, such as restricting the age for consumption of such goods. Tobacco and alcohol consumption are the most evident examples. In such cases, a Pigovian tax goes a long way to reduce consumption. Deliberate policies to encourage merit goods are also common when manufacturing of such goods is not profitable for private organizations. Clean energy initiatives would fall in this category. Carbon tax has increased from ₹50 (~$1) in 2012 to ₹400 (~$6) per tonne of coal in 2016.[9] This has made renewable energy use attractive to businesses. Labour laws are another such example. Most countries have laws that discourage child labour by punishing its practice with heavy penalties and even imprisonment. On the other hand, employing handicapped persons is encouraged through policy-driven subsidies.

Keeping in mind the situations that call for intervention, three key questions need to be answered by policymakers before they venture into making policy.

Coming back to the key questions

The fundamental and sharp questions are: Is there a market failure? Is there a case of public goods? Is there a case of merit or demerit goods? These are the only questions that can establish a rationale for policy intervention. If these questions fetch a no there is no role for the state.

If yes, does the proposed intervention address the market failure or need for intervention? Sometimes, hastily proposed, poorly-thought-through solutions do not address the claimed problem at all. If yes, do we have the state capacity to effectively implement the proposed intervention? Often an idea might be sound but the state might not have the tools for its effective implementation and enforcement.

Answers to these questions will also help prioritize policies. More pressing issues can be addressed ahead of the less important ones, depending on the extent of market failure and the extent of possible, effective intervention.

Once it has been established that a condition for policy intervention exists, it is important to understand the ingredients of a good policy. So, we know we want a policy. Now, what should this policy include and exclude?

'How' should policy intervene?

Unfortunate as it is, we know that even policies made with the best intentions and addressing the most important issues are likely to fail in the details or during execution and implementation. How do we avoid such failure? A study of the dynamics that lead to failure and the corrections that are possible will shed light on the ingredients of an ideal policy.

Many policies fail to accomplish their fullest potential because they do not go to the root cause and thus do not fix the issue at the root. Instead, they make do with just addressing the consequences of a situation. Quite often, a quick fix of the symptoms is preferred to a deeper study of the real causes. Policies are used as superficial band-aids to manage the current issue. In its attempt to address present concerns, this attitude often overlooks long-term implications. A good policy would be one which is deliberated in depth to plumb the root cause of the current situation.

In the recent past, some Indian states implemented a strange policy to tackle the issue of low grades scored by students.[10] The new policy got rid of exams in every year of school except the last year. This resulted in lower grades in the final year and in lowering the quality of education through all grades because the teachers were no longer interested in teaching students who were going to pass anyway. After all, there was no way to check if the teachers were doing their job. If the policymakers had taken a deeper look, they would have realized that the true cause for the low passing rate was a badly designed and managed education system and education policy.

Therefore, before all else, a good policy ought to address the root cause of a problem.

Anybody who has dealt with policymakers and enforcers knows that even the best policy can prove to be worthless if lopsided power is accorded to the enforcers. As an example, public policy is rightly used to ensure that every citizen pays their dues in the form of taxes and duties. However, according unchecked power to tax officials to enforce these laws results in harassment of people and misuse of authority. Therefore, it is critical to have proper checks and balances. A good policy should incorporate accountability along with authority, or else the damage the implementation of such policies cause is far more than the good it intends to bring. This emanates from the well-known economic concept of 'public-choice theory'. The theory calls for an economic analysis of the objectives of politicians and administrators. No matter how famous or reputed a person is, when they are hired as an official in a government agency, there will be a gap between their personal interests and the public interest.

Public-choice theory forces us to change our outlook towards authority. It calls for a change in our expectations of wanting our bureaucrats and politicians to be spotlessly incorruptible. The wait for the ideal, selfless politician and administrator is indeed futile. Instead of hiring a competent and benevolent person to head an institution and leaving all the decisions to them, this theory recommends that policies diffuse concentration of power. It is important to create forces of accountability so that politicians will serve the people and not pursue their self-interests.

From the public-choice perspective, all policymaking is marred by conflict, and conflict is the normal state. Differences between citizens and agencies are considered normal and healthy. In fact, it is encouraged so that these differences play out in the public domain. Thus, the call for checks and balances that are rooted in the systems and processes of a policy itself.

Having made sure that enforcers do not take advantage of the system, policies should next take a look at the far-reaching impact of incentives as a method of policy intervention. One of the biggest ideas in economics is that people respond to incentives. So incentives are often used to promote a desired behaviour. However, it is dangerous to design incentives in the hope that they will have the impact as expected. It is human nature to optimize and get the best out of incentives or to wriggle out of the impact of disincentives. It is the policymaker's job to have as watertight an incentive as is possible, to discourage its misuse.

To curb the menace of a growing cobra population in Delhi during colonial rule in India, the British announced a monetary reward for cobras caught and brought to the authorities. This gave birth to a new profession—breeding cobras! People bred cobras so they could be brought to the authorities. This did nothing to reduce the infestation by cobras in the city. What's more, when the authorities found this out and withdrew the reward, the cobra breeders set the newly bred snakes free.[11]

Another common example of unintended consequences is when a law is heavily tilted in favour of one stakeholder. Many laws are geared towards protecting the consumer. In doing so, the producer or service provider is disregarded to such an extent that they lose interest in providing the product or service.

For instance, rent control is an often-adopted government mandate to protect tenants from exorbitant rents. A maximum ceiling on rent disallows landlords from charging high rents. This is to ensure that a large population has access to accommodation at affordable rates. The intentions were noble, no doubt. But in the 1990s, Maharashtra's rent regulations ended up reducing the per unit rent from ₹1200 in 1940 to ₹12.12 in real terms.[12] It was economically untenable for landlords to maintain their properties, and this resulted in the rapid deterioration of buildings.

As an unforeseen consequence, many owners withdrew their properties from the rental market. Fewer people bought property that could be rented out. This unavailability of property led to the development of the many slums of Mumbai. The informal slums fetched better rates for the landowners too. Others who did not wish to live in slums were forced to buy properties because rental accommodation had become scarce. This shortage of rental accommodation also led to an increase in congestion in the city, which caused hygiene and sanitation problems.[13]

This phenomenon is not restricted to densely populated, developing countries. Rent control legislations have led to similar consequences across the world. The War Emergency Tenant Protection Act was introduced in New York after World War II, to protect against war-related housing shortages. Like any other policy that introduces price control, this one was counterproductive too. Housing shortages were created because of legislation that was made to address the very issue. Landlords weren't able to make money from their properties because they weren't able to meet rising expenses, such as fuel, refinancing and repair costs.[14] A paper on the impact of rent control in San Francisco mentions that the landlords who came under the legislation reduced rental housing supply by 15 per cent. This caused a hike of about 5 per cent in rents across the city.[15]

So, for all the good intent behind the government's attempt to provide relief to tenants, in reality tenants suffered a greater economic burden.

These examples highlight the fact that in designing incentives, policymakers have to be chess players. They must be able to anticipate the behaviour of self-interested stakeholders. For one, initial data analysis may show certain patterns that must be addressed by policy. But when a policy is designed to address those patterns, people re-optimize their activities, and the patterns change. And the cycle continues. Therefore, historical data to make policy changes has limited utility.

Secondly, incentives are also linked to the 'public-choice' theory. The point is that politicians and bureaucrats are not benevolent; they are self-interested actors. They too respond to incentives. Policymakers have to keep this dynamic in mind when framing incentives.

The reality is that a policy will invariably have a cascading effect on many aspects of society. It is a constant challenge to guess how stakeholders will react to a certain change in policy. Sometimes, irrespective of incentives or disincentives, just by themselves policy interventions have unintended consequences.

All these examples point towards minimizing curbs on free market forces to avoid unintended problems, especially as far as economic policies are concerned. Every time we interfere in the workings of a free market, we have to be mindful of the adverse consequences. In this seemingly unending balancing act, it is important to deliberate over situations that truly call for government intrusion.

Countries have faced repercussions whenever they have tried to meddle with free market forces. This has been seen when nations try to peg their currency to a predetermined range of rates. This is to avoid fluctuating exchange rates. So, instead of allowing the nation's currency to respond and adjust to the market, the government intervenes by buying or selling their currency to maintain the said fixed exchange rate. This is what Great Britain saw in 1990.[16] While within its boundaries, the peg system worked, but when hit by global recession in 1992, the British economy couldn't hold up. The system was one of the causes for the drastic rise in unemployment in Britain.

Unintended consequences come in many forms. The challenge is that actions, reactions, plays and interplays are simultaneous, many of which work against each other. Our facts and analytical models are incomplete. We know less than we think we know. Hence we make errors. We suffer from confirmation bias and lose objectivity; we tend to look for facts that support our positions. Also, some policies work in the short term, but create undesirable impacts in the long term.

Further, the ideal technocratic plan can never be implemented in the real world. Political considerations win. Our frail management systems result in an intervention which diverges substantially from what was originally intended.

In line with holding a broad outlook towards incentives and their unintended consequences in general, a holistic look at policies is imperative. Most laws are conceived with a rather defined and restricted mindset. By default, we are wired to consider the impact of our actions in a rather narrow fashion. Due to functional reasons, limitations of our mind and stringent turf-line specializations, it is easier to look at one sector at a time. This is a 'partial equilibrium' thought process. Real-world economics, however, works on the basis of 'general equilibrium'—all stakeholders interacting on an economy-wide scale.

Governments ought to look at the nation as one whole, not only in terms of its geography but also in terms of the far-reaching implications of a law meant for one section of the society when used or misused by another section. Policies, therefore, need an all-encompassing reach. Almost no policy works in isolation. Implementable, efficient regulation will have to begin and end with a bird's-eye view of its impact.

Prioritization—not always a chicken-and-egg problem

When we speak of many policies interacting with each other, we also need to consider which one takes priority. Is there a logical order in which policies should be approached? The prioritization of policies has three dimensions—economic considerations, political economy considerations, and sequencing in the construction of state capacity.

The guiding rule of thumb is that interference with free market forces should be kept to a minimum. For instance, in the case of trade reforms, managing exchange rates and protecting local producers are both policy interventions. How do we pick one over the other? A floating exchange rate should be encouraged before protecting local producers and traders because it is more in line with a free market economy.

Similarly, policymakers should consider subsidies against trade restrictions. In a free economy, international trade should be free-flowing too. However, most nations try to protect domestic producers. Usually this is done in two ways, either by providing support to domestic production through subsidies or by protecting domestic producers through restrictive foreign trade policy. Our contention is that it is better for the principles of free economy to prevail by encouraging foreign trade. In this case, if domestic companies have to be subsidized temporarily, so be it.

Another guiding principle for prioritizing policies is that of least coercion. When two alternative tools have similar outcomes, a good policy would go for the one that uses the least coercion. Use of force is always problematic and very often expensive. Economic reasoning helps us understand the root cause of market failure. Using minimum force by focusing the intervention at the source of the market failure helps in its enforcement and implementation. Sometimes, this principle of 'least coercion' could be at cross purposes with our fundamental principle of addressing the 'root cause'.

Consider the problem of antibiotic resistance. The market failure in this case is that the misuse of antibiotics by some people increases healthcare costs for everyone in the form of increase in health insurance premiums or increase in the price of the medicine itself. The public at large could be denied swift and rapid solutions for simple illnesses because of anticipated misuse. The state could intervene by subsidizing the cost of medicine for certain people who cannot afford it. The other option is to go to the root cause—the abuse of antibiotics. In this case, a subsidy doesn't meet the purpose. Only in cases where going to the root cause is inefficient would focusing on 'consequence' be used—as a second-best option.

Political economy is another valuable source of insight for prioritization of policies. In a given situation, the established incumbent has little incentive to support policy change. Policy actions that open up the economy are a good first step because they reshape the incentives of the local elite in favour of taking on the domestic barriers to high productivity.

The third dimension of sequencing lies in the construction of state capacity. Our first objective should be to establish easy objectives for state capacity and fully succeed in building this capacity. Only after this is done should we tackle problems that are more complex. As an example, it is better to first build a single-rate GST with a low GST rate, and achieve full mastery over this, and only then consider more complex possibilities, such as high or multiple rates.

If a policy addresses the root cause, incentivizes appropriately and takes a holistic approach to policymaking, it will necessarily promote competition, bringing more value to society in its wake.

Creative destruction

Competition pushes firms to cut costs, to innovate and to deliver the best bargain to customers. Companies constantly try to adapt to changing consumer needs and to the potential of technology. Obviously, some companies will falter and go out of business. Traditionally, to avoid mass failure, we look at bailouts as a policy intervention. We need to reconsider this approach.

In the truest economic sense, failure of a company frees up labour and capital that can be used in more productive companies. Naturally, when some firms go out of business, it is hardly a reason to celebrate. However, the key is that the birth and death of firms is healthy and desirable. Termed as 'creative destruction', a well-functioning bankruptcy process needs to be in place for the transition to be palatable to all. Bankruptcy at the level of firms or individuals is intertwined with business cycles. In good times, many firms do well, whether they are capable or not. Recessions, however, bring out the true mettle of companies, weeding out the ones which cannot survive. This is a cleansing process. Similarly, firms that start operations during the trough of a business cycle are usually more capable. Both firm creation and firm destruction are required for a sound ecosystem of companies.

Therefore, good policy requires a progressive outlook that supports entry of newcomers and competition. By default, politics favours the incumbent and leads us to stagnation, because one industry after another gets locked up by a few powerful incumbents. The power of the state ought to open these closed systems, especially those of public-sector units (PSU). In India, privatization of PSUs like Air India, the national airline company, or SAIL, the steel consortium, is necessary to promote competition. Public-sector players have deep pockets and soft budget constraints, and this distorts competition and leads to inefficient allocation of national resources.

This invariably leads to taking sides—there are parties which gain more than others. Incorporating the all-important, social cost-benefit analysis within the policy itself is a good guiding principle. Costs are not just monetary in nature. Their first element consists of the direct costs borne by the government. The second element is not necessarily measurable. Policies cause inconvenience to citizens and are an intrusion into their lives. Against this, we have the claimed benefits. Policy has to ensure that the benefits to society outweigh the costs.

In the end, was policy effective?

A formal, regulatory-impact analysis in terms of social cost-benefit analysis for every legal instrument is a healthy practice. This is of particular importance when the power to write regulations is given to unelected officials. This analysis has to bear in mind that the calculations for such analyses are notoriously vulnerable to changes in assumptions.

Even so, there are strong reasons for such an analysis. First, the very act of conducting the analysis forces the decision makers to improve their understanding of the problems. The release of documents showing the cost-benefit analysis of measures taken helps improve the policy process as the assumptions will be critiqued. Second, with all its imprecision, a cost-benefit analysis can block some egregiously wrong initiatives. While cost-benefit analysis does not guarantee good outcomes, blocking blunders would be a huge contribution in itself.

Any rule that is implemented will require a post facto analysis too, a 'sunset clause', so to speak. This calls for a review of policies after a predetermined period. Again, this has to be provided for in the policy itself. Every law or regulation should state its objectives at the outset. After a certain period has elapsed, it should be possible to empirically examine whether these objectives were met. This empowers the authorities to strike down interventions that did not deliver on their objectives. Backing out from failed interventions releases much-needed resources. This also forces policymakers to articulate policy objectives with better clarity. Another reason to keep an eye on the impact of policies is to keep interest groups in check, tying in with the 'public-choice' principle. A periodic review of policies would also ensure that lobbying by powerful and wealthy persons doesn't take away the very essence of a policy.

Some policies might have a delayed and/or long-lasting impact rather than an immediate one—this ought to be taken into account in such an analysis. For instance, a law that legalizes abortion might see a decrease in crime rate only years later and thus should not be judged based on two-year, or even five-year changes in crime rates. The states in the US that allowed abortion saw a decline in crime rate eighteen years after the law was passed. To further strengthen this hypothesis, a study found that the five states that made abortions legal in 1970 saw the declines earlier than the ones that passed the law in 1973.[17] Therefore, some laws will require even more patience on the part of the authorities and society to allow them time to come to fruition.

It is evident that cost-benefit analysis, post facto analysis, a system of checks and balances—all require the discipline of recording numbers on the go. So far, the success of policies has not been measurable because of lack of quality information. For a good policy to encompass all the features we have described so far, data collection will have to be incorporated in the policy itself.

What will we analyse if there is no data?

Our ability to undertake rational analysis and post-mortems of policy initiatives is heavily dependent on availability of information. Consider the problem of air quality in India. How bad is air pollution in the country? What is the root cause? What are the interventions that can make a difference? When interventions were undertaken in the past (e.g. shifting taxis to CNG), did they deliver useful results? Making progress on these questions requires fine-grain data on air quality from thousands of locations in India. At present this data does not exist. Our own experience while conducting research for this book led to dead ends every once in a while owing to lack of data. For instance, Indian employability data was elusive. Let alone research for a book, how will we tackle employment concerns through policies if we do not have the necessary data? We therefore need to establish sound public data sources before we can consider using them.

Fortunately, in other arenas India is geared towards being data-rich. The success of the Aadhaar system to distribute subsidies is just a starting point. Karnataka's Bhoomi programme—an initiative to digitize all land records in the state—had technology at its heart, but this technology was used for policy, enabled by government implementation. The policy goals for developing and implementing Bhoomi were clear—get the land record data in order. The government made administrative support available at all levels. A government officer championed the project and saw it through to completion. Without these ingredients, Bhoomi would not have succeeded.[18]

In order to have sound policies in place, we need sound, contextual data. Very often, in the case of large populations, the world has changed before the collected data can be used. After all, collecting usable, quality data takes time. For example, it is impossible to get any estimate of the magnitude and type of skill gaps that need to be addressed by policy. Data poverty is particularly acute when it comes to policymaking at the state or local levels. It might be well worth the cause to include independent think tanks and private companies in conducting the necessary research.

While all the factors considered thus far are necessary constituents of good policies, there is scope for making policies even better. Further steps can be taken to smoothen and improve the process of policymaking and policy acceptance. There are well-known roadblocks to good policymaking. These hindrances come from both the public at large—who, whether incentivized or disincentivized, try to game the system by taking advantage of the loopholes—and from the people placed in authority who misuse their power. The situation worsens when vested interests collude to form the business-bureaucrat-government nexus that is not in the interest of the end consumer.

One of the reasons is that transparency in policymaking has been rather elusive. However, when policies are formulated and implemented in a transparent manner, they have a much greater chance of acceptance and achieve better outcomes. A prominent example is the potentially contentious policy issue of sharing of taxes amongst states in a federal system like India. Revenue sharing between the

Centre and states, as well as amongst the states, has been accepted by both the Centre and states, precisely because these fiscal transfers were formulaic and were arrived at on a fair and transparent basis.

One way to at least begin to get over this complexity is to communicate better. Human beings do not like unpleasant surprises. Hence, if we do not want policies to shock citizens, which might lead to policy reversal, we must prepare them by consulting the maximum number of stakeholders and by explaining to them the pros and cons of a policy. When prices of petroleum products increased sharply in 1997, the rise went through smoothly because the ground was prepared for over a year through debate and discussion across different forums.

That public policy is an important lever to support desirable transformations is evident. Its interplay with the other levers is of equal importance too.

Policy, the economic catalyst

As we have seen to some extent in this chapter and will soon see in much more detail in our discussion on the fourth lever of the STEP framework, 'Economic Model', policy plays a pivotal role in managing costs and increasing demand for a product or service. Therefore, the 'Economic Model' lever can receive catalytic support from timely policy interventions.

We would like to repeat that policy intervention is an important instrument to implement solutions to any major problem. It is a blunt and strong instrument. However, the tendency to use it too quickly and without too much thought leads to many unforeseen problems that become difficult to control. Therefore, this instrument deserves a great deal of forethought and deep study before it is used even if it makes economic sense at first glance.

Policy: In a constant race with technology[19]

By definition, innovative technologies are new. Therefore their impact is hardly known before they percolate deep into the society. On the other hand, policies, by definition, are reactionary in nature. Therefore, technology always outstrips policy.

The concept is hardly novel. The benefit of personal cars brought unanticipated deaths by accidents. Through traffic rules, policy attempts to contain this hazard. High crop yields through the use of pesticides led to a deteriorating environment, which has led to bans on harmful pesticides.

In today's times, connections with family and friends brought about by social media has led to the inadvertent spread of fake news. Little did we realize that WhatsApp and Twitter could create massive social descension. As is appropriate, the world has now woken up to this danger. Many governments are rushing to introduce apt policies to protect their citizens.

However, with the exponentially multiplying influence and growth of technology into the very fabric of society, policymakers have to be ever more vigilant. Relatively nascent technologies will inevitably play dramatic roles in the future. Though introduced with good intent, they are likely to have undesired side-effects too. Wearables and implantables, the Internet of things, connected homes and smart cities, will change the way we live, how long we live, the quality of our long lives, and so on. But they will also put another layer of our privacy out of our control. These are in-the-face examples of the assault on privacy and security. A rather subtler example is that of free storage of digital data for one and all. Who can guarantee that private companies will not survey stored emails, photos, and the like?

AI and the Internet of things, along with robotics, will make unemployment the most gruesome problem of our times. Who will balance the benefits they offer through cost reduction, increase in productivity, etc., against the jobs they take with them?

Moreover, the supercomputer in our palms, which is likely to use all of the above technologies, is the biggest boon we know. But who is working to keep them from being used to manipulate societies—à la fake news created to influence people's political and social thought processes?

Clearly, public policy has a role to play in keeping technology aligned with social good. Although, ideally, policy should be ahead of technology, the truth is that it never is. It is, however, important that the lag between a technology's advent and relevant protective policies is kept to a minimum to keep the undesirable byproducts of technology at bay.

Learning from mankind's experiences in the centuries gone by, policies should at least attempt to be up-to-speed with technology and predict what can go wrong, to the extent possible.

Yes, policy becomes a game between politics and society

Most examples in this discussion on policy have highlighted this issue—policies get formulated in the realities of political economy. Public policy interventions always have winners and losers; they will have consequences for the distribution of income and wealth, and these conflicts will be played out through democratic politics. There is a role here for philosophy, politics, intuition and experience, over and beyond sharp economic analysis.

In any economy, change means changing the current power equations. In any environment, the incumbents who tend to dictate policies have greater power than the rest. To bring in policies that rebel against their interests entails political costs, which most political decision makers are unwilling to incur.

This is what links the 'Policy' lever to the next STEP lever, 'Social Engagement'. Getting socially desirable policies implemented calls for enormous social pressure. This becomes even more pertinent as we gear ourselves to solve the imposing problems of our times—the 3Es. Such pressure can only be generated through intense social engagement. Active citizen engagement can pressurize governments to bring about desirable regulations. The next chapter elaborates on the importance of people participation, when used in conjunction with other levers.

SEVEN

Lever 3 of 4
Social Engagement—The Power of People

Nelson Mandela would not have been allowed to swim in certain sections of South African beaches because of the colour of his skin, let alone vote in elections—as recently as 1994. That is just twenty-four years ago. Consistent resistance by large sections of the population across the globe led to withdrawal of the repressive apartheid policies in South Africa.

Women across the world gradually began getting voting rights in the early 1900s, with countries such as Switzerland giving suffrage to women as late as 1971. None of this would have come about were it not for the suffrage movement across the globe.

Back home, while gender and race weren't an issue of contention as far as voting rights were concerned, the caste system was a huge social evil that had to be fought. It is social movements across the board that got people from the so-called lower castes equal opportunity in education and employment.

Before the term 'eco-friendly' came into vogue forty-five years ago, some Indian villagers, mainly women, embraced trees to keep them from being chopped down. The 'Chipko' movement originated in a small village in north India and spread across the world—before the Internet age. It saved many a tree and inspired environment-friendly laws in many nations.

And in more recent times, the #MeToo movement resulted in hundreds of thousands of women and men revealing their traumatic experience of sexual harassment within a span of a few weeks. A movement which led to many perpetrators of sexual crime being fired from positions of power and authority.

The reality is that any established structure tends to benefit some people more than others, based on their power, wealth or such other deemed superiority. As elaborated in the previous chapter, the benefiting group has a vested interest in maintaining the status quo and in resisting change. It is quite common to see these benefiting groups act against the interests of clean energy, environment-friendly production and dignified, gainful employment for human beings. Given this situation, changes to the established structure can happen only when they are backed by a huge social force. This is where 'social engagement' comes in as our third lever for change—where the society, people like you and us, are actively engaged in making change happen.

Very often, there is an economic benefit to be had by a larger section of the society in engaging with a transformational solution. That is when this larger section easily takes to new solutions. WhatsApp, for instance, could achieve scale because the cost of communication reduced substantially for the user. This benefit was multiplied many times over by WhatsApp's ease of use and the quality of communication it enabled. Therefore, it is easy to see why such a change would be adopted by the people at large.

However, some aspects of solutions related to energy, the environment and employment are such that not all people can easily perceive or appreciate the direct benefits. So, there are two things at play—not enough people are directly better off because of these changes, and established benefiters of damaging activities lobby to maintain the current state of affairs. This is exactly why social engagement is even more crucial for successful transformational changes.

To understand how to attract wide participation in any movement for change, we would like to consider some major changes that have been successfully effected through social engagement. An analysis of such social movements will help us identify key elements of success, which we can replicate or tweak to make our own efforts fruitful.

What is a successful movement?

Success in the context of social movements is a little fuzzy. The success of a technological solution can be binary—it has succeeded if it has reached a certain number of users or is economically self-sustainable. Economic models or policy changes too can be measured using precise parameters for success and failure. In these areas, the extent of success or failure could be different for each stakeholder, but it is clearly definable. Assessment of social movements, though, is relatively analogue. To answer the question, 'Is this social engagement successful?', one must first define a successful social engagement undertaking.

We define 'success' as a sustainable, long-term change. Unless the change is self-perpetuating and permanent, let us not announce victory.

In this sense, Gandhiji's freedom movement achieved success. However, the other Indian movements, such as the one led by Gandhian socialist Jayaprakash Narayan or the more recent anti-corruption movement led by Anna Hazare, cannot be termed as successes.

Consider Gandhiji's 'Quit India' movement. What was the aim? To make the British leave India. Did the British quit India? Yes. Are they ever going to come back to India to rule the country? No. This, to us, is success. It brought about a sustained, long-term change, meeting its clear, predefined goals. On the other hand, the movements by Jayaprakash Narayan and Anna Hazare, which set out to rid society of corruption, did not result in a corruption-free society and cannot be called successful.

However, we don't cast these last two examples as 'failures' either. Far from it. 'Not successful' certainly does not translate to 'failed'. They have added value because they brought fragmented groups of people together. The movements gave marginalized people, wronged people a voice. They made them believe that change is possible, even if it is in the future. They moved the needle in public discourse and brought the issue to the mass media. They created a social conscience. They were a step in the right direction in the journey of social rejuvenation. They were certainly useful and critical, but we would not call them 'successful'.

Now we can draw lessons from both successful and valuable-but-not-successful social movements. The dos and don'ts for the changes we seek through social engagement will depend on the distinction that emerges from studying the full spectrum of some movements. Towards this end, we take a look at some of them.

What makes for a successful revolution?

The key features of the Indian Independence movement were: a high degree of need for change felt by a large number of people; a leadership with a strong belief in change and staunchly committed to their demand for change; and a clearly identified purpose—independence from British rule. And there were iterative, structured efforts towards achieving this goal. As discussed earlier, this is a successful movement because it led to a long-term change that is not going to be retracted.

Another example of a successful movement is Chloe Maxmin's 'Divest Harvard' campaign. Chloe has been a climate activist since she was twelve. As a student at Harvard University, she started a campaign against the university's endowment funds investing in fossil-fuel companies. Her stand was on moralistic grounds— how can their school support industries that degraded the environment? This movement gained momentum and spread to form an empowering network of 70,000 participants over two years.[1] In the fall of 2012, Harvard students passed a referendum demanding that the university divest its holdings worth $31 billion in the fossil-fuel industry.[2]

By 2014, oil prices dropped, and divesting from traditional energy companies started making economic sense too. The State of California too passed a legislation in 2015–16 that required two pension funds to sell their investments in coal companies. The London School of Economics divested some of the endowment funds it had invested in coal and oil companies too.[3] Therefore, the need for change felt by a large number of people, a leadership with strong belief and commitment and a clearly identified purpose are all present in this movement for divestment from fossil fuel companies.

In India there were many good-but-unsuccessful movements—apart from the ones led by Jayaprakash Narayan and Anna Hazare—that led to visible collective action. In the state of Bihar, Vinoba Bhave's land reform campaign of 1951, the Bhoodan movement, aimed at persuading landowners to donate a certain percentage of their land to landless people. The condition was that the recipient could use the small piece of land as their residence or to grow crops, but could not sell it. The objective of this movement was to secure 50 million acres of land for donation. This was a sixth of the total cultivated land at the time. The movement culminated in a law called the Bhoodan Act, creating a central land bank and putting the government in charge of distribution. But just when it appeared that it would succeed, interest in the movement began to wane.[4] By 1957, only 4.5 million acres of land was received in donation. Of this, only 650,000 acres were distributed, to around 200,000 landless farmers, each receiving land in the range of 0.5 acres to 3 acres. This further fragmented ownership of land. In 1999, the state of Bihar dissolved its Bhoodan committee because it wasn't able to distribute even half of the land it had collected in thirty-eight years.[5]

To understand why this happened, we have to go back to the origins of the movement. On a visit to communist areas in Andhra Pradesh, with the intention to spread the message of non-violence, Vinoba Bhave visited a community of 'untouchables'. This community said they would like to own a certain amount of land to thrive through their dire situation. The leader wondered if others in the village could do something for their distraught brethren, since the government was not in a position to help. At this meeting, one of the local landlords offered 100 acres of land. This gradually evolved into the Bhoodan movement.

As it stands today, though, land assigned to the landless is often encroached on by people with clout in the government. In 2011, 2.3 million acres still lay undistributed in the land bank. There are no official records of the land and its allocation. However, some reports suggest that 50 per cent of the land today has been encroached on. In fact, it is reported that this land is being distributed to corporate houses for industrial and housing projects.[6] Thus, this movement cannot be called a successful one.

Similarly, the various road-blockade protests across the globe achieve little. From the protests by women against US President Trump to the protests by Dalits and Marathas in India for job reservations, and to demonstrations in the Middle East (except in Tunisia) against the governments there—protests bring the injustices in the news for a day or two, but don't really lead to any meaningful outcome. Again, undeniably, they create awareness and bring debate into our living rooms. However, no clear parameter comes across as successfully accomplished.

In analysing these examples and a few others, a pattern emerges. A study of this pattern is important to identify the components of a movement that stays sustainable in the long run. We can compare and contrast the successful campaigns with the not-so-successful ones to know what clicks.

Breaking down successful movements

While we go through these basic characteristics of successful movements, we should keep in mind that the cause-and-effect association between the parameters might not always be obvious, despite the correlation. However, the contrasts point to glaring differences between successful and not-successful endeavours along the said parameters. Also, none of these features can work by itself. They have to work in cohesion to create success.

Clarity in thought and execution

To begin with, by definition, the results of a successful campaign have to be sustainable and long-term. We find that campaigns leading to such outcomes had clearly defined, measurable, time-bound goals. We saw this in the Quit India movement; to get the British to leave India was a clear goal. In the case of the two anti-corruption movements, tangible goals weren't clearly defined at the outset.

Similar comparisons have been drawn between the Occupy and Otpor movements.[7] Occupy was a campaign against social and economic inequality, led by a group of young activists in Manhattan. Otpor, on the other hand, was a similar Siberian group that was protesting against the Milošević regime. Occupy didn't achieve much; however, the Otpor movement overthrew the president's government. In fact, the activists from the Otpor movement also trained other rebels in Ukraine, Georgia and even Egypt.

While it might not have been the sole reason, Otpor had a clear objective—that the country be rid of Milošević. However, the goals of the Occupy movement were difficult to identify. All of us have a list of things we don't like about the system we live in. However, that list alone isn't going to make for a successful change. We also need an accompanying list of the changes we want to see. Unless activists have a transparent, lucid goal to work towards, what will our day-to-day activities in the movement look like?

It also makes better sense to break the goal down into smaller, more achievable sub-goals. In the Salt Satyagraha, Mahatma Gandhi chose a small issue which affected a huge population—the salt tax. He contended that a fight for freedom from the salt tax would unite the entire population towards the ultimate goal of complete freedom from British rule. Protesting the salt tax became a primary focus of the Indian independence movement because this small step was necessary to lay the foundation for the bigger fight.

A universally felt pain-point

As a corollary, the defined problem ought to be a problem common to many. Oppression suffered by the common population on account of a tyrannical ruler inevitably results in a revolution. Similarly, a problem that pinches citizens inevitably results in disruptive solutions from the business world. This includes problems that no one was complaining about in the first place. In solutions like Uber and Jio, there was no perceived problem until it was solved. However, once solved there is no going back. Thus, if Uber and Jio were to disappear, commuting problems and unavailability of cheap data would become commonly felt problems, which in turn might lead to social engagement campaigns.

This leads us to the question—how many people does it take to make a problem 'common'? It is impossible to predict when a revolt will begin and, more importantly, when it will gain mass momentum. How many users does a product or service need to have to be considered successful? How many protestors make for a successful social movement? Of course, the answer is, there is no definite number.

Surely, the success of social movements is clearly a matter of scale. When it is a technological or economic model, this scale is relatively easy to define. For instance, Jio is willing to incur a loss for a certain period of time until it achieves a certain scale. Scale, in this case, is a matter of funding. In other instances, even without one big investor, the end consumer clearly sees a direct benefit. The move away from taking a cab instead of driving your own car is such an example. The automobile industry is witnessing a disruption through social engagement—there is a revolutionary change in how people are beginning to think about commuting. The concept is gaining popularity because users see value in hailing a cab over owning one. Sure, some of such moves might fail even though they achieved scale initially. But the question is, when there is no organizational funding and there is no direct benefit to the users, how does one arrive at the specific number for one's own social engagement campaign? What is the magic number?

Here, we would like to borrow from a concept in science—critical mass.[8] This is defined as a tipping point beyond which a technology or process can sustain by itself. This phenomenon is observed in a wide variety of fields such as nuclear physics, medicine, and even in social movements. A disease is said to have become an epidemic, for instance, when it has affected more than a normally expected number of people. A meme is said to have gone viral when it has reached so many people that the growth of its reach is exponential.

Along similar lines, a technology can be said to have achieved critical mass when not owning or knowing that technology becomes a hindrance or an inconvenience for normal citizens in their community. In such a case, early adapters convince others in their influence circle to try the new technology, forming a positive feedback loop. The rise of the Internet, the spread of the mobile phone and the ubiquity of WhatsApp are all cases in point.

One can generalize from this understanding to say that critical mass is when the reach of a particular concept extends from the expected few to the unexpected many— from early adapters to sceptics. There is a huge chasm between the two that needs to be filled before we can see successful change. Understanding the peculiarities of the change we want to see and identifying this chasm often guides us about ways in which to engage with stakeholders to arrive at a desired change. This understanding is the catalyst which can change a small protest march into a successful social engagement. Of course, change is not linear, and ups and downs are to be expected.

Also, no revolution starts with a million sign-ups. Very often, progress happens step by step, sometimes starting from just one person rustling up support for a cause. And after gaining some momentum, even the naysayers begin to take notice.

While no concrete number can be assigned to 'critical mass', according to Boleslaw Szymanski, director of a research project at Rensselaer Polytechnic Institute, it takes only 10 per cent of the target population to form the critical mass that can bring about sustainable change. The research showed that once a concept gains an unchangeable interest from more than 10 per cent of the target group, it spreads like wildfire.[9]

No large 'loser' group

Just as indispensable as critical mass of supporters or 'winners' is for a movement, the consideration that there are no large numbers of 'losers' is imperative too. Any movement that may result in a large number of losers is bound to lose steam in a short time. In that sense, it is essential for a movement to bring success to all or at least to a vast majority and to keep losers to a minimum. Successful social movements have never created a large 'loser' base.

For example, in our drive towards organic farming, there is likely to be a large loser base—conventional farmers. If we were to design a social engagement programme to make organic farming popular for the environmental advantages we think it brings, there will be a large number of traditional farmers who will lose their livelihood. Most traditional farmers are unlikely to have the tools, funds, know-how, etc., needed to adapt to organic farming. Organic farming as a movement will face significant resistance because we are creating a large base of losers. In India's freedom movement too, Mahatma Gandhi did not have 100 per cent support. There were people who did not want freedom from the British. However, since the losers were fewer than the total number of 'winners', on account of the promise of freedom for the country, the movement saw success.

Keeping a movement from negatively impacting any large group of people is a call on the conscience too. It can be thought of as a core value of the movement. Similarly, successful social engagement ventures have shared values at stake. It is these basic principles that guide the movement towards its predefined goal. We can think of this as a shared conscience. Yet again, there is a learning from the contrast between the Occupy and Otpor movements. Otpor formed well-defined training systems that inculcated the core values in new participants. Well-trained, inspired, determined participants themselves go a long way to sustain a successful change. From Civil Rights protestors in the US to Satyagrahis in India, the participants were known to maintain composure while facing police. All of these were missing in the Occupy movement.[10] The shared value of not giving in to pressure by the authorities was common to the successful social engagement movements.

Converting naysayers

Another common feature seen in successful movements is that they managed to convince the non-believers about their cause. For this to happen, there is a prerequisite though. The movement itself has to be open to constructive debate. It has to be accepting of contrarian views.[11, 12] It is convenient and easy to assume that there is no other opinion rather than to allow a healthy discussion. But a campaign can be successful only if the people who drive it are open-minded. We have to recognize disagreement as our opportunity to overcome resistance.

Here again, a sub-pattern emerges. Successful movements begin with a small group of allies, then move on to embrace people who are most likely to be receptive to their point of view, gradually increasing their circle of influence to cover the neutral or even parties opposing the cause.

For instance, Martin Luther King's 'I Have a Dream' speech was not just referring to the problems of African Americans. When listeners, irrespective of race, saw value in his argument for the nation as a whole, the movement gathered momentum beyond just the limited community.[13] It was indeed a non-African-American, a person who did not stand to benefit directly or positively from the movement, who finally signed the Civil Rights Act. Today this kind of campaigning might not be as structured as the one led by King, but we do see feminist movements with male participants and LGBTQ movements with support from people of all sexual orientations.

Successful movements identify and garner support from not just individuals or groups, but also from other cogs in the wheel—the other organizations in the ecosystem—to bring about ultimate change. These other organizations would be enablers, such as authorities in law and administration, influential journalists in the media and government agencies. Their support means people within these institutions see value in the desired change. In the Otpor movement, protestors were trained to not provoke police officers. This made the police officers appreciate the core value the protestors were fighting for. When faced with the situation of having to shoot the protestors, the police chose not to.[14] This is certainly a bigger success than blocking a road, picketing or violently protesting against the police, which only tend to aggravate the institutions in power.

Simple leaders, high thinkers—who pass the values on

Among the features of successful movements, one theme trumps them all. The one name, the visionary, the person whose name makes it happen—the leader. Most successful movements have a leader at its helm. Very rarely does diffused leadership do the job. While having a leader is not a defining feature of a successful movement, the characteristics of its leader certainly are. Mahatma Gandhi, Martin Luther King Jr, Nelson Mandela—their names inspired trust. Even the simplest study of their stories highlights their well-rounded yet simple personalities. They had a strong ethical foundation and were totally committed to their cause. They led frugal lifestyles and were attuned to the needs of the community. They were excellent communicators and were tolerant and open to new ideas. Most importantly, they were not arrogant about their ideology. And yet, none of their successful movements lost momentum after they passed away. Despite their strong leadership, their movements were person-independent.

The monumental changes that the problems of our times need, ask for exceptional leadership. However, this doesn't mean we wait for people with the required skills to become leaders. Instead, a successful movement should groom enabling leaders. The average baseline of leadership skills will have to be pushed up through training. Conversely, social movements are known to give birth to leaders too.

In today's times the leadership also has to be well acquainted and updated with the cutting-edge technology that relates to the movement. For instance, India's Bharatiya Agro Industries Foundation (BAIF) which was established in 1946 by the Gandhian, Manibhai Desai, is led by a group of professional social workers who draw from the latest technologies in the world to breed cows. Dr Abhay and Rani Bang's work in the interiors of Maharashtra involves the use of the latest health practices for the betterment of the communities they are involved with.

Having said that, a strong, well-intentioned leader doesn't necessarily guarantee success. The requirements of successful transformations through social engagement sound insurmountable and call for a lot of grit. However, there are changes around us that are making decentralized social engagement movements possible. Technologies that enable communications have changed with the changing times and have made the communication end of social movements far easier. It is an enormous relief for mankind today that social media has made it so easy to communicate, to lead, and to generate critical mass.

Engaging society has never been easier

Social engagement today is truly far easier than it ever was. This is owing to three resources that we seem to have more of now than ever before—technology, time and money. The reach of technology is wider today, people have more time, and there is more money flowing into social movements.

The hashtag world

In the third quarter of 2017, Facebook had 2.07 billion monthly active users.[15] That is well over a quarter of the world's population. WhatsApp's 1.3 billion[16] and Twitter's 330 million[17] sound minuscule in comparison, and yet they constitute 17 per cent and 4 per cent of world population, respectively. Even accounting for fake and duplicate business accounts, these are huge numbers. In addition, many WhatsApp users wouldn't be actively engaged on Facebook or on Twitter, and vice versa. Yet we do see content move from one platform to another, making their combined reach rather mind-boggling. And we haven't even spoken about other popular platforms. This reach has led to some successful social movements.

2014 saw people from across the world give themselves a bath with bucketfuls of ice water. Celebrities, politicians and athletes posted videos of themselves doing this. In just two-and-a-half months, 1.2 million such videos were posted on Facebook, and the 'Ice Bucket Challenge' was mentioned 2.2 million times on Twitter in just two weeks.[18] Why were so many people participating in such an absurd act? They were creating awareness about a little-known but prevalent disease, Amyotrophic Lateral Sclerosis (ALS). Could millions of people pouring ice-cold water on themselves really create awareness? Well, the English Wikipedia page on ALS, which used to fetch an average of over 160,000 views per month, saw views rising to almost 3 million in August 2014. Similar increases were seen on the Spanish and German Wikipedia pages too.[19] After the Ice Bucket Challenge, the ALS Association received almost $42 million in donations from more than 739,000 new donors in the first three weeks of August 2014. By the end of the month they had collected $100 million.[20]

2017's #MeToo movement is an example of how easy and quick it is to reach out to huge populations. Actress Alyssa Milano asked people to reply to a tweet of hers with the phrase 'me too' if they had been victims of sexual assault. The word spread, and the phrase converted to a hashtag that crossed over to Facebook. The hashtag reached eighty-five countries and was used in 1.7 million tweets.[21] It was #balancetonporc in France, #YoTambien in Spain, #وأنا_كمان and #وانا_ايضا in Arab countries. Facebook reported that 4.7 million people around the world used the tag in over 12 million posts, comments and reactions—in twenty-four hours![22] And yes, men got involved on the right side of the argument too. While this campaign might be shrugged off as armchair activism, the issue did take its toll on the assaulters. Well-regarded popular celebrities have been fired from their jobs. Within two months, ninety-eight sexual offenders, including one woman, faced action for alleged sexual assault.[23] The #MeToo movement received the TIME 'Person of the Year' award.[24] Without a leader, and without a clearly defined objective, the movement achieved unimaginable momentum and reasonable impact. What would social media be able to achieve if the efforts to engage people are better directed?

A lesser-known fact is that there was another 'Me Too' movement that began in 1997 by an African-American woman, Tarana Burke. Why did we not hear of it? It can be argued that it lacked the celebrity backup that MeToo 2017 had. But it is also because social media didn't exist then.[25]

At this point, we have to acknowledge the downside of social media too. The enormous amounts of data collected are going to be put to use, and not necessarily to good use. Everything we do online—purchases, holiday bookings, searches—leaves digital traces. We can be physically tracked even when we think we are offline, even when our location is turned off, through our mobile phone service's cell tower information.

So, while one social campaign on Tinder focused on getting more people to vote, there were other companies that analysed data from Facebook 'likes' to customize advertising for political campaigns, such as for Brexit or for the presidential elections in the US.[26]

Certainly, there is cause for worry.

A PhD student of psychometry at Cambridge University launched a survey-based Facebook app which could tell the user's personality type. These results were compared to the user's Facebook likes, shares and posts. The database was big enough to form correlations between personality type and the kind of things a user shared or liked on Facebook. There was a reverse correlation too; online likes and shares pointed towards the user's personality type. Soon enough, it took all of sixty-eight Facebook likes for the self-learning algorithm to predict demographic and personality aspects such as skin colour, religion, sexual orientation, intelligence, and cigarette, alcohol and drug use with more than 85 per cent accuracy!

Yes, a social media user's political affiliation can be guessed with considerable accuracy too. So an introvert (from a psychology survey), angry (Facebook's 'angry' option) person could be correlated to an undecided Democrat. An analytics company, Strategic Communication Laboratories, specializes in using this data to influence elections. When this information is combined with disjointed data, such as the kind of land or car you own, or your club and church memberships, very fine, micro-targeting becomes possible. So a highly customized message can be sent to each voter at a far lower cost than mass advertising.

So far, we don't see the problem—targeted marketing has its advantages. The advertisers get more bang for their buck. Targeted advertising fetches 63 per cent more clicks and more conversion to sales than blanket advertising. The users don't have to wade through lots of information and, instead, see more products that they need or like. Sounds like a win-win situation. But very soon, such targeting becomes nasty. A user who is an undecided Democrat now sees specific posts about the Democrat candidate based on the user's skin colour or religion. This post could be true or fake, but if the opinion it expresses is against the voter's beliefs, then this voter might abstain from voting, or might even vote Republican.

This was a known aspect but was not talked about much until recently when it came to the fore when a whistle-blower leaked the details.[27] Mark Zuckerberg, Facebook CEO, is being held accountable. So, while we can say that one person is sometimes enough for social good to come about, we do not know how many technology companies have taken advantage of the trusting public at large.

We are, however, in a stage of transition. Companies like Facebook and Twitter realize the potential damage and are working on it. For instance, they are being more responsible in trying to filter out fake news from real news. This is another iteration in correcting the side effects of our activities.

Gamification

Like hashtags, video gaming, commonly thought of as a menace, is being put to good use too. There is a huge opportunity to create concrete impact by turning awareness and educational processes into games—virtual or augmented reality games that create awareness and prompt positive action. From disease prevention to waste segregation, gamification can be used to gather and spread information.

University of Washington's Centre for Game Science, along with their biochemistry department, created an online puzzle related to protein-folding. The objective was to find a protein structure that fit the researchers' criteria to solve an imposing problem related to AIDS. It took only ten days of fierce competition between 240,000 people from all over the world to find a solution.

Opower, a company that works to engage customers in energy-efficiency solutions, gives users a comparison of their energy usage data with their neighbours' and the community's. They also provide milestones that users can aim for. As a result, participants are consuming, on an average, 2 per cent less energy than they earlier did. In 2012, this led to savings of over 1 terawatt of energy globally, translating to $120 million in utility bill savings, and decreasing pollution equivalent to what 100,000 cars would produce. The company went on to be acquired by Oracle.

And these are examples from just one list of top ten social gamification ventures.[28] There is a lot more work that can be done by individuals and businesses. It is a matter of applying our creative juices to use gamification to solve individual problems. Fortunately, we as a global population now have the time to make these things happen too.

Longer lives, more leisure (to engage in social movements)

We might not find it true on a day-to-day basis, but it is so—we have more time on our hands than before. For one, functional lives are longer today. In the 1960s, India's life expectancy was around forty-one. In 2015, it was over sixty-eight.[29] Similar increases in life expectancy have been recorded across the world. So, in the 1960s, many people didn't live too long after retirement, but today it is common for men and women to live a good ten to fifteen years of vibrant and productive life after retirement. Many senior citizens are choosing to give back to society by engaging in a social movement close to their hearts. Indeed, it is not just years being added to life, but more importantly, life being added to the years.

For the younger population too, working hours have reduced. The five-day workweek is a concept not even a century old. In 1890, an average workweek was about sixty hours. Today a workweek longer than forty-eight hours is considered worth studying and corrected. International Labour Organization reported that only 22 per cent of the total workforce surveyed worked more than forty-eight hours a week.[30]

Moreover, those of us who do work longer hours also spend a lot of our time at work in non-work-related activities such as social media or chatting. Would it be surprising to find out that a huge percentage of the #MeToo posts happened during working hours? Therefore, the younger and more energetic population has the time to get involved in social movements. Not only do they have more time, the part of the younger generation that is getting richer faster also has the willingness to engage in social causes.

The compassionate capitalists[31]

Many of the 80 million millennials—children of baby boomers—will soon own wealth worth $40 trillion as the older generation passes away. And this generation is interested and engaged in transformations that will be better for the planet and the people. This generation seems to believe in its own brand of capitalism; they want economic systems that heal and nurture the planet instead of systems that just extract profit from its degradation. There is indeed growing social pressure on governments to make regulatory changes to the way we use our earth. This attitudinal change is here to stay.

Moreover, some of the biggest foundations in the US have been created by tech entrepreneurs. From Microsoft's ex-CEO, Steve Ballmer, and his wife, Connie Ballmer, to Jeff and MacKenzie Bezos, tech entrepreneurs are generously donating to social engagement endeavours. Given the kind of resources in terms of money, hearts and minds we have at our disposal, truly fundamental changes are possible.

In 2010, Warren Buffett and Bill Gates announced a campaign, the Giving Pledge, to get the billionaires of the world to commit at least half of their wealth to social causes. As of 2017, the campaign has 173 pledgers—aged thirty to ninety, and from twenty-two countries. By 2016, $365 billion was pledged. To put this in perspective, in 2014, donations by all charitable foundations in the US together amounted to $53 billion. The causes range from poverty alleviation, disaster relief, global health and education to medical research. While 'the Pledge' is only a moral contract, it encourages the thought of philanthropy and gives some direction. The pledgers come together once a year to discuss new ideas for maximum impact.[32]

Through the Pledge or otherwise, Mark Zuckerberg and Priscilla Chan have committed 99 per cent of their total wealth ($36 billion, 2017) to charity. With such monetary resources, philanthropy can be bold, take risks and incubate new ideas. With the greatest minds of our world behind these funds, they can be applied to creative solutions.[33]

And it is not just the billionaires, the non-billionaires might not have the money but they have the energy and the will to volunteer for causes they strongly believe in. Some of these causes relate to energy, environment and employment. People do go out of their way to spread awareness about related information. The campaigns for organic, vegetarian food serve as an example for environmental causes. The push for EVs aims to reduce fossil-fuel usage. The movement for local produce is a cause closely associated with the livelihood of local farmers. This is a welcome trend.

As you might have noticed from our discussions on social engagement, public policy and technology, a theme emerges. Whatever positive change we could bring about so far, going forward we will be able to do more, better and faster. The job of spreading awareness about a development or an opinion was left to newspapers earlier, but it can be done much faster today because each of us can do it. People were busy thriving in the short lives they had; today it is possible to live longer, more meaningfully productive lives. This environment is conducive to voluntarism, it is conducive for people young and old, rich and not-so-rich, to engage in causes they believe in.

So this is the best time to make social movements possible. We have the time, money and technology to make it easy. We also see the sprouting of leadership in movements for social change. And we have dire needs in the three problem areas—energy, environment and employment—to keep us engaged. So, we think we have all the ingredients to create successful social movements. It is important to pool them together to achieve success.

Social Engagement and technology: A love–hate relationship

Technology: By the people, for the people

So far, we have considered technological advances as 'external' to society and have examined their acceptability and widespread use through social engagement. Often, we witness innovation that spreads through a different mode of social engagement. This is when ordinary grass-root innovators create technologies that germinate from very local needs and address a smaller community's issues.

Mansukhbhai Prajapati, from Gujarat, India, created Mitticool, a clay refrigerator. In this home-made refrigerator, water from an upper chamber seeps through the side walls and cools the lower chamber, where food can be stored for days together. The first viable version of Mitticool, priced at ₹2000 (~$30), was sold to people from his own village. It became an instant hit. Demand for the clay fridge exceeded his expectations, and he had to scale rapidly. He moved from an artisanal craft to an industrial pottery process. He trained and hired women in his new factory. His product was sold all over India. He was even featured in *Forbes* magazine as being amongst the most influential rural Indian entrepreneurs who had made a big social impact.[34]

Interestingly, Prajapati has impacted all 3Es. Mitticool consumes no electricity and thus does not rely on non-renewable sources of energy. The clay fridge is 100 per cent biodegradable and produces no waste during its lifetime; this is as good as it can get for the environment. And his mass production, industrial pottery process provided meaningful employment to several rural men and women.

We thus have in Prajapati, a trained potter, who studied only up to grade ten, an inventor of the epitome of an innovation that is by the people, for the people. His innovation gained social engagement, first in his village and then in the entire nation.

Prof. Anil Gupta, considered the father of the grass-roots innovation movement in India, has summarized in his book a database of not just one Prajapati but thousands of potential Prajapatis.[35]

We think of such innovations having a 'firefly' effect. It is not just one blazing sun but thousands of fireflies lighting up to create local impact.

When 'social engagement' hinders

The social engagement lever is powerful by itself. In fact, it is so powerful that it is as capable of promoting good causes as it is of throttling them too. For instance, activism against stem cell research, for the perceived problems it can bring along, has stalled it in the US. As mentioned in our discussion on socially sustainable innovation, AI is facing such opposition too. Genetically modified produce and nuclear technology are other technological advancements that face such resistance. It is indeed technology, then, that has to prove itself worthy of acceptance. This is how the EVs of our times are garnering more and more support among the laypeople. This is how the lever of 'social engagement' from the STEP framework intertwines with that of 'technology'.

A force to reckon with

The impact of social engagement grows manifold when it is used with the other levers to address the problems related to the 3Es, and augments the other levers of the STEP framework. For instance, the promise of technology is compounded when the technology is 'owned' by as many people as possible. Information and communication technology wouldn't be as remarkable if it benefited only computer scientists. Its wide accessibility has made stakeholders out of laypersons such as fishermen, farmers and citizens wanting to access land records. Likewise, as we saw in the beginning of this chapter, social engagement pushes for policies that society needs. At the same time, public policy itself can get society engaged to make transformations successful. The war against plastic, for instance, is becoming a policy push that engages even a reluctant citizen into action. Similarly, a society can be engaged more easily and willingly if it makes economic sense to everyone involved.

We will address this next, the last lever of the STEP framework—Economics.

EIGHT

Lever 4 of 4
Economic Model—Doing Well by
Doing Good

Good economic sense underlies virtually all successful solutions. Indeed, even the other three levers of the STEP framework need to make economic sense. Expensive technology cannot in itself be transformational for the general population. At the very basis of public policy lies the need to use limited resources for the greater good of all. Social engagements might not entail direct financial rewards but will work towards adding value to lives. In fact, as a community of economists, scientists and business people we ought to consider getting economic models to answer questions of social responsibility too—a move from CSR 1.0 to CSR 2.0 of sorts. We will come back to this concept in a bit.

The point, though, is that, in some sense, the economic model is the very basis of almost anything and everything we do. It is indeed the basic premise of a free market economy. A good solution need not necessarily solve an economic problem immediately. But it certainly has to be economically sustainable in the long term. When it comes to our three global challenges of energy, environment and employment too, we need to convert every solution into a commercially viable business for it to have impact. The problems are many, with an equal number of armchair solutions. They all fall flat without action. And any actionable solution has to have economic merit.

This economic viability is not one-dimensional. All stakeholders have to see a value proposition in it. No change can sustain itself unless it is economically sustainable for all involved. At the very outset, the product or service has to be priced at levels at which the consumer sees value for money. A consumer will seek a positive answer to 'Is it worth it?'—a cost-benefit analysis of their own. At the same time, the producer of a solution will eventually seek profits so that they can continue the business.

Therefore, the value the producer offers must be such that consumers will voluntarily pay for the product or service; and this payment should be enough for the producer to survive and to prosper. Only when these two sides of the transaction seem fair to the participants will a business sustain in the long run.

Of course, this does not apply to just the main producer and end user; each intermediary step in the process will have a giver and a taker, who both need to see value in the proposition. Each action in the value chain has to make economic sense for all the entities involved, and for a long period of time. An ideal solution would either reduce cost or increase value and would see benefits accruing to all entities along the transactional chain. In our model, this distribution ought to be fair across parties.

In a sense, a sound economic model is the ultimate test of any solution that seeks to address the problems of energy, environment and employment. The three levers we have discussed so far have to ultimately result in the creation of a sustainable economic model. The conditions today are ripe for possible solutions, which were until now economically unviable. This is on account of the interplay between one or more of the three levers of the STEP framework—technology, public policy and social engagement.

Reduce costs or increase value

We believe that conditions are propitious now for cost reduction and increasing value on account of the trends in the three levers. In this chapter we discuss how cost reductions come about and how the value a user sees in a solution rises such that the solutions become economically viable. Before that, though, let us consider a few illustrations.

In the war-ravaged Darfur region of Sudan, circa 2005, women and girls from refugee camps walked up to seven hours a day over unsafe territory to gather tiny quantities of fuelwood from scouring the barren land around.[1] Alternatively, they traded their meagre food rations for fuel. Once acquired, this fuel was used to make inefficient open fires that were highly polluting. Dr Ashok Gadgil, a scientist at Lawrence Berkeley National Laboratory, California, reckoned that energy-efficient stoves could be very useful for this community. He developed a stove that used fuel efficiently, cut down fuel expenditure dramatically and reduced environmental pollution. Most importantly, this stove made women and girls less vulnerable to violence because the need for them to step out reduced with a reduced need for firewood. Not only were these stoves priced at a level that made sense to this community, they were also financed in ways that were attractive to the buyers. Their purchase could also be cancelled if they malfunctioned. All these extra services sweetened the deal for the buyer.

Another example is that of land records in the state of Karnataka, which we talked about in the chapter on 'Public Policy'. Land records, especially in rural areas, are important for the rights and livelihood of the inhabitants, and for access to loans and insurance. In India, land records were maintained, issued and updated manually. As one would expect, there was rampant corruption and inefficiency in this system. At the turn of the twenty-first century, computerization of these land records was undertaken under a programme called 'Bhoomi'.[2] This had to be financed through a manifold increase in the price people had to pay to access records to ensure the economic sustainability of the programme. However, once the computerization was rolled out, the number of farmers insuring their crops nearly tripled. This increase in demand led to affordable premiums, making crop insurance more efficient on the whole. People were now even more keen to update changes in landownership because of the technology's transparency. Earlier these changes would often stay unrecorded. Now the number of ownership-change requests received by the administration jumped by 85 per cent in just two years. A bureaucratic tangle that obstructed inclusiveness for all was transformed into a transparent, impartial and accessible system. Despite the hike in price of a public good, the Bhoomi programme, which completed computerization in March 2002, was a huge success because the security and opportunities it afforded to users were well worth the price.

On the other hand, there was LifeStraw, a personal, bottle-sized water filter that filtered the most contaminated water. It was an excellent, easy-to-use mechanism, but it was also very expensive. One study showed usage rates at a meagre 13 per cent in the villages in which it was introduced.[3] A perfectly helpful and necessary solution couldn't sustain because of its unviable price point.

In both the successful cases, the solutions were designed to create a definite economic incentive for their potential users. However, as with LifeStraw, for more than one reason, many beneficial solutions are not accepted by consumers—especially those that address the issues of energy, environment or employment. Now, if the consumer is not willing to pay for a solution, then who will? This is when a community looks to the government to step in. As we will see in just a bit, this stepping in can be the right move if certain criteria are met. Otherwise though, seeking government help is fraught with many problems.

Dear government, please help—but not yet

The first constraint to approach governments, of course, is that of limited resources, especially when compared to the number of claimants. Many projects are vying for governmental resources, and a large number of them may have to go without the support. So, from amongst the large number of claimants, we all know, those with higher political strength, win. The government's limited funds, therefore, are often allocated not on the basis of need, but on the basis of the political strength of the claimant. This is as true of the developed world as it is of the developing world.

The misuse and inefficiencies of lopsided political or bureaucratic power are behavioural issues that require a systemic change from within. The harsh truth is that relief rarely reaches the right pockets. Since the powerful are the biggest beneficiaries usually, the needy cannot depend on the government for their requirements— at least not completely. In our experience, seeking government funding or procurement cannot be our first resort. Only after certain conditions are met can we seek government aid.

First, reduce costs

Let us now turn to the mechanisms used to reduce costs. Fundamentally, in an efficient and competitive economy, costs can be reduced in two ways—by increasing the scale of operations or by changing the technology of production and distribution. In the chapter on 'Technology', we discussed at great length the ability of technology to bring low-cost products to the market. The other method to drive costs down, that of economies of scale, warrants an in-depth discussion.

Assuming producers do their best to keep variable production costs at a minimum, the only way they can make satisfactory profits is by distributing their fixed overheads over a large number of units. The world around us is full of success stories that wouldn't have been possible but for scale. Indeed, solutions that are not sustainable at a smaller scale can become so at a larger scale. For both physical and digital products, scale is a key determinant of cost. If scale can be increased, costs can be brought down. However, in the initial stages, when a product is being scaled, costs continue to be high. During such periods, losses are a natural result. The critical question then arises: How does a business tide through this initial phase of loss?

When digital assets increase the value of their platform it is largely done through incurring fixed costs. The larger your proportion of fixed costs to your total costs, the larger your user base will need to be. For instance, a part of Google's revenue model is based on the number of advertisements clicked by users who browse the site for search results. If the database Google offered to its search engine users were a small one, it would obviously have fewer users, and even fewer users who clicked on advertisements. Advertisers would then not be interested for lack of eyeballs. However, the reality is that billions of people use the engine, so advertisers are more than willing to pay. The economics work out because of scale. This is true of Facebook, Airbnb, Uber and the who's who of the digital world. Their scale is intrinsic to their platform's value.

For physical products, on the other hand, the good old reduction in production costs brings scale in most cases. The higher the volume of production, the lower the costs, and the lower the costs, the higher the volumes. Internal combustion engine (ICE) cars are cheaper than EVs because they are made in large numbers. ICE cars are made in large numbers because they are now cheaper, because of which they are in huge demand. As EVs become cheaper, their cost-attractiveness will lead to an increase in their scale of production, to further cut down their costs. EVs need to get into this virtuous circle to be able to truly beat ICEs. However, in the initial stages, EV makers will incur significant losses, as we have witnessed in the case of Tesla.

In addition to these basic requirements of economic sustenance through scale, new innovations have to sustain a learning curve too before they can reach the desired scale. As first-time users of search engines, we needed time to reach a comfort level with the required operations of this new beast. Today, as seasoned users, we don't think twice before reaching out for our phones to check a spelling. This learning curve was essential for Google to achieve scale.

An experimental project taken up by SEKEM, an Egyptian organization that works on bringing sustainable, cultural renewal in the country, serves as another good example.[4] Their innovation was radical—turning a stretch of desert into an agricultural strip. Their vision was to create a community in the area that not only grew organic food but also had its own medical centres, schools, etc. SEKEM had to fight the scepticism of both the farmers and the government. Only after years of persuasion and practical demonstrations of their processes were they able to convince all the stakeholders that the biodynamic agricultural system they proposed was actually feasible. Their perseverance, confidence and knowledge helped them gain scale bit by bit. As a result, today they have the support of both the farmers and the government for their other, newer ideas too.

In contrast to Google's learning curve, SEKEM built confidence gradually, by helping the government and the farmers negotiate the learning curve. SEKEM brought the elusive scale by making the other stakeholders see additional value in the project when there was no more room to reduce costs.

So how do you lower costs without a large demand? How do you increase sales if you cannot lower costs? If you innovate, scaling can become difficult. And if you scale, you may find it difficult to focus on continuous innovation. The cost-scale and innovation-scale cycles are only two of the many day-to-day challenges a business faces. The ability to balance these two cycles and to overcome the other hurdles that may come in the way is necessary for a business to achieve scale. This is where goods made for the social good—solutions that solve the problems of energy, environment and employment—need a nudge. This nudge can come from a few places.

While this is not a management book and therefore not a guide for businesses to reach scale, we would like to share a few ideas about the role various players can take on in order to help innovative solutions achieve scale.

Now the government can step in. And step out

This is where we see the government playing a pivotal part by means of public procurement to drive scale. As alluded to earlier, we are not addressing the bureaucratic and political motivations. But we can surely find ways to maximize the use of limited resources amongst the many claimants for government funds. Precious government revenues cannot be endlessly used to subsidize potentially good concepts. A solution will thrive only if it has an intrinsically viable financial model. Once that can be proven, and especially if the solution can solve a social problem, a business can approach governments.

As we did in the chapter on public policy, we would like to point out that this is not a call for continuous and permanent support from the government. On the contrary, and at the risk of repeating ourselves, we re-emphasize that the government ought to wean itself out as soon as the solution it funds has reached a predetermined scale. The UJALA procurement drive mentioned in the chapter on public policy did exactly this. Government procurement gave LED lamps just the right momentum to scale to a self-sustainable level.

Here is an illustration of the mechanism: assume that the cost of producing 100 units of a socially desirable good is $2x$, and the calculations say that when production reaches 10,000 units, the costs can be halved to x. Assume also that at x the market will be ready to consume the produced units and the producers will be able to run their business independent of government funding. In this case, the government should step in at the beginning to fill the gap, considering that we want this good to be accepted because of its social benefits. However, once the scale has reached the sustainable level of 10,000 units and the costs have reduced to x per 100 units, government support should be tapered off. The idea is not to support the product but only to make it self-sustainable. There are other nuances to be understood here, though.

Traditionally, public procurement support has a tendency to go for only lowest-cost, low-risk solutions, low-margin players and mature technology. Innovation is not welcomed, let alone rewarded. In part this is due to competing objectives and bureaucratic barriers that public procurers face, which discourage risk-taking. Governments must move away from this and create bold, transparent and innovative public procurement policies.

Innovations are products of creative interaction of supply and demand. Both 'supply-led' and 'demand-led' approaches can have an effective role to play. Governments incentivize supply by funding national research and technology organizations. They create part-financing schemes and provide financial incentives, such as weighted tax deductions, to spur industry-led research and development. Besides making supply-side initiatives, governments can not only be the biggest, but also the most influential and demanding customer. This would be a demand-side push.

A demand-side push could either be made through public procurement *of* innovation or public procurement *for* innovation to meet national objectives. Procurement *of* innovation would involve providing public funds, at least in the pilot stages, to have the innovations scale with speed. This initial financing will lead to a product or service being brought to the market. This would generate customer feedback and establish a market for the new product; now it can attract private financial backing.

On the other hand, public procurement *for* innovation would involve creating an enabling market for an innovation. The government approach could be based on three pillars.

First, government could act as the first buyer and early user for small, innovative firms, helping them to manage risk by getting them the initial revenue necessary for survival. As a buyer the government can also provide customer feedback to help refine the innovation. This will be a step towards making the product effectively competitive in the global marketplace. Based on a survey of 1100 innovative firms in Germany, it was found that public procurement is especially effective for smaller firms in regions under economic stress. There's a lesson here for developing countries.

Second, government could enforce regulations that can successfully drive innovation, either indirectly by altering the market structure and enabling funding, or directly, by boosting or limiting demand for particular products and services.

Third, government can set standards that can create market power by creating demand for innovation. Agreed standards will help mitigate the risks for early adopters and innovators, thus increasing investment in innovation.

The standards should be set at a demanding level of functionality without specifying a predefined process or solution. By not prescribing a specific route for innovation, new solutions are bound to flourish.

Many nations have drawn up innovative public procurement policies for boosting global competitiveness. China has truly aggressive policies for public procurement. Members of the OECD (Organization for Economic Cooperation and Development) have also taken a big lead. Almost 80 per cent of OECD members are reported to have taken measures to support innovation procurement, while 50 per cent have developed an action plan. Since 2011, more than a third of European companies have sold an innovative good or service as part of a public procurement contract they won.[5] More specifically, Germany has created a new Agreement on Public Procurement of Innovation, by which six federal ministries—interior, economics, defence, transport, environment and research—will promote innovative procurement.[6]

As a keen reader might have observed, the two levers of 'public policy' and 'economic model' have merged. This is inevitable. Indeed, this goes to prove that a STEP lever cannot stand alone and has to work hand in hand with the other levers for the 'leapfrogging to pole-vaulting' model to work.

Private funding or impact funding to only be sustainability funding

Other than the government, venture capitalists and private equity investors can take on the role of providing the nudge required for scale. This would, of course, be limited to for-profit activities. Tesla, Google and

Facebook were all funded largely by venture capitalists during their initial phases. In the case of for-profit entities too, the idea is to offer private funding only till a certain scale is achieved. For instance, a firm already funded by a venture capitalist might want to enter a new market. The venture capitalist could insist on restricting the funding to one geography, or insist that the promoter achieves success for their product or service in one locality before getting funds for the next. Based on this success, a trajectory for funding can be determined. The time and extent of funding support for the market under development can be limited to a predetermined point on the trajectory that all parties agree on. This is what we would call sustainability funding—financing only to the extent needed to take an immature market to maturity, in terms of scale.

Another and a relatively newer source of money for achieving scale is philanthropy funding. We spoke of this kind of funding in the context of social engagement. This kind of 'impact funding' lies between government and private funding. Foundations across the world are encouraging small firms which are taking on pressing global issues, from health and sanitation to environmental initiatives. The well-known Bill and Melinda Gates Foundation promotes development of new, low-cost technologies in agriculture, electricity and other areas. Over the years, these foundations have gained experience in risk-tolerant, patient, social-impact investments. Investment by such foundations not only reduces individual risk but also acts as a catalyst to attract other private and government funding. In fact, taking this a step further, TPG, a private equity giant, raised $2 billion for an impact-investing fund with the help of the rock star Bono.[7]

Both provision and procurement of such funds are becoming innovative too. In India, Jankidevi Bajaj Gram Vikas Sanstha (JBGVS) helps rural households by 'filling' the time gap between making an expense and receiving a promised government reimbursement grant. Under a Government of India scheme, certain qualifying rural households get ₹10,000 (~$150) for constructing a toilet. This payment comes through as a reimbursement. The rural households do not have the funds to build toilets and wait for reimbursement. For obvious reasons, they would resist borrowing money too. JBGVS, a trust run by the Bajaj corporate group, began its work in the city of Pune. They not only help households with the application process, but also help them procure low-interest loans till the government funds come through. This process has helped build 10,000 toilets in 150 villages.[8] In fact, this is an example of a private philanthropic fund helping a government scheme achieve scale.

Redefining economic sustainability

As you would recall, while elaborating on the ASSURED Total Innovation framework, we referred to one 'S' as economic, environmental and social sustainability. Also, as mentioned in the discussion on social movements, this is a good time to experiment with economic models too because the ecosystem is open to commercialization of not-so-profitable ideas. There is a growing consensus amongst corporate executives, investors and the general public that no business can focus on profits alone, and that business performance should be evaluated after taking into account factors beyond profits. This idea has been put across by many people in many different ways.

Attention to the new challenges of the past few decades have resulted in a welcome change in value systems. These shifts in attitude are causing a desirable change in the very definition of an economically sustainable model. Is an innovation an economic success if it causes pollution? Is it an economic success if costs were reduced by downsizing human labour? These are the questions being asked by stakeholders. Setting up and achieving economic models that are sensitive to such matters is becoming easier, because receiving value rather than monetary benefit is gaining importance among both givers and takers.

Gradually but surely, investors, including shareholders like you and us, are demanding changes in the way investee companies operate. They are also willing to take a hit on their returns on investment and to redefine success. In addition to the traditional profit-and-loss bottom line, companies are also measured against the social metrics of their impact on people and the environment.

The discussion so far centred on reaching cost-effective scale. The other side of the equation consists of techniques to increase the value of a product or service. Here we see some aspects of social engagement coming into play. Customers are willing to pay more for ideas that appeal to them. From organic food to eco-tours and vacations, customers accord special consideration for concepts that they feel passionate about. Employees too are known to let go of cosy, secure jobs to work for companies working in environmental or social fields at 30 to 40 per cent less pay. Of course, this requires them to have some financial surplus so that they can afford to let go of monetary benefits for something else that they value more. Most of them certainly have the means way beyond mere survival.

That brings us to the new breed of millionaires we referred to in the previous chapter. This generation is aghast at the condition of the environment and the poverty in the world. Fortunately, they are coming into money through their innovations and inheritance. And most importantly, they want to invest it responsibly. From divesting from socially irresponsible companies to actively participating in impact funding, this generation wants to do good. Based on a very broad definition of socially responsible investment, one study estimates that this kind of screening was applied to $8.7 trillion invested in the US—this amounts to 20 per cent of professionally managed funds. This is a bump up from 11 per cent in 2012.[9] Demand for holistic accountability is only growing.

Shifting attitudes—of individuals, businesses and governments

Also, the new trend of 'asset-light' and 'information-heavy' businesses are easier to finance and create sustainable economic models for, because the capital investments they require are lower. From Uber to Amazon to Airbnb, none owns assets but has a huge number of asset owners who have become participants. In fact, these businesses have reached such a scale that they are taking steps towards owning their own limited assets.

CSR 1.0 to CSR 2.0

All these factors add to the case of doing business, which also takes care of environmental and social concerns. It is easier now than it has ever been to come up with a sustainable economic model.

One suggestion in this direction is our own; Mashelkar suggests that the corporate social responsibility (CSR) practices followed so far can now change to keep up with the times.[10] Thus far, surplus profits have been ploughed back by companies into a foundation or a trust and used for philanthropy. This is 'doing well and doing good'—CSR 1.0. However, to create greater social impact, the private sector ought to 'doing well by doing good'—CSR 2.0. This makes 'doing good' intrinsic to the business. Activities like manufacture of affordable medicines, affordable 'green' products, etc., would fall in this category.

Going back to our definition of excellence, businesses ought to aim for affordable excellence; this would cater to the rising aspirations of people with fewer resources. Products and services have to be affordable yet excellent. The idea of an economic model, which combines profit with a purpose, a larger social purpose, has been popularized under different terms such as 'creative capitalism',[11] 'creating shared value'[12] and 'compassionate capitalism'.[13] The basic approach, though, is to create a new sustainable economic model—doing well by making profits while doing good for the society.

Policy push to do good

Public policies can also alter the economic model for good projects without the government having to pull out funds from its own pocket. For instance, governments may heavily tax alcoholic beverages but may subsidize milk. This can be taken a step further to create an economic model for good ideas. The principle of bonus-malus, which rewards bonus (desired) behaviour and penalizes malus (undesirable) behaviour, can be used to generate funds for innovative solutions to current problems. France already does this by applying an environmental tax on vehicles, based on their carbon emissions. At the same time, a tax credit is allowed for car emissions below a certain level. The tax credit is therefore financed through the environmental tax itself and without the use of any other kind of funding.

This discussion leads us to a framework: producers as stakeholders have to invest in technology; the government as a stakeholder has to create and implement appropriate policies; the masses as stakeholders have to converge to make change happen when there is resistance from other stakeholders; and eventually, the solution has to make economic sense to all.

We will go on to discuss a few success stories to examine the role played by each lever of the STEP framework of the 'leapfrogging to pole-vaulting' model.

NINE

Leapfrogging to Pole-vaulting
Creating Radical Yet Sustainable Transformation

Innovative solutions to problems in the areas of energy, environment and employment hold the key to the future of humanity. We need transformational changes in these three areas for humanity and planet earth to coexist. We have seen such reshaping changes being enabled through a change in technology, a policy initiative, a revolution that erupted in a society or through concepts that made economic sense for all the stakeholders involved.

However, disruptions that have stood the test of time are the ones that used all four levers in conjunction. While each of the levers might not have made an equally vigorous contribution in each of these successful disruptions, we observe that none of the levers had been completely ignored either.

We demonstrate the power of the four levers working in conjunction using two illustrative initiatives from India—the White Revolution and Aadhaar. Each initiative had its origins in a different lever, but both ultimately needed the support of the other three levers to achieve sustainable success. Each of these dramatic programmes has benefited a huge section of the community it operates in.

The White Revolution

Only seven decades ago, Indians queued up early every morning to get their family's share of milk for the day. If a festival was around the corner and you needed extra milk for the celebratory pudding, the additional milk requirement would have to be applied for in advance. This sounds like anecdotal nostalgia today because we have milk delivered to our doorstep every day. However, this was the stark reality of those times.

Milk production in India went up by almost two-and-a-half times in the one-and-a-half decades from 1974.[1] This increase in production was also backed by an increase in the number of producers, from a handful of villagers to a nexus of 90,000 village cooperatives across 170 districts in twenty-three states.[2]

At a micro level, a milk producer in the 1970s had very small profit margins and had no incentive to increase yields. Today margins in milk production are between 15 and 20 per cent because of the incentives created by the cooperative system. This system has also established ancillary industries. Only 10 per cent of dairy equipment is imported today, the rest is all produced indigenously.[3] A heartening 10 million people have been touched by this cooperative movement. At the same time, consumers have benefited from a guaranteed quality supply.

The reality of India's dairy industry is that it is largely traditional, local, informal and very fragmented. Milk producers are small farmers, and some of them are landless agricultural workers. They rely on family labour to collect and deliver milk to the market or directly to their consumers. Eighty per cent of the milk produced in India comes from farms consisting of only two to five cows. This is as true today as it was seventy years ago.

What has changed then? How were milk shortages eliminated across the country? Where did the change begin?

The challenges were many. Small rural milk producers could not deliver their produce to the cities. Middlemen increased the price, a fraction of which reached the producer. The perishable nature of milk made it even more difficult for producers to fetch a good price for it, as the commodity had to be sold very quickly.

Three movements—the AMUL (Anand Milk Union Limited) model in the little town of Anand in Gujarat, the Indian government's Operation Flood and Bharatiya Agro Industries Foundation's (BAIF) efforts—came together to make milk an abundantly available commodity in the country. A bird's-eye view would tell us that this boiled down to many factors that worked in a circular fashion. The creation of cooperatives of producers who sold directly in the market cut out the middlemen and brought the fragmented producers together, leading to savings. Policymakers saw merit in this concept and made empowering policy changes. At the other end of the spectrum, profits from the cooperative system enabled technology-led storage and preservation of milk, which in turn led to higher yields, reducing losses and further increasing economic merit. Let's understand the role of each of these individual factors.

The AMUL model began with Dr Verghese Kurien's vision. In the mid-1950s, he organized the milk producers of Anand district in Gujarat into a private cooperative. The singular aim of this model was to maximize productivity and profit for producers. The AMUL model got fragmented producers together to form cooperatives, in which each producer enjoyed both ownership and decision-making power. This made the individual milk producer a part of the entire chain—from production to consumption.

While this would bring economies of scale, it still wouldn't necessarily result in higher milk yields. These producers weren't equipped to use the latest technologies or supply-chain management models. So Dr Kurien got the cooperative to employ professionals who had the required know-how. They would be accountable to the leaders elected by the members of the cooperative—the milk producers.[4] Now, supported by technical and managerial experts, producers could collectively decide their business policies, adopt modern production and marketing techniques and receive other services that they would never have been able to afford or manage by themselves.

In 1964 Prime Minister Lal Bahadur Shastri, after a visit to an AMUL cooperative, wanted the model to be replicated throughout the country. He wanted to 'flood India with milk'; and thus originated Operation Flood, a government-backed initiative to change the way milk was produced, distributed, and even consumed in India. This became a procurement system that used rural production to satisfy urban demand.

In 1965, the Government of India created the National Dairy Development Board (NDDB) to promote and support dairy cooperatives. The board would provide extended services to producers, improving dairy technologies, veterinary services and cattle nutrition. The founding chairperson of NDDB was the redoubtable Dr Kurien.

Coincidentally, the European Economic Community had granted dairy aid to India in the form of skimmed milk powder and other milk products. With a long-term vision, instead of just distributing these products NDDB decided to 'monetize' the aid. They decided to sell the products received as aid and invest the profits in capital-intensive but essential infrastructure, the National Milk Grid System (NMGS). This became the world's largest rural development programme.[5]

The NMGS was a three-tiered structure. Milk producers from a cluster of villages became members of a village cooperative society by buying its shares. Many such societies owned district unions. The district unions bought milk from all its member cooperative societies and was responsible for processing and marketing the produce. The technical know-how provided by the cooperative societies often came from the unions. The district unions of a state formed a state federation, which made sure the milk had a market and managed distribution. Some federations also manufactured animal feed and supported other union activities.

This created a structure where the milk produced by a small milk producer in a remote village could be sold in a town far, far away. This small milk producer now got a fair price and had dependable infrastructure that reduced costs and increased production. What is more, this landless producer was an owner in the entire process, from end to end. Their wants were heeded by the entire chain. At the same time, the consumer too got milk at reasonable prices.

Operation Flood was seen as a tool to foster development by generating employment, which brought regular incomes to millions of rural households. This twenty-five-year programme was established in three phases; it began by linking eighteen milk sheds and four metropolitan cities. By the end of the programme in 1996, it had 173 milk sheds and included over 72,000 dairy cooperatives. The spectrum of services expanded to include veterinary first-aid, healthcare, feed, artificial insemination services and member education. Research in animal health and nutrition was also encouraged during the last ten years of the operation.[6]

Independently, in 1967, among other developments, Manibhai Desai's organization BAIF brought fresh technology in cow breeding to the country. It was his quest to solve the productivity issue that saw the cross-breeding of Indian cows with imported cows. BAIF also had veterinarians visiting the farmer at his doorstep to resolve animal-health-related problems. Interestingly, this was more a decision of economics than of convenience—if a cow were to be sent to an artificial-insemination centre in the closest town, she might have lost heat, and the effort and expense would have been wasted. Instead, a doctor who took the insemination kit to the village could service a request within eight hours. These solutions, which were revolutionary for the time, saved the villagers a lot of money.

Let's examine the roles played by the four levers in the White Revolution.

Technology was involved each step of the way

The very first problem was that of increasing productivity. Traditionally, in India, the bovine species were used for farming activities. This meant bulls were preferred to cows.

This also meant low milk yields. In Europe, horses tilled the farms while cows were bred to produce more milk. As farming became mechanized, it reduced the need for bulls in farming, which made cows available to produce more female than male calves, thus increasing milk productivity. This was one aspect of technology that led to a larger number of milch cows.

Indian milk yields were very low. This meant selectively cross-breeding indigenous cows with high-yield breeds from Europe. Hybrid cattle was therefore BAIF's answer to the yield problem. Artificial insemination by cross-breeding Indian cows with European bulls led to cows with high milk production. This was a highly technical and delicate process. It involved skilled manpower and advanced technologies such as semen washing, cryo preservation and insemination. BAIF established the whole chain, from European labs and farms to Maharashtra's cowsheds. However, these new breeds were more vulnerable to disease because their genes were foreign to the Indian environment. This called for proper nutrition, care and veterinary services, which BAIF also provided.

Such innovations were made in the Operation Flood programme too. Each step of the milk industry process, from conception of the heifer to getting the milk to the consumer's fridge was reinvented. Technology saw the process through, from production, collection, chilling, pasteurization, packaging, marketing and delivery. And innovation continues in the industry. Bulk chilling machines are making life easier for small farmers by allowing flexibility in collection and delivery of milk to the cooperative while also allowing them to produce more milk.[7]

Policy gave the all-important nudge

Creating the NDDB and facilitating Operation Flood under NDDB's wing were both policy initiatives. Again, the National Milk Grid was a government initiative. It still exists and is still supported by the Government of India. In fact, the very basis of collection and distribution—the creation of cooperatives—in the first place was a policy intervention the government could have chosen not to support. That the government allowed cooperatives as legal entities made the system's existence possible.

On their part, state governments in India announced a minimum price for milk to ensure steady income to farmers. The milk offered by a member had to be accepted by the cooperative society as long as it met the quality standards. This assurance allowed farmers to take up dairy as their main line of employment. Quality standards are also the government's way of protecting the consumer.

The government also rolled out various subsidy schemes to develop the supply chain consisting of collection centres, chilling centres, etc. Special incentives were also given to cow rearing rather than to buffalo rearing. Moreover, dairy income was, and still is, tax free.

Policy support is also as much about what a government does as it is about what it doesn't. Faced by shortages, the government could have just allowed imports, which would have taken over the local markets. But instead, the longer-term vision was supported.

The very essence of cooperatives is social engagement

Could there be a more successful story of social engagement than millions of farmers, irrespective of caste, gender and class, being included in one cooperative society? These cooperative societies also brought about a sense of ownership and social cohesion. The objectives of all three movements were clear—better income and increased milk yield. The very fact that the central government just did some hand-holding, leaving the core action to the farmer collective, is a testament to the extent of social engagement.

The cooperatives not only fixed the rules for their society together, but also fixed their problems together. There was a collective response to issues, such as low yields or substandard feed, instead of bureaucratic buck-passing.[8]

Most importantly, it wouldn't be an exaggeration to say that the White Revolution wouldn't have happened were it not for staunch leaders like Dr Verghese Kurien and Manibhai Desai. Dr Kurien applied his knowledge from his American degree. Even though he was only finishing up a mandatory requirement of his scholarship when he went to Anand, it was his inherent vision for social good that made him think of a system that did not allow exploitation of small farmers at the hands of self-serving businessmen. Manibhai Desai, on the other hand, was always guided by Mahatma Gandhi's principles. He questioned the orthodox ways of society and was flexible in his methods, which made way for greater social good.

The economics worked out for all the stakeholders

The very beginning of Operation Flood, launched in 1970, was an economic innovation. This initiative cleverly used loans from the World Bank.[9] Monetizing the food aid received in kind was a master stroke in creating finances that led to a cycle of income for all the stakeholders involved. This made government-funded agricultural research possible too.[10]

The smallest of individual producers could benefit from the economies of scale that the cooperative structure brought. Incomes doubled for landless farmers.[11] Getting rid of middlemen saw a bigger proportion of the final milk price reaching the actual producer. The increased productivity of cows led to more income for individual families. Hybrid cows produced about four times more milk than indigenous Indian cows. Operation Flood's well-researched supply-chain management and capacity building, from creating trucking networks to chilling plants and refrigerated vans, involved expenses that were completely out of reach of the individual farmer. Let alone fancy management, even a market was out of reach for this farmer. Moreover, compared with the delayed cash flows earlier, this system brought cash to the farmers within a couple of weeks of sale of their produce.

And the success continues

Having understood the factors that contributed to the success of the White Revolution, it is evident that the holistic and integrated approach to production, distribution and sale of milk created capabilities that were otherwise elusive. One contributing factor depended on the other for its success. Technology seeped its way through every aspect of the value chain, but it couldn't have done so without policy support, and this would have been impossible without the three-tier structure that enabled social engagement. Empowerment of the individual farmer through more income and decision-making power fed the next cycle of transformation. This participative approach fostered social ambitions and gave rise to a new era of political leadership from the grass-roots level. And the good story continues.

It has been two decades since Operation Flood as a programme concluded. Yet milk production in India continues to increase, and more and more producers are coming into the fold of this campaign. By 2008, 13 million participants, including 3.7 million women, were part of the cooperative society network. Sure, there is more work to be done. Even so, Operation Flood did revolutionize the industry. BAIF itself provides services to over a million rural families spread over 12,000 villages in seven states, across all agricultural activities.

As alluded to earlier, the White Revolution has done its bit in reducing income inequality in the country, and it has been an inclusive process too. By 1984, 72 per cent of cooperative members were small and marginal farmers, a majority of them from the minority castes and tribes. The biggest victory is that 60 per cent of Operation Flood members are landless or small farmers who hold less than 2 hectares of land. Today India is the largest producer of milk in the world.[12]

So successful is this setup that India is replicating the model for other commodities such as fruit, vegetables and even vegetable oils. Indeed, China, the Philippines, and Sri Lanka are also examining the success of Operation Flood to learn from its design and implementation. Right from using food aid for development rather than for short-term humanitarian purposes to its long-term attitude to income generation—this model is an example to follow. More specifically, today India has indigenous knowledge in all aspects of animal husbandry, nutrition, animal health, breeding, management information systems, dairy engineering and food technology. And this expertise can be used all over the globe.

Another Indian project can be thought of as a world leader. Aadhaar is one of the world's biggest biometric ID project. Its implementation is another example of a successful combination of the four levers.

Aadhaar[13]

In 2016, we could have said that India stood on the cusp of a digital revolution. Today one can say without any ambiguity that we are right in the midst of one. Unimaginable scale was achieved at great speed by India's biometric identity system, Aadhaar. Its genesis lay in the idea of creating a system to smoothen the process of subsidy deployment to marginalized citizens. In addition, the central database could be used by national security agencies for proactive threat monitoring and investigations, and by service providers for providing prompt services.[14] Over 1.12 billion Indians have been brought on to the system since its inception.

The system was first launched in 2009, and the first Aadhaar number was assigned in September 2010. However, for many reasons it didn't gain momentum. A Unique Identification Authority of India was set up in 2016 to carry the work forward.[15] The Indian government invited Nandan Nilekani, co-founder of the Indian IT giant, Infosys, to pioneer and champion a transformative initiative which would touch every Indian's life. He successfully conceived and deployed Aadhaar, 'the biggest social project on the planet'. He put together a team of like-minded people whose singular aim was to serve India's unserved. The power of identity makes every government scheme accessible to each eligible Indian.

This bold initiative now enables large-scale, technology-enabled, real-time delivery of welfare services. Aadhaar is estimated to have saved $9 billion in fraud and wastage for the government by eliminating fake and duplicate names from beneficiary and employee lists. Almost half a billion people have linked their bank accounts with Aadhaar to get benefits. Until March 2018, the government has transferred benefits of about $12 billion to bank accounts electronically in real time. This has made the Direct Benefit Transfer scheme the world's largest real-time cash transfer scheme by any government.[16]

While at conception the motivation was to efficiently imburse subsidies, the applications are limitless. The government itself is at the forefront of using the possibilities that Aadhaar affords. The Jan Dhan Yojana, a government scheme, made it extremely easy for anyone, especially those without the resources to maintain a minimum balance, to open a bank account. With 21 per cent of the adult population of the country having opened a Jan Dhan account, the scheme has become an unrivalled global example of financial inclusion.[17] In fact, it boasts an entry in the Guinness Book of World Records for having opened 18.6 million accounts in just five days.

The objective of linking the bank account number to the Aadhaar number is to make the account easy to operate using the ubiquitous mobile phone. Together, this trinity has been popularized under the acronym, JAM. Today 92 per cent of the Indian population have an Aadhaar number, the country's biometric identity.[18] 95 per cent of Indian households have at least one bank account,[19] and

36 per cent have phones with Internet connectivity[20]—the most crucial link.

Outside of this, Aadhaar has brought convenience to the middle-of-the-pyramid consumer. Aadhaar allows KYC processes to be accomplished in a few minutes, compared with the days it took earlier.

These quantifiable and non-quantifiable benefits have all come about as a result of the four levers working in tandem.

The Aadhaar initiative was conceptualized by policymakers!

As mentioned earlier, UIDAI was created with the objective of issuing a unique ID, called Aadhaar, to each Indian. This statutory authority was established under the ministry of electronics and information technology. Prior to its establishment as a statutory authority, UIDAI was functioning as an office attached to the Planning Commission, now NITI Aayog. Along with setting up the system for issuing Aadhaar numbers and authenticating records, the security of identity-related information is also UIDAI's responsibility.

The system received a more-than-adequate push from the authorities during each step of the process. This is at the heart of the project's speedy and gigantic success.

Technology—the very defining factor

Issuing a unique identity to every citizen has an underlying implication—that the process should eliminate duplicates and identify fakes. In addition, once issued, the identity should be quickly, smoothly and cost-effectively verifiable and authenticated. ID generation involves systems that can receive new requests, capture data, do verification and make amendments. An authentication system allows use of the ID in a KYC process. Swift and seamless authentication calls for speedy querying of the database. At this level the system has to be capable of detecting fraud too—from registering non-existent applicants to misrepresented information to impersonation. Such a system by default requires appropriate security and privacy insulations through access control. In addition, the system provides statistics and allows administrators to access reports and check grievances. Parallelly, the regular citizen ought to be able to access his or her information at will.

And this is just a cursory glance at the processes involved. Each step along the way requires technological backing, which has obviously been provided, or else the system would have fallen flat before it began.

No economic fortunes made, but enormous value created for all

Considering that this is a government project, it is the taxpayer's money being put to use. At one end, establishing and maintaining the database calls for capital and operational expenses, such as biometric terminals, software development, consulting, and recurring database management and support costs. At the other end, integrating Aadhaar with various government schemes also calls for expenditure. This includes the cost of providing incentives to banking channels for programmes that involve payments through banks.

UIDAI's annual budget works out to ₹2000 crore (over $300 million). This cost could be recovered either through taxes or by charging users such as service providers who use the system for customer authentication. While the debate on cost recovery is yet to be settled, a cost-benefit analysis projects that the government can receive a return of about 53 per cent on its investments over ten years.[21] This analysis has included the costs mentioned above and has calculated the benefits in terms of integrating Aadhaar with various schemes and reducing leakages. For instance, Aadhaar has saved the government ₹15,000 crore (~$2.4 billion) a year in liquefied petroleum gas subsidies alone.[22] The government has estimated that the Direct Benefit Transfer scheme has expanded significantly and helped save around ₹83,000 crore (~$13 billion).[23]

As far as the end user, the Indian citizen, is concerned, the costs are zero and the benefits many. For the bottom-of-the-pyramid subsidy beneficiary, it is the difference between receiving the benefit and not receiving it at all. For the next layer of the population, the so-called middle class, the benefits have to be calculated in terms of the time they saved—the hours spent in queues and days spent waiting for a service.

Social engagement—from the greatest minds in the country down to the last beneficiary

That over 90 per cent of the country's population is on the system more than showcases the level of social engagement. If indeed most Indians did not have faith in the system and were not convinced of the benefits that would accrue to them from being part of it, Aadhaar could not have accomplished the feat that it has.

An ever-improving system

With a technological venture of this nature, there are bound to be glitches. It is technology, there are bound to be hackers, and there will be bugs. An ever-vigilant process must keep track of and fix these hackings and bugs. Aadhaar is still not ubiquitously accessible despite its one-time registration process having been declared successful. Registration for benefits, for instance, still requires many creases to be ironed out. Fingerprints and iris scans become outdated as citizens age. The process for updating such information has to be in place without causing inconvenience to the citizen. Glitches in matching the beneficiaries with their Aadhaar numbers may lead to citizens being treated as bogus Aadhaar holders.[24]

For the Aadhaar applications to come through, just having an Aadhaar number is not enough. Only when the entire infrastructure is functional—mobile connectivity, electricity, functional POS machines, UIDAI servers and fingerprint recognition—will benefits accrue to the intended beneficiaries. In addition, privacy protection is essential to make the system more trustworthy and secure.

Even so, we know that these issues are not being overlooked. And these issues cannot undermine the success so far. As we speak, bank accounts are actually being used by many financial entities to create credit histories of individuals, which can then help them secure microfinance, make savings, get sachet-insurance, education, and so on. Just as India jumped from difficult-to-get landline phone connections to ubiquitous mobile telephony, Aadhaar has the potential to pole-vault India into the next phase of financial inclusion. It will allow millions of people to become part of the mainstream economy and provide them access equality, notwithstanding the income inequality.

These successes of the White Revolution and Aadhaar highlight the fact that if social good is kept at the heart, the four levers can indeed make it possible for people to progress together as a community. Sure, all four levers might not be equally important in every project. However, the ones that were needed to a lesser degree might help a project attain further scale or help it speed up. But certainly every one of the levers is needed for any programme to be sustainable in the long run.

Interestingly, both the White Revolution and Aadhaar projects required 'pole-vaulting' thinkers and innovation leaders like Dr Kurien, Manibhai Desai and Nandan Nilekani. Not only did they create projects on an enormous scale but they also planned their execution meticulously. Even while the success of the White Revolution and Aadhaar can be attributed in large part to government support, businessmen have to keep in mind that they must move from leapfrogging to pole-vaulting, seeking help from government only as a last resort. Business persons can certainly attempt transformation on their own.

With these inspirations and our own aspirations, we will now take a look at two areas where we have applied the 'leapfrogging to pole-vaulting' model. Any model worth its mettle will be able to stand tall and hold its ground in the real world. The problems picked to demonstrate the efficacy of the model are critical problems the world faces—solid waste management and mobility. One fights the problem of pollution on the ground while the other addresses air pollution. Globally, the former is largely under the purview of the public sector, whereas the latter is completely driven by private enterprise. And while one calls for immediate and transformative action, the other is witnessing exceptional transformation already. We believe that solid waste management is in dire need of a 'clean revolution' and that mobility can become today's great, grand 'green revolution'. In both cases, we have successfully applied the STEP framework along with the ASSURED Total Innovation framework to arrive at solutions that have the potential to pole-vault us into a new, cleaner, environmentally amiable world.

TEN

A Clean Revolution
Solid Waste Management

Contrary to popular belief, an ideal world would be densely urban, with fewer people living in its remote corners. The shift by human beings to cities has had the subtle effect of making our forests denser and the hills grassier. This is because people are moving away from those areas. On the other hand, cities are better equipped to provide facilities to their citizens. Mere economies of scale make that possible. Increased population also leads to better talent because of competition and peer learning—be it in literature, art or scientific advances. Whether it was Rome, Florence or Paris of ancient times, or London and New York of today, cities have been the foundation of human progress.

Moreover, cities have a subtle positive impact on human interaction. Urban areas allow for formation of new social structures, breaking the feudal social frameworks often found in villages. In the Indian context, for instance, in Mumbai's crowded trains, the commuter's caste is indistinguishable and untouchability unthinkable. In contrast, generations of so-called lower-caste communities often continue to be treated despicably in villages.

Unfortunately, in our cities we get beaten by unorganized urbanization. Unplanned and unadministered urbanization—and not urbanization itself—lies at the root of many global concerns. Managing our urbanization better would mean better management of transportation, public spaces, natural resources, waste, and so on. We need mindful urbanization that will accommodate the changing nature of our future cities.

The catastrophe called unmanaged waste

As desired, more and more people across countries are moving from the interiors to bigger cities. The world's urban population is expected to increase by over 66 per cent by 2050. India alone is expected to add over 300 million new urban residents.[1] However, the cities are not growing at the same pace in terms of facilities for this influx of citizens. Many of the biggest cities of the world are bursting at the seams, their infrastructure not being able to cope with their increasing population. Almost the same quantity of resources such as water are being stretched to serve disproportionately more people as the years wear on. Sometimes, even when facilities such as public transport, recreational amenities, education and health facilities grow, the pace of growth is nowhere close to what is required to keep up with the population growth. This, in turn, has a ripple effect on a vast range of issues ranging from pollution to crime.

Amongst this plethora of issues arising from rapid urbanization is the matter of solid waste management—

another urban system that has lagged behind population growth. Solid waste consists of the everyday items we discard into our trash bins—the garbage we create with every packet of wafers, every plastic water bottle and all the food we throw away. This is the garbage that is inefficiently collected and inadequately processed. This is the garbage that burns in the air we breathe, flows into the water we drink and becomes patches of plastic in our oceans.

Solid waste accumulation is an especially aggressive problem in cities because they generate more per capita waste than villages do. However, we must bear in mind that high population density also allows for efficiency in resource use, financial economies of scale and technological innovation. With that hope in mind, let us take a 360-degree view of the nature of this problem.

Urban solid waste: Unimaginable quantities, undesirable quality

Of course, there is more to our garbage story. At a very superficial level, taking a look around will tell us how much waste we create. And while there can be efficient waste disposal, there isn't. Littering is an issue of equal importance, but just the amount of waste that humans generate and don't dispose of adequately is mind-boggling.

Currently, an estimated 62 million tonnes of municipal solid waste is generated in India every year. Taking 1991 as the base year, growth in waste generation is outpacing population growth by two to three times every few years.[2] So, in addition to an increase in waste generated because of the growing population, people are also generating more waste per person than earlier.

To make matters worse, only about 23 per cent of waste collected is processed. This includes waste transported to landfills and other waste that is disposed of in environmentally friendly ways. Most landfills lack appropriate design and operational processes, making them mere dumping grounds. Other than these environmental issues, they are a nuisance for the people living in their vicinity and are a serious health concern. At current dumping rates, by 2031 India will require 1240 hectares of land per year to accommodate the 165 million tonnes of waste generated. This would translate to 66,000 hectares of land—more than six times the size of Paris—holding 10-metre-high piles of waste in the next twenty years or so.[3]

From 1950 to 2013, the plastic produced globally went up from 1.7 million tonnes to 300 million tonnes a year.[4] All the plastic produced so far still lies somewhere on earth, letting out toxic chemicals into its ecosystem. Much of the waste collected flows into rivers and oceans. About 5,000,000,000 tonnes—5 trillion tonnes—of plastic is floating in our oceans![5] Most of this debris consists of plastic products such as bags, bottle caps, water bottles and Styrofoam cups.[6] From bears in the mountains to dogs and cows in the cities and villages, discarded plastic is affecting the health of these animals and is even running some of them down to extinction.[7]

Not just the quantity of waste, but its composition too is changing with growing urbanization. Earlier, wet or biodegradable waste in Indian cities would account for over 75 per cent of the total waste produced. Gradually, this has reduced to less than 50 per cent in some cities. This is at best a very rough guess, because assessments of waste composition in India can get misleading very quickly. For instance, such estimations are made at landfills, but India has a huge informal waste collection system that does not make it to the landfills.

Another rather positive contributing factor to waste generation in India is the traditional habit of a frugal lifestyle. While plastic bags, boxes and bottles might not find their way to the landfills, they are stored and reused indefinitely, and this waste cannot be measured. India's waste-generation rates are therefore lower than those of other low-income countries, and much lower than those of the developed world. However, this is changing with changing lifestyles. Especially in the cities, we are witnessing a move towards increasing use of disposable plastic. Packaging material and per capita waste generation is increasing by about 1.3 per cent per year in the larger Indian cities.[8]

India's waste composition too differs from that of the developed world. The more developed a country, the less is its organic waste. Organic waste contains the least calorific value. While organic waste is reducing in the larger Indian cities to 50 per cent of the total waste, the statistic is still encouraging compared with the 28 per cent for the OECD countries.[9] Non-organic waste has more stored energy that can be used as fuel. If non-organic waste is used to create fuel, it solves a waste management problem, along with providing power. This calls for customized waste management systems for India, because the incineration or gasification plants that produce electricity in OECD countries will not be profitable, given the small and scattered amounts of non-organic waste generated in the country.

From the global perspective, the problem of waste management in India might seem less significant than it is in the rest of the world, but the country still has waste management issues that need immediate attention. From the Himalayas to the coasts, garbage is omnipresent. While tourism is the lifeline of many of the northern states, it is also becoming a nuisance in terms of littering. Trekking trails across the Himalayas have become trails of instant noodles packets and plastic bottles. Even worse, used tissue and toilet paper is dumped right next to campsites. In addition to waste-management issues such as littering and pollution, cities and non-urban areas are short of resources to manage their growth too. They need economically viable solutions, soon.

So, as the country is transforming at a quicker pace with every passing day, the nature of the waste it generates is changing too. As encouraging and desirable as progress is, we cannot ignore the concerns such development generates in its wake. The quantity and quality of waste we generate is one such concern that will be unsurmountable if we do not heed to it right away. It is not just about the appearance of our cities and country; it is, more disturbingly, about our health and that of our children. This issue of managing waste is akin to the alarming 'food shortage' situation in the country from the 1950s to the 1960s. Solid waste management calls for an operation as significant as Operation Flood and the Green Revolution, if not an even more aggressive one.

The gravity of this situation has prompted us (the authors of this book) into action. Our work in this area has seen great success in the city of Pune, India. More importantly, we contend that the model we created can be scaled for application across the entire nation. With the right push it can lead to a Clean Revolution of the

2020s. Indeed, if applied across the country, we envision this model to lead to a spick and span country that has an environmentally sustainable solid waste management system—in not more than five years!

Our learning: Aiming for civic forests

This chapter is a distillation of our learnings from a solid waste management programme that we designed and continue to run for Pune city. Our inspiration has been nature itself. In an untouched forest or on a mountaintop, everything you see around you is reused, recycled. Can we apply the same principle in a city? Can we not reuse and recycle our waste? Can our concrete jungles not become civic forests? Then came some pressing questions. Do we have the required technologies? How do we get people engaged? After all, a lot about waste disposal in India concerns participation by the individual on the ground— each citizen of the city. Can these processes run without continuous external funding? City funds cannot be engaged indefinitely. Can the processes and technologies be cost-effective for all involved?

We thought it possible

From 2004 to 2006, one of us, Ravi Pandit, was the president of the Mahratta Chamber of Commerce, Industries and Agriculture (MCCIA), an organization that works to improve the commercial prospects of Pune to make it a leading industrial town. In order to attract commerce, a city has to be liveable, and one of the steps to make a city liveable is to make and keep it clean. During Pandit's time with MCCIA, the chamber established

Janwani, a platform that deals with problems faced by the city's citizens.

Janwani initiated the 'zero-garbage ward' project in one of Pune's suburbs, Katraj. This model aimed to turn a *prabhag*—an administrative division of the city, a ward—into a self-contained unit with respect to municipal solid waste disposal. We thought of each ward as an urban forest. A forest where all the waste generated within its geographic bounds was processed in that ward itself. We wanted to devise a self-sufficient system that would locally recycle waste to create a new type of value. This would avoid transportation to a central landfill too. Following this vision, the model implemented in Katraj, was a resounding—but a very hard-earned—success.

The achievements of this focused drive became evident from the numbers. Door-to-door waste collection in Katraj grew from covering 30 per cent to 90 per cent of households, while waste segregation grew from a mere 10 per cent to 70 per cent of households. Waste collectors grew from twenty in number to forty-five. From having no wet-waste processing plants, Katraj now has five new biogas plants. And the number that says it all is the waste tonnage that makes it to the landfills; whereas earlier Katraj sent 10 tonnes of waste every day to the landfills, it now sends only 2 tonnes. Today, the 'zero-garbage ward' project has been rolled out in twenty wards, covering almost half of Pune. Another twenty wards have awarded contracts to Janwani. Door-to-door waste collection in the wards where the model has been implemented stands at 88 per cent, and segregation stands at about 80 per cent. We see our model's success as a reinforcement of our belief that if waste collection and segregation are implemented well, then we are a step closer to managing urbanization well.

The journey

In 2011, Pune Municipal Corporation (PMC) partnered with Janwani, SWaCH Cooperative, KPIT and another company, Cummins India, to develop and implement the 'zero-garbage ward' model in the city. The public–private partnership developed an innovative system. While PMC continued to be responsible for duties such as street sweeping and industrial waste collection, the new model sought to change waste collection at the household level. The idea was to change people's perception of waste and to get them to treat it as a valuable resource. In seven years, Janwani has established a comprehensive and well-documented system.

The model also intended to decentralize solid waste management and incorporate the hitherto informal waste collectors into the formal system. Two key challenges faced by every Indian city—collection and segregation of waste—had to be addressed. By achieving optimum segregation of waste and selling dry waste to scrap dealers through waste collectors, landfilling had to be brought to a minimum.

But before advocating change in behaviour among the people, we had to understand the current patterns. There was next-to-zero awareness about waste segregation. For our model to work, waste had to be segregated at the household level. In this context, an average Indian household had to be educated about the ABCs of waste segregation. Even in affluent, well-educated families, dry vegetable waste, such as onion peels, was considered dry waste and a wet milk packet was considered wet waste. Only if education translated to correct, practical segregation could advanced technology, stringently implemented collection processes, transportation, treatment and disposal bring the required garbage revolution.

Before implementation of Janwani's model, house and shop owners handed their garbage over to an informal waste collector. Typically, this waste was unsegregated, leaving its segregation into dry non-biodegradable and wet biodegradable waste to the waste collector. Since such after-the-fact segregation was time-consuming, it was never done. In effect, unsegregated and therefore difficult-to-dispose-of waste was passed on to the waste disposal system.

Therefore, only once the new model educated the waste creator, and each household and commercial property owner segregated the waste properly, would the rest of the model be implementable. Then, it would need to bring economic value for the waste collector, the local government body and the waste disposal organization, if any. The ward-level waste disposal plant would need to employ appropriate technologies too.

In 2011–12, the 'zero-garbage ward' model initiated a pilot project for one ward in Pune—Katraj, the biggest ward in PMC, with about 30,000 residents. It represented a perfect demographic mix of a developing town. Modern housing societies sprawled along with *gaothan*s, areas that were villages earlier. Katraj is home to slums and to low-income and middle-income groups too. Any solution that addressed the varying constraints of this diverse group would be a good starting ground for further customization of the model in other parts of the city and indeed, in other cities of the country or even the world.

The first issue—the residents' waste disposal behaviour—called for a major shift in attitude among the citizenry. With corporate and other volunteers pitching in and providing a personal touch to popularizing the process, the project started gaining support, and residents began making the necessary changes.

Waste collectors collected segregated waste at each doorstep. They then further segregated the dry waste into non-recyclable and recyclable waste and transported the waste to predetermined collection points. In addition, they reported non-segregating and non-paying households. Therefore, a waste collector had to be incentivized to encourage both waste segregation and collection. This was done by a combination of user fees and income from recycled dry waste.

Irrespective of income level, residents were to pay a nominal ₹10–₹30 (~¢15–¢45) monthly user fee directly to waste collectors. This held households and waste collectors responsible for waste collection and segregation. Waste collectors sold the wet waste to an authorized agency at ₹1 (~¢1.5) per kilogram. Dry waste, after finer segregation, was sold to authorized scrap recyclers, fetching rates varying from ₹3 to ₹22 per kilogram, depending on the type of waste. Garden waste could be converted to biofuel, while biomedical and construction waste went to specialized disposal plants.

To get the segregated waste to their final destinations, technology was used to prepare an optimum collection route for the collecting trucks. Once this collection route was established, the collection points were defined keeping in mind the quantity of waste collected and the distance that the waste collector had to travel with the collected waste. Waste from the collection points was picked up by the trucks for disposal. For waste disposal, clean and energy-efficient systems had to be set up using good economic policies.

The lessons from this pilot project were simple and heartening. It proved to us that a socially acceptable and economically viable solid waste management programme could be implemented. At the social level, it would require micromanagement during waste segregation because this segregation was key to the programme's success. Segregated collection had to be facilitated at the resident's doorstep. From an economic standpoint, the waste collectors would earn from user fees and dry-waste collection; waste-plant operators would earn from tipping fees and sale of byproducts; and municipalities would benefit from savings in transportation and manpower. And, of course, there was the non-monetary benefit to all, of having a clean city.

Companies such as Persistent Systems, Cummins India, and KPIT took charge of wards as a part of their CSR programmes. In fact, corporates have become an integral element of this model. Apart from providing financial support, these companies have encouraged their employees to volunteer. Over 10,000 volunteers from these companies put in countless hours to make the project a success. KPIT's employees voluntarily invested significant time and effort in this initiative too, something we are very proud of.

Since its success, this model has been ISO-certified. It is the first Indian waste management system to receive the certification. Its process manual outlines practices and monitoring systems to make the model sustainable and easy to replicate.

Based on the Katraj success, PMC decided to replicate the model in more wards. The collaborative, research-based and result-oriented approach has been customized for other wards, according to their demographics and socio-economic composition. Between 2015 and 2017, the model was implemented in twenty wards, covering almost half of Pune—or over 1.5 million people! Currently, we are looking at covering the rest of the city.

The 'zero-garbage ward' model: A perfect example of STEP levers working in tandem

Our belief in the importance and interdependence of the four levers—technology, public policy, social engagement and economic model—was fortified by the success of the 'zero-garbage ward' model. We would like to highlight the invaluable input of each of the levers.

Social engagement: Overturning apathy

People participation was by far the key to the model's success. As mentioned earlier, the public at large was indifferent to garbage disposal etiquette. Overturning this apathy was the biggest bottleneck to our success. Over 1900 individual volunteers, 10,000 corporate volunteers and the Janwani team collaborated to conduct over 1200 social engagement and awareness initiatives. From distributing bins for waste segregation to door-to-door awareness campaigns to street plays and rallies—no stone was left unturned by the volunteers, who were the leading force.

And the campaign was not just one presentation or one play. The approach for small commercial setups had to be different from the one used for the residential slums, which was still different from the one for the more affluent areas. A nuanced understanding of each group's attitudes and reservations led to a customized outreach strategy.

For instance, high-income households did not mind the monthly ₹30 (~¢45) fee, but they were just not motivated to segregate their waste, even if it meant training their domestic help. For this group, the simplicity of the required behavioural change was highlighted against the disproportionate benefits it brought, such as environment-friendliness. Films and talks on the cascading impact of segregation were used for this group.

For the gaothans, the already established vigorous political dynamics had to be catered to. Puppet shows and street plays had content specifically tailored for the group. Other than these specific steps, general outreach efforts—such as the screening of short films in cinema halls and information pamphlets for the housing society noticeboards—were made too.

But for the involvement of thousands of volunteers to the actual engagement of each household—from the educator to the educated—without the participation of people from end to end, the model would have failed at its very inception. Or it might not have seen such immediate success.

Public policymakers: Moral and practical partners

It must not be forgotten that the 'zero-garbage ward' model was a project in partnership with the city's municipal corporation. Were it not for the support from the political leadership and the administrative setup, the model could have failed, despite clear social and economic benefits. Successive mayors of the city supported the drive, and key corporators actively participated in its vision and implementation.

This support was not only social and conceptual. The city administration took practical steps too to get the project going. For instance, the Municipal Waste Handling Rules, 2000, emphasizes segregation of garbage, making non-segregation of garbage an offence. Policies that require a user fee for waste collection and those that impose a fine for non-segregation of waste have been successful.

The authorities have been very receptive to suggestions for both implementation and enforcement. Amongst its many other initiatives, Janwani helped PMC to prepare by-laws for sanitation and waste management. As a result, regulations mandating segregation of garbage at source for residential buildings and composting facilities within their premises itself, came into force. Janwani assesses composting units and compiles the data for rebate calculation. This has made enforcement more efficient. Janwani also played a crucial role in simplifying compost registration and inspection processes. Also, Janwani has now been given the authority to issue notices to violators and to fine them for non-segregation.

The model's success will continue to depend on support from the policy and regulatory sphere. We are now looking at garnering equally enthusiastic support beyond the city. Some suggestions from the model have already been included in the Union budget (2013–14), and Janwani is also on a Maharashtra state-level committee for solid waste management. Both Janwani and PMC have received awards and international recognition.[10] To name a few, the ICON SWM Award for Excellence in SWM (2012), the Vasundhara Award by State Pollution Control Board (2013), and the Dubai International Award by UN-Habitat (2015).

While this pilot project could not have worked without the strong support from the authorities, it is time now to take it to the next level. We will need more stringent enforcement of segregation and incentive schemes need formalization. At the same time, detrimental policies will have to be dealt with. For instance, in the prevailing system, a tipping fee is paid to the waste management plant. Inadvertently, this has become a source of inefficiency. The plant operators receive tipping fees for the waste they collect instead of the biogas and electricity they generate. Left unmonitored, the operators show an exorbitant amount of waste as accepted but don't treat the waste. They just throw it back into the city's drains. Similarly, housing societies are given a 5 per cent property tax rebate for installing in-house waste-treatment facilities such as composting pits. But there are inadequate checks to see if composting actually takes place. Also, the complex administrative procedures are not encouraging for the residents.

Surely, there is more work to be done, but the support we have received so far is indicative of the willingness of local authorities to be a part of this waste management revolution.

Technology: Working hard in the background

This brings us to the role of technology in the 'zero-garbage ward' model's success. A bird's-eye view of the model might make the role of technology almost invisible. However, it has played an understated role by being at the root of the model's functioning.

The model deployed technology with two very specific purposes—for collection and monitoring, and for decentralized waste disposal. GPS systems were extensively used to optimize collection routes. Mobile apps too were used for monitoring the 'chronic' spots, places where citizens tend to throw garbage. The municipality used mobile apps for grievance redressal too.

Economics: Unmeasurable cleanliness and good health; measurable income and savings

The beauty of the 'zero-garbage ward' model is that it makes perfect economic sense for everyone involved. There are costs to poor solid waste management. Improper segregation leads to improper disposal, causing environmental hazards. Litter impacts public health and affects the usability of public amenities like roads, footpaths and parks. On the other hand, fuel, fertilizer, plastics and metals are all valuable materials that can be recovered from waste. Effective solid waste management brings real economic benefits to the society at large.

As mentioned earlier, the model required citizens to pay a user fee. Initially, however, Janwani paid the waste collectors, and households were not charged at all. Soon we realized that some of the waste collectors were not working on schedule or weren't picking up trash daily. Within two months we switched to the user fee system. This incentivized waste collectors to collect waste from as many households as possible. This step—the primary collection of waste at the household level—had long been problematic. A simple user fee provided enough value to all stakeholders to enable the change.

At a rupee a day, the fee was insignificant for most residents, especially for the value it brought—a clean neighbourhood. Moreover, some of the most exhilarated feedback to the Janwani model has been, 'The value of our homes has increased after this project implementation!'

Indeed, we were concerned if low-income households would be able to afford even the minimum user fee of ₹10 (~¢15) per month. As it turned out, in Katraj, slum residents disposed of waste in waterways, bringing mosquitoes and health problems. Slum dwellers in Katraj were willing to pay the fee because it kept their area clean, reduced the incidence of disease and, with it, hospital expenses. In 2017, Janwani successfully tested a different economic model for slums in another ward. Janwani supported this slum financially because some residents could not afford the user fee. While fees were collected from willing residents, Janwani chipped in for the rest. Janwani supervisors had to keep a keen eye on the waste collectors' work. One would think a voluntary user fee would see most people content not to pay. But, to our surprise, the proportion of properties willing to pay the user fee rose from almost zero to 52 per cent in three months. As it turned out, once trust was in place and residents were sure of timely garbage collection, they were willing to segregate their waste and pay. Interestingly, the gap funding was much less than PMC's spending on maintaining cleanliness in the area.

Over and above the collection fee, waste segregation brings extra income for the waste collector. Unsegregated waste is useless. However, when segregated, both dry and wet waste generate income. Dry waste can be recycled, which means an additional income of about ₹10–₹15 (¢15–¢22) per kilogram for the waste collectors. Wet waste can be processed to give fuel, fertilizer, or both.

The model has also demonstrated the economic viability of each of the technologies used in waste processing. They have a payback period of three to five years. In case of shortfalls, a tipping fee based on output of waste disposal, instead of one based on waste collected, would be charged.

Also, despite having to dole out this tipping fee, the urban local body ended up saving money as a result of reductions in transportation and staffing costs. The 'zero-garbage ward' model, if implemented citywide, is estimated to save the city about ₹50 crore (~$7.7 million), or 40 per cent of its current solid waste management costs, annually. All stakeholders, including the city itself, see economic value in this system.

The 'zero-garbage ward' project demonstrates that application of all four STEP levers can decisively solve a serious problem. The interplay of the levers is evident. This experiment in Pune is like a successful laboratory experiment, which now needs to be rolled out across the country.

At the national level, the potential advantages of such a system are monumental. A business research organization, NOVONOUS, estimates that the Indian waste management market will be over $13.5 billion by 2025.[11] Since this market is largely unorganized, there is huge potential to create value. Moreover, Janwani's experience has demonstrated that if applied across the entire country, the model can create over 2.6 million jobs, impacting over 13 million lives.[12] Also, when solid waste is not segregated, it results in methane emissions. Over 100 years, inappropriately treated waste results in twenty-five times more harmful emissions than when it is appropriately segregated and processed. Considering that India's solid waste is estimated to produce 29 per cent of the country's total emissions—almost twice the global average—by 2020, reducing solid waste emissions can lead to a manifold reduction in the harm they cause.

Even as we are proud of all that the 'zero-garbage ward' model has achieved, we are raring to do more. It is indeed not only possible to implement this at the city and state levels, but we also see a national garbage makeover in the offing. We see this transformation in some of

Pune's wards only as a stepping stone towards nationwide implementation.

Every ward a zero-garbage ward—in five years!

Indeed, Janwani is not the only organization working on solid waste management. Across the world, different methods are being tried to manage urban waste. However, the message is the same, and the mechanism too. From Alappuzha (earlier Alleppey) in Kerala and La Pintana in Chile to Montejurra in Spain and Alaminos in the Philippines; from citizen-led models and user-fee-led models to NGO and corporate involvement; from subsidies, incentives and public procurement of recycled produce to technological support and detailed guidance on composting according to nutrient content—many minds are at work to solve this issue of solid waste management. As is rightly so.

Within India itself many initiatives that work towards better solid waste management have begun to take root. While a couple of towns in Kerala and Tamil Nadu have government-led programmes, the one in Solapur, Maharashtra has a private programme. And these are only a few examples.[13] Clearly, people are realizing the significance of waste segregation and its appropriate reuse or disposal. We see these organizations as partners with the same passion as us, all working towards the same goal.

Now it is time to take waste management programmes to the national level. All the methods used by different agencies ought to be studied, curated, tweaked, executed and enforced. Each organization would have invariably used all four levers. In fact, it was heartening to see that Indore, which was recently awarded the cleanest city distinction in India, has made use of each of the STEP levers effectively to achieve waste segregation.[14] Ideas to augment each of the four levers can be picked up from all the organizations working in this area. Having implemented a successful model for over 550,000 households, we believe that Janwani's model can be treated as a nucleus, which can be further enhanced by the knowledge and experience of various other outfits who have worked in the area.

Also, when one seeks to implement any model at the national level, many more options become available in each of the STEP levers. A nationwide campaign, by definition, can have the force of the central government behind it, thereby getting more people from each city involved. Also, national budgets allow for investment in cutting-edge technologies that are out of reach for a municipality.

We believe the 'zero-garbage ward' model can be implemented at the national level. Easy replication has been Janwani's vision from the very beginning. Thus, the insistence on standardized-yet-customizable processes. The detailed methodology, from identification of the NGOs and corporates for collaboration, and planning and implementation, have all been well documented. So the groundwork is ready.

Any practical waste management solution would have three clear objectives: to reduce the quantity of waste generated; to increase waste segregation, organize waste collection and transport to disposal plants; and to dispose the waste in scientific and environment-friendly ways. In order to implement this model across the nation, we propose an examination of waste management from the perspective of the STEP levers.

Nationwide social engagement—so very doable!

Beginning with what we think is the most influential lever for the 'zero-garbage ward' model—social engagement. We believe that at the root of our model's success is creating awareness. Once residents are willing to participate in segregation, the focus can shift to the other cogs in the wheel. While at the city level we operated a door-to-door awareness model, at the country level, the model can gain momentum with media campaigns and public outreach campaigns.

Learning from the 'zero-garbage ward' model, the importance of volunteers cannot be underestimated. We believe that with the involvement of a few full-time professionals and supporting volunteers, the solid waste problem can truly be solved for the entire country. We propose one full-time professional for every 10,000 residents, which would mean 37,000 full-time professionals for the country's urban population and another 83,000 for residents of rural municipalities. We estimate that this entire initiative will cost the government a little over ₹2850 crore per year (less than $500 million), which is extremely affordable, considering that Pune's annual budget for solid waste management is ₹530 crore (~$80 million).[15] In the worst situation these costs can be recovered through local taxes at a mere ₹110 (~$1.7) per year per family![16] (Teach For India and SBI fellow programmes are successfully running such drives in areas other than waste management, using full-time employees.)

In addition to the employment opportunities, 900 million volunteer hours would be required to address the waste management requirements of 300 million households. Over five years, this would translate to 1.15 million volunteers spending about three hours a week on this programme. Yes, very doable—this is less than 0.05 per cent of the population. Especially, considering they can also come from 140 million school students, 3.5 million scouts/NCC/ NSS cadets and the roughly 3 million corporate employees. Rotary clubs and spiritual and religious organizations are often eager to pitch in too. In fact, since these organizations have hundreds of thousands of willing followers, it should not be too difficult a task for them to mobilize volunteers to keep their own environment clean.

It certainly helps that there is a general consensus amongst citizens that the problem of waste management needs immediate attention. Very importantly, no stakeholder stands to lose by solving this problem. This need for a change in society has all the ingredients required to make a social movement in waste management successful.

Collectively, we need to make a guided effort. We need a completely new way of thinking that makes us ask every time we make a purchase: How much of this will end up in the waste bin? Are we minimizing single-use items? If the waste is going out for recycling, does it really end up being recycled? What can we do to make sure the recycling is appropriate?

The time is ripe for such a movement, because globally, new technologies are being developed to attack each aspect of the problem—from reducing generation of waste to effectively reusing waste that has been generated and to disposing waste appropriately.

The technology to scale already exists

Scientists are at work across the world tackling the problem at its very inception. A company in California has developed edible water pouches to replace water bottles. Just like we eat the cone with our ice cream, we can now eat the pouch that holds our drinking water.

However, in areas where there is no escape from waste generation, attempts are being made to make the waste either recyclable or easily decomposable. At the household level there are solutions such as in situ composting of waste, or organic kitchenware in place of disposable plastic. Many start-ups are currently involved in producing such kitchenware. In addition, new materials are being developed to replace Styrofoam, a disposable material that takes thousands of years to decompose. This new material is already being used by companies like IKEA and Dell in their products and packaging.[17]

Another area of constant research is bioplastics. These are 100 per cent biodegradable materials, similar in strength and versatility to regular plastic. These are already being used in agriculture, textiles, medicine and packaging. They are gaining popularity in the western world for ecological reasons. They reduce one's carbon footprint, lead to energy savings, do not use non-renewables for production, produce less non-biodegradable waste, do not contain harmful additives, and do not change the odour and taste of food. Hemp is being used to make a composite material that can replace plastic packaging and plastic products. Hemp grows really quickly without the use of herbicides and with very little pesticide.[18] Currently, the cost of bioplastics is slightly prohibitive; however, economies of scale can work their magic if there is initial funding support. Such avenues also generate employment.

A circular economy, in which one industry uses the waste of another as input, can be formed. Technology can intervene to find new ways to convert waste into something of value. Centralized biogas or bio-CNG plants can be used for commercial and bulk wet-waste generators. Meanwhile, the non-recyclable dry waste can be converted into fuel using available technology.

Technologies such as thermal liquefaction can take care of waste disposal. Of course, to facilitate collection and transportation of waste, technology solutions can aid with route optimization apps. Public participation can be encouraged through mobile apps that allow citizens to point authorities to areas that need to be cleaned up.

Since 2011, 260 projects from thirty-four countries have been undertaken to reduce plastic waste. Some of these projects work on scooping out plastic junk from the bottom of the ocean. Other companies, such as Adidas, use recycled plastic in their products. And of course, there is a constant effort to discover new methods of converting waste into new biodegradable plastic—from developing bacteria capable of digesting plastics to microwaves that can break plastic down quicker.[19]

Technologies are aplenty; we have to pick the ones that fit the Indian context, suit our purposes and make economic sense to us.

Making the economics work for each citizen

As described earlier, the economics works out for all the stakeholders involved in the 'zero-garbage ward' model. However, at the national level, it is important to make the financials even more lucrative for everyone.

Waste collectors are the foot soldiers for a sustainable waste management programme in India. Without them the entire system will crumble. While the income model has been detailed earlier, we further implore that the user fee be different for different households, based on their capacity to pay.

We propose a ₹30–₹50 (~¢45–¢75) range for non-slum areas and ₹10–₹20 (~¢15–¢30) for slum areas. Densely populated slums mean more households in a given area, thereby equalizing collections from non-slum and slum areas from the waste collectors' point of view. Waste collectors can earn more than ₹16,000 (~$250) per month.[20] And this from just a four-hour day job; the waste collectors then have the second half of the day free to employ themselves elsewhere.

Waste treatment plants, when operated professionally, can be profitable ventures. The focus should be on value addition and productization of waste rather than just waste disposal. Information technology should be used for real-time performance monitoring. A mini-biogas unit could earn a net profit of ₹15,000 (~$230) annually on a capital investment of ₹50,000 (~$770). A dry-waste recycling plant could earn as much as 19 crore (~$3 million) per annum, at an initial investment of 2 crore (~$300,000) and annual operating costs of ₹8 crore (~$1.25 million).

These earnings also depend on what the end product substitutes. For instance, if the end product from recycling is converted into pellets for burning in a boiler, it substitutes coal, which costs ₹6 (~¢10) per kilogram; and if it is converted into compressed fuel used in a public transport vehicle, it makes ₹48 (~¢72) per kilogram. However, if the waste is converted into biogas that is sold as a substitute for LPG, the earnings are ₹61 (~¢92) per kilogram.[21]

As is evident, each of the STEP levers needs constant and progressive support from all-important public policy. And this support can come in the various ways described in the 'Public Policy' chapter.

Give-and-take relationships: policy and the other three levers

Other than the benefits outlined earlier for the municipal corporation in terms of savings in transportation costs and landfill costs, the 'zero-garbage ward' model's public–private partnership model can include sharing of the initial capital burden with a private partner. The municipal council need pay only the viability gap. Governments can also get support from corporate and philanthropic funds. The savings in costs can be to the tune of ₹950 (~$15) per tonne for transportation and approximately another ₹950 per tonne in tipping fees paid to disposal plants. Tipping fees payable to centralized processing plants halve as a result of reduction in waste. Salaries reduce by ₹44 crore (~$6.8 million) per annum. For a city the size of Pune, this leads to savings of about ₹70 crore (~$10.7 million) every year.

In addition, the municipality has avenues to earn additional income, which can finance other desirable schemes needing an initial nudge. Yes, the bonus-malus model can be used to fund the viability gap. For instance, certain technologies, like bioplastics and organic kitchenware, may need initial government support. This could be in the form of subsidies or through mass public procurement, as in the case of the LED light bulb project in India, mentioned earlier in the book. Funding for these projects can come from taxing plastics and other materials that we wish to replace.

As an example, the Indian plastics industry is estimated to be ₹1 lakh crore (~$15 billion) in size.[22] Given an annual growth of 10 to 11 per cent, a cess or tax, similar to a carbon/green cess on coal, of even 1 per cent can generate a corpus of ₹1000 crore (~$150 million). If this money is deployed for dedicated research on environment-friendly materials such as bioplastics, cheaper bioplastics might not be a distant dream. Like any other bonus-malus model, this one will make eco-friendly technologies affordable and accessible on the one hand and make plastic costly on the other, arresting its rampant use.

This is where the 'Economic Model' lever begins to blend with the 'Policy' lever. While bonus-malus is a policy initiative to aid economic viability of desirable projects, many other policy tools can be used to similar effect. From accelerated depreciation for waste management production equipment, reducing the tax burden on the manufacturing companies, to incentive schemes for organic fertilizers derived from biogas and composted organic waste, waste can actually be treated much as we treat agriculture in terms of policy breaks and support.

Similarly, policy will also have to be used to get the public engaged. Here policy push is required at two levels. At the national or state level, a broader philosophy of waste management and general guidelines have to be established. At the municipal level, in the cities, a more detailed policy drive will be required.

Swachh Bharat Abhiyan (Clean India Mission), initiated in India on 2 October 2014, the birth anniversary of Mahatma Gandhi, was a good starting point at the national level. Some of the activities undertaken by the mission, such as the vigorous drive to build toilets and the cleaning of the country's most revered river, the Ganga, are extremely important initiatives. Akin to the Ice Bucket Challenge discussed in the 'Social Engagement' chapter, the prime minister called out on the country's top celebrities to start a 'chain campaign' using social media. It did create some awareness and inspired citizens to participate in the cleanliness movement, but the movement lost steam soon afterwards.[23] That it created awareness was a great first step. However, it turned out to be a symbolic launch which did not lead to action. The efforts need more structure for the scheme's long-term sustenance.

We must revive such initiatives into more sustainable campaigns through well-planned, coordinated actions. This will mean a dedicated administrative support structure, with competent officers taking the lead. We propose that Swachh Bharat be conducted on the lines of the Pulse Polio Campaign, which has been very successful in eradicating polio from India.

Public policy can also help desirable technologies take hold; it can also use technology to make the implementation of any project easier. As mentioned earlier, the government can invest in new technologies till they hit the necessary scale. In the matter of waste management, policy can also encourage use of recycled material by supporting manufacturers who develop such technologies. Alternatively, governments can make recycled content mandatory for plastic products, thereby driving research in technologies that can do so.[24] This is already being tried in other countries. Sixteen US states have legalized hemp production for commercial purposes, and twenty states allow research and pilot programmes that use hemp as a material to substitute plastic.[25] Authorities can also use technology to create customer response centres that invite suggestions through public participation.

Thus, public policy can actually be used to encourage each of the other levers, and each of the other levers can both influence and be used by governments to create the desired effects. In fact, policy can be used effectively at each stage of the waste management process—generation, segregation, collection and disposal.

Currently, waste management in India is governed by a series of rules and regulations under various pollution control acts. These laws are geared towards reducing pollution by waste, but do not specify guidelines for waste management. Considering the potential for both industry and employment in waste management, dedicated and holistic waste management laws that cover management and financial aspects are necessary.

This policy initiative will have to begin at the beginning. In our model of waste management, the first step is to reduce the quantity of waste generated. Punitive measures and taxation policies can play a major role here. To curb the manufacture of certain products that can create harmful waste, such as plastics, a top-down approach will have a greater impact than a bottom-up effort that begins at an individual citizen's conscience.

To encourage waste segregation, the government can create an enabling environment for start-ups through promotional schemes for micro-waste management activities. We found that the more decentralized and micromanaged the waste segregation system was, the better it worked. Government policies to promote micro-scale initiatives will help to generate sustainable, full-time employment too. National-level competitions with awards and recognition for the best-performing state/city/district/village, similar to the Sant Gadgebaba Gram Swachhata Abhiyan of Maharashtra, will go a long way in making each area a better version of itself.

Such broad national policies will have to be supported at the local level by bringing in day-to-day rules and regulations like Pune's by-laws. They will include detailed guidelines for collection, transportation and disposal of waste. Simple steps such as serving notices to households that fail to segregate garbage will go a long way in compelling citizens to be more compliant. Location-specific incentives to ensure timely and segregated collection of waste will have to be implemented through laws too.

One of the biggest hurdles to success in the case of the 'zero-garbage ward' initiative lay in convincing all the partners that their participation was worth their time, energy and effort. As illustrated earlier, Janwani and its partners used various methods in their outreach campaign to heighten awareness about the project and its value to the locality. Local bodies can take the lead and help spread the word using their authority. This can be done in many ways. Detailed notifications, language-neutral signboards, use of print and visual media, rallies and awareness campaigns in schools are a few of them.

These are only some ways in which the STEP levers can come together for implementation of a viable, sustainable waste management system at ward, city, state and national levels. We are sure that as more minds apply themselves towards this cause, there will be even better results. As it stands today, we are already seeing a positive impact of our model on the three major parameters of success, the 3Es: Energy, Environment and Environment. And there is potential to do better.

The 'zero-garbage ward' model: A powerfully positive impact on the 3Es

When extended to the national level, the model can have a forceful impact on all 3Es, and we see a cleaner, more productive country. At the outset, waste when properly managed can be a renewable source of energy. Load centres that are close to cities can supply power with minimum technical losses. At present, India has 114 megawatts of waste-to-energy installed capacity.[26] The ministry of new and renewable energy believes that urban waste can create about 1500 megawatts from solid waste.[27] While electricity can be generated from dry waste, vehicular fuel can be created by scientific management of wet waste.

As expected, these sources of energy have a positive cascading impact on the environment. The first of these is a reduction in emission of harmful gases. Open dumping of waste pollutes groundwater and also causes a significant reduction in soil nutrients such as nitrates, potassium and phosphorus. Open dumping also makes it much more difficult to recycle and reuse waste. Well-designed, properly covered landfills with an adequate collection system can enable sustainable disposal of solid wastes and further their use as an energy source. According to one estimate, currently only 20 to 25 per cent of landfill gases can be recovered, while the rest of the gases escape into the atmosphere. Properly engineered landfills can enable utilization of 30 to 60 per cent of the emitted gases. These recovered landfill gases can be used as a direct source of energy and power generation, or can even be upgraded to vehicle fuel.[28] The other environmental benefits of a well-functioning solid waste management system are reduced soil pollution and availability of organic manure for agriculture.

The newer avenues of waste management will be a source of employment too. Direct employment will come in the form of waste collectors and employees needed in waste processing units. On the other hand, recycling will be an indirect source of income for scrap collectors.

The 'zero-garbage ward' model's experience shows that two waste collectors can cater to a population of 800 to 1000. Considering the population of 1.2 billion Indians, a nationwide implementation can create 2.4 million jobs, impacting 12 million livelihoods.[29]

It is evident that when the STEP levers come together to solve the problem of solid waste management in this manner, they can effectively address the 3E problems. The solution that has emerged in the form of the zero-garbage model and the one that we propose for scaling it to a national level are indeed ASSURED Total Innovations.

Since it satisfies the economic model for all stakeholders, it is Affordable for all involved.

That we could transition from one ward to twenty is proof enough that it is Scalable. In fact, we are in a position where we are raring to go, to scale it to the national level.

By definition, it is a solution that is environmentally sustainable. When tweaked to local requirements, it is also a solution that is socially and economically Sustainable.

The very basic idea was to make the entire process of solid waste management, from generation to disposal, as easy as possible for everyone involved, making User-friendliness an integral part of the solution.

Having understood the nitty-gritty of the problem, and given the right support system, we are positive that we can implement it effectively across the country as Rapidly as in five years!

This is because it is a solution that achieves Excellence, involving and taking care of the people at the bottom of the pyramid in a transformationally Distinctive manner.

Indeed, when we look ahead five years down the line, we see an India where there is no plastic on the shores of Mumbai or on the Himalayan slopes. We see all Indians actively participating in segregation and recycling waste, not just for a clean India, but also to see themselves as the world's leading force to create a truly cyclical economy. We see many Indians dignifiedly and gainfully employed through this and similar projects. We are now, more than ever, convinced that all of this is possible in India. Because this is a changing India. The iron is hot and we can strike at the right time. Yes, we envision a Clean Revolution in the making. A Clean Revolution that is relevant to our own generation and the many to come.

ELEVEN

Today's Green Revolution Transforming Mobility

From the time our ancestors started walking on two legs to our ventures into outer space today, mobility has been an intrinsic part of our evolution. Were it not for our urge to move from one place to another for survival and to satisfy our curiosity to explore, our species would not have moved out of our birthplace in Africa. But for this deep desire to move, we would not have invented the wheel, let alone produce engines that would sail, drive and fly us. Further, as humans unlocked new technologies and new sources of energy, these were incorporated into the current forms of transportation to change the face of this sector. These innovations in transportation have reduced the time, risks, costs and inconveniences associated with travel, allowing humans to cross cities, countries, and the planet itself.

Improvement in mobility has played a dominant role in almost all economies of the world for the last century and a half. National economies are dependent on the country's ability to transport not just humans, but also goods, from place to place. Transportation is thus key to a lot of what humans do. It has encouraged migration, shaped the architecture of cities and towns, changed societies, influenced culture, created and grown economies, fostered job creation. In a nutshell, it has changed every aspect of life.

While we have taken huge strides in marine and air transportation too, and their importance cannot be exaggerated, the role of ground transport in changing our lives is the most prominent. We have come a long way when it comes to mass public transportation on land. And within ground transport, automobiles—cars and commercial vehicles—have played the most dominant role in shaping modern human life.

For the purposes of this book we have chosen the automobile industry as our focus in the area of mobility. At present, by all indications, the world of cars and public transport is in a state of phenomenal transformation. The next few decades will be nothing like the last century. As much as efficient and affordable transportation is essential for a vibrant economy, it brings its own share of problems. The energy needed to power transportation has posed problems that concern us all. Today we might find it difficult to believe that the automotive industry was welcomed in New York as a technology that reduced pollution! The air in the city in the 1910s was unbreathable because of the overbearing stench of horse excreta. And yet, today, we are back to square one, with an even bigger problem at hand.

The present shift in the mobility industry calls for an accessible, environmentally sustainable and affordable energy system to power transport. In the pages ahead, we explore one such vision: a world where transportation is built around clean vehicle technology, driven by energy sources that are clean, and creates employment and equitable access to economic opportunities for all.

Going forward, we urgently need to look at this industry differently. Is it possible to look forward to a world of transportation that doesn't pollute our cities? A world in which some nations do not rely on imported energy, which is the cause of much of the political instability in this world? Can we look forward to energy sources that do not involve oligopolistic production by a few, even though the sources are consumed by many? Can we have energy sources that are independent of the inefficient technologies used today?

This is certainly possible. We can cut petroleum consumption drastically. We can create a new transportation industry that is more inclusive, one that enables more people to participate both in creating and sharing value. Again, this is not idealistic fantasy, but a very possible reality.

We are witnessing changes in physical infrastructure and public transport systems; we are seeing 'servitizing' of transport through information technology, and smarter cargo networks and changes in human behaviour underlying the new age of transportation. These are all a part of our future reality.

Each of these areas and more are important, exciting, and has tremendous scope for innovation. In fact, the last time we saw change of such magnitude in the automobile industry was when Ford introduced the Model T over 100 years ago. This made cars affordable for the common man, revolutionizing the industry. Not since then has the industry changed as much as it is changing right now. This is why we are so enthused about the transformation in this industry—which we are very much a part of.

For the purposes of applying our 'leapfrogging to pole-vaulting' model, we will focus on innovations related to vehicles.

Before that though, let us try to understand the current situation in the industry as it relates to the 3Es.

Road transportation: An omnipresent contributor to the 3Es

The energy demand–supply story

Any discussion on the auto industry cannot begin without a discussion on the fossil-fuel industry. These two industries have taken strides in lockstep. Oil has been the fuel of choice for this industry so far. Except for electric cars, which constitute less than 1 per cent of new auto sales worldwide currently, all other automobiles run on oil. Each problem enumerated in the 'Energy' section of the 3Es chapter—from controlled supply and pricing, to increasing demand and the impact of energy extraction on the environment—will also present itself in the energy problems related to the automobile industry. Other fallouts of the automobile industry's reliance on oil, such as overdependence of some countries on imports, skewing the international power dynamics, and the widening urban–rural divide in terms of both energy production and consumption, become integral to the discussion too.

Indeed, as far as the use of energy resources is concerned, the automobile industry is at a breaking point. Due to the increasing difficulty of access to depleting energy sources, increased costs and, most importantly, alarming environmental consequences of our current energy consumption patterns, the need for new energy sources is now more pressing than ever before. India's energy import bill in 2016–17 was about 26 per cent of its total import bill of $384 billion.[1] This proportion is only likely to increase, given the desired economic development and ever-growing urbanization in the country.

As far as the refineries in India go, they are operated by a handful of organizations. As it stands today, the energy setup for transport currently enables very limited participation—and therefore employment—along its value chain. And this is true of almost all non-OPEC countries.

Production: A health hazard for the planet and its inhabitants

It is important to underscore the disastrous impact of drilling itself. One might have heard about the hazards entailed in natural gas extraction. Oil and gas drilling also carries many hidden costs. For instance, the water brought to the earth's surface during such extraction carries dissolved solids, heavy metals, radioactive materials and other substances of a toxic nature. This water is not usable and is not easy to dispose of either. And to think that a single shale gas formation requires not only millions of gallons of water but also thousands of gallons of chemicals. To make matters worse, the producers do not disclose the names of all the chemicals they use. Independent studies have found 630 to 750 chemicals in such gas products. And only about 350 were traceable. These chemicals can cause neurological damage and cancer, and can adversely impact the hormonal and immune systems of humans and animals.[2]

It must be remembered that oil wells are not stand-alone structures; they need access roads, processing facilities and other infrastructure, which have their own impact on the ecosystems around. For instance, between 2001 and 2005, there was an 82 per cent decline in the population of the sage grouse, a unique species of bird, in the Powder River Basin in the US. This was directly correlated to coal-bed methane production in the vicinity. Many gas resources are often found in virgin, unexplored areas, thereby leading to disturbing a fresh ecosystem.[3]

Another aspect of oil drilling is that it often happens in the hinterland or far out in the ocean, where employees find it very difficult to access health facilities. This has resulted in untreated injuries and even deaths. Between 2008 and 2012, there were thirty-four deaths and 1436 injuries, and sixty oil spills at US offshore drilling rigs.[4]

Consumption—exacerbates the looming environmental concerns

In addition to the environmental impact of digging, energy consumption systems are wasteful and harmful too. For instance, the ICE used in most vehicles today is extremely inefficient, especially when load, road and speed conditions vary.

This wastefulness, combined with the inherent chemistry of fossil fuels, contributes to the environmental and health problems discussed in Chapter 2. Energy resources are increasingly inaccessible, climate change increasingly grim, and the costs of local air pollution shocking, to say the very least. The Global Commission on Economy and Climate recently reported that premature deaths from air pollution alone cost India up to 6 per cent of its GDP.[5]

And the road transport sector can be held responsible to a great extent for these tragedies. This sector accounts for almost 63 per cent of the total consumption of petroleum products.[6]

Most Indian cities have high levels of various types of air pollutants, from carbon monoxide to particulate matter. It is estimated that the transportation sector accounts for 70 per cent of this pollution. Road transport alone is responsible for almost 95 per cent of the carbon dioxide (CO_2) emitted by the transport sector. While accounting for only 17 per cent of the total energy consumed, this sector accounts for 60 per cent of greenhouse gas emissions in the country.[7] At present, fourteen out of the twenty most polluted cities in the world are in India.[8] As India continues to develop, more and more smaller towns are going to be impacted by transportation.

In addition to the environmental hazards of using vehicles the way we do, automobiles have an indirect impact on other aspects of our lifestyle too. To begin with the obvious, traffic congestion is responsible for loss of man-hours and peace of mind. The way we manage transportation causes loss of life and limb too.

The subtler impact—loss of money, time, and life itself

The direct impact of vehicular air pollution on our health can be seen in the form of respiratory diseases and the like. We also know of its impact on our planet through global warming. Though we all suffer the indirect impact of transportation, this impact is not reflected in the GDP and other such metrics.

Ironically, air pollution in the road transport industry is worse when traffic is not moving. The environmental damage caused by inadequate infrastructure and planning is only one part of the traffic congestion problem. In 1998, New Delhi alone wasted fuel worth $300,000 every day as a result of vehicles idling at traffic signals! In 2010, this per-day number stood at about $1.6 million, and in 2015, at $23.5 million. Likewise, expenditure due to traffic congestion in the United Kingdom is expected to increase by 50 per cent annually from the 2014 numbers, to $33.4 billion ($91 million per day) by 2030. The United States is expecting to see a similar rise, and will see losses of $186 billion ($510 million per day) by 2030.[9] But the numbers for Delhi alone are about 26 per cent of the numbers for the entire UK, and 5 per cent of numbers for all of the US in 2030! And these numbers don't include loss of productivity in hours spent by the citizens, which can be monumental by itself. Another Indian city, Bengaluru, loses 600 million man-hours annually on this score.[10]

When the congestion is not too bad, road accidents lead to disability, if not a toll on life. Globally, 1.3 million people die every year in car accidents.[11] In 2017, there were 146,000 fatal road accidents in India. While this is a 3 per cent drop from 2016, it still amounts to seventeen deaths every hour.[12] Counter-intuitively, about 38 per cent of these deaths happen on roads other than national and state highways.[13]

The silver lining—employment. For now

Given all these factors, the current state of road transportation in terms of energy consumption and environmental destruction is so bleak that it calls for a complete overhaul of how resources are extracted and used in this industry. In terms of employment, though, the industry stands at a relatively favourable position—so far.

From mining to the roadside automobile repair centre— spanning manufacturing, road construction and logistics— transportation, across its value chain, is amongst the largest employers. In fact, in its heyday it was the symbol of middle-class prosperity. Road transportation also results in investment in roads and is responsible for viable and sustainable suburbs, all of which create employment opportunities of their own.

The Indian automotive sector alone employs over 29 million, making it one of the world's largest employers.[14] India ranks at the top in production of tractors, second in two-wheeler and bus production and fifth in heavy truck manufacturing—to name a few of its rankings in this sector.[15, 16] More importantly, for every two-wheeler produced, direct and indirect opportunities are created for one person; every three-wheeler produced creates four jobs, every car, six, and every truck, thirteen! With India being one of the largest manufacturers of vehicles, the impact of this industry on employment is very encouraging. Moreover, India's logistics industry is expected to grow at a compounded annual rate of 10.5 per cent, and employment is expected to grow at almost 8 per cent, which is currently at 22 million.[17]

Even as the number of jobs has been increasing so far, as discussed earlier, the quality of life has gradually taken a beating in some aspects. The very character of employment has become mostly tedious and dull, while some jobs like mining and night-time truck driving are dangerous too. As is the truth of our times, some of these jobs are now being taken over by mechanization and robots. Except for tyre repair, even the roadside mechanic's job is at stake. With puncture-proof tyres, we might soon not need a human for changing tyres either. Self-driving cars by themselves are expected to lead to job losses of between 12 and 15 per cent, and this loss will be quick and extremely disruptive.[18]

So, employment can be considered as a strong but weakening interest fighting the other two Es. The fact is, as individual incomes increase in developing countries which progress along financial and other metrics, vehicles on the road are on the rise, and they are choking our cities and towns. Healthcare costs have increased, and so has time wasted in idleness. In addition, public spaces, which can be used for other purposes, are wasted on parking. The situation is grim.

Even so, new technologies and innovative asset-sharing trends have compelled us to take a downside-up look at the industry. These new innovations have their positives and make an unyielding case for examining the industry with completely fresh eyes.

Towards this direction, we can ask some fresh questions. How can we transform this industry so that it becomes clean and has more distributed sources of energy? Can these transformations also lower the demand for materials and minerals? At the same time, could these solutions bring about greater income and more egalitarian distribution, while also reducing accidents and freeing up urban spaces? With this new paradigm as the goal, we shall pit the industry's present and future against the STEP levers.

STEP—driving us towards transformation

Technology—undreamt-of developments, inconceivable potential

In the last decade, every aspect of the industry has seen enormous technological advances. Today, as we stand at the cusp of change in this industry, three major aspects are witnessing hitherto unimagined innovation: the manner in which our vehicles are powered, or the fuel they use; the manner in which we commute, a shift from ownership to shared riding; and the manner in which we drive that is not drive at all, because automated vehicles won't need us to. Each of these shifts has far-reaching impacts that are going to take us by surprise. Let's take them up in turn.

Powering engines

As an alternative to petrol and diesel, which are an environmental menace, we are already using CNG and bio-CNG, which produce relatively less pollutants. But, slowly and surely, electricity is becoming the new but pollution-free oil. The massive move towards EVs is extremely relevant to urban transportation, even more so because an increasingly large part of humanity will live in urban areas in the decades to come.

The obvious questions to ask next are: How is this electricity generated? How is it stored? How is it used?

Newer and cleaner technologies are the answer to each of these questions. Very clearly, if a vehicle runs on electricity, it does not produce any emission where it is used, namely, in the car. But how can we say that EVs do not harm the environment if the electricity they use is generated by burning coal or oil? Therefore, in the first place, the source of energy used to generate the said electricity has to be considered. If energy generation is clean and if it burns cleanly, we obviously have an environmentally clean solution.

In the recent past, there has been a move away from generating electricity using coal and gas to using renewable sources, such as the sun, wind, waves, geothermal sources, to name a few. These sources of energy don't require fossil fuels, and are therefore certainly clean. Right now, price parity between electricity generation from fossil fuels and electricity generated from renewable sources is on the horizon.

This brings us to the issue of electricity storage for EVs, which use electricity for power instead of petrol or diesel. EVs are either battery electric vehicles (BEVs) or hydrogen fuel cell electric vehicles (FC-EVs). BEVs store energy in the battery which is converted to electricity as needed. FC-EVs, on the other hand, store hydrogen in the vehicle and convert it to electricity through a fuel cell.

Currently the world is largely focused on BEVs and the infrastructure around charging BEVs. Battery costs are the largest component of the price of the electric powertrain, the mechanism that transmits the drive from the engine of a vehicle to its axle. The burning question of the hour then is: How do we make batteries for BEVs affordable to the common person?

In the recent past, most innovation has been directed towards increasing the energy density of the battery— making a lighter battery store the energy required by an average vehicle to cover a distance between two fuel stops. Every time you drive a car, you consume the electricity stored in the battery. Like your phone, when the battery drains, it will have to be recharged before you can use the vehicle again. The longer it takes to recharge the battery, the less convenient it is to use a BEV. After all, it is rather pointless to own a car that takes half a day to charge for every 150 kilometres of driving. Across the globe, efforts are also being driven towards increasing battery capacity.

The second characteristic of a battery is its power density. The higher the power density, the less time it takes for a recharge. An ideal battery should have high energy density as well as high power density so that once charged, a vehicle can be driven a long distance, and once discharged it can be recharged quickly. Unfortunately, the world has not yet reached a stage where a battery, an affordable one, has the right energy density and power density.

The energy and power requirements of a car make lithium-ion batteries the current choice to store energy. Lithium provides the required energy density. However, current lithium batteries are expensive and take a long time to charge, unless one compromises on the life of the battery. But newer technologies are progressively allowing for longer and longer drives between two recharges.

Battery technology is moving at a pace at which both these goals will be achievable in the next five to ten years. How efficiently a battery is used depends on the electronic system which guides their charging and how the battery discharges in the running of the car—the battery-management system. KPIT is playing a role in addressing battery-management issues and is deeply engaged in this work globally.

Even within various aspects of BEVs, the world's focus is on electric personal car where the key concern is 'range anxiety', the driver's worry that their car will suddenly run out of battery. So, all efforts have been directed at ensuring long ranges that enable long-distance drives. However, personal cars are not the only vehicles that run on the road. Already in cities, the trend of people moving away from personal cars is apparent, an encouraging trend we will discuss soon.

Driving patterns in the case of heavily used vehicles such as cabs and buses are very different from those for personal cars. Typically, a bus drives a known distance along its route. In India, almost 100 per cent of urban bus routes are less than 35 kilometres, one way, and the bus stops at the end of this route for about twenty minutes before travelling the same route back. So distances are short, making the twenty-minute break available for a quick recharge. Rental cars or three-wheeled rickshaws have similar driving patterns—short drives followed by short rests. These vehicles would need quick battery recharge but do not need high-energy storage capacity at any point. A low energy density battery that has a quick recharge time, which is not very expensive, and has a long life can be the perfect solution for an electric urban public transport vehicle. We contend that such a vehicle does not need a lithium battery.

The world requires chemistries other than lithium, and which will be far more relevant for countries such as India. Such alternatives will counter the other problem related to the materials that lithium-ion batteries use—lithium and cobalt. Both these materials are rare, and are available in only a few countries. One of the problems with current global energy supply, as described in Chapter 2, is that fossil fuels are controlled by a few countries, making most of the rest of the world hostage to the oil-producing countries. We suspect that dependence on lithium-ion batteries will lead to a similar situation. Lithium and cobalt will be the new oil.

Both these materials are required not just for BEVs but also for phone and laptop batteries, making them an essential part of today's energy mix. And of course, this adds to the increase in demand for the two materials too. This demand is likely to increase sevenfold in the next seven to eight years.[19]

Next, the supply of lithium and cobalt is limited. While a few countries mine cobalt, Democratic Republic of

Congo (DRC) supplies two-thirds of the world's cobalt, with no other country contributing more than 10 per cent of world supply. Cobalt production in DRC is infamous for its illegal mining, and child labour is a major humanitarian concern too. Similarly, over 76 per cent of the world's lithium is supplied by Australia and Chile, while Argentina and China supply almost 20 per cent.[20]

As a corollary to the rising demand and restricted supply of these materials, their prices are increasing. Cobalt more than doubled in price in 2017 alone.[21] And since battery prices have dropped to 10 per cent of 2010 levels, the cost of lithium and cobalt needed per lithium-ion battery has risen to 70 per cent of their total cost. The lithium-ion battery could make up about 50 per cent of the total cost of a BEV. So the cost of these materials is central to any further reduction in EV costs. We are confident that it is possible to move away from lithium-ion batteries. KPIT believes that we need to explore other battery chemistries, and is working on such solutions.

This brings us to our other contention, that FC-EVs—EVs not dependent on batteries at all—are a more appropriate solution. BEVs are most appropriate for urban drives. When you drive a BEV, you are actually carrying the battery around—the battery's weight in a Tesla is over a tonne. If you want to drive a long distance, you will obviously have to carry a larger battery, and your vehicle will be heavier. This makes BEVs an inadequate solution, especially for long-distance drives. The world has been looking at hydrogen fuel-cells in this context.

In an FC-EV, you carry hydrogen along with a fuel cell. The fuel cell uses the hydrogen and converts it to electricity, which runs the vehicle. When hydrogen is so used, you get only water as effluent. So this is possibly the

cleanest solution for driving a vehicle. You don't carry
a lot of weight around and you emit nothing other than
water. While one can use FC-EVs in cities too, the solution
is particularly relevant for travel between cities.

Recognizing these advantages, many countries are
now joining a hydrogen mission—promoting the use
of hydrogen as the right fuel. International automotive
companies such as Toyota, Honda and Hyundai are
currently running trials of FC-EVs. We too believe that this
is the right way to go. This technology can be affordable
and will certainly be very clean. We are working on FC-
EVs and are attempting to bring them to an acceptable
price and mileage range.

Of course, FC-EVs cannot run without hydrogen.
Hydrogen can be generated from natural gas, water or
biomass. Hydrogen generation from natural gas is a
well-known process. However, you need natural gas for
this purpose, which, unfortunately, is generally available
through the fossil-fuel route. This would have the same
demerits as oil. Making hydrogen from water is the next
option.

Some countries are considering converting water into
hydrogen through use of peak extra power generated
from solar energy during times of bright sunshine, or from
wind when there are strong winds. The extra electricity
generated during this period can be safely stored in the
form of hydrogen and can be used for running FC-EVs.
In such cases, the cost of hydrogen can be very low. Many
countries are relying on this method for their hydrogen
economics. This hydrogen will be available wherever
the sun shines or the wind blows—which is practically
everywhere in the world. Right now the technology to
convert water to hydrogen is capital-intensive. However,

as the share of renewable sources goes up in the total mix, more hydrogen will also become available at lower costs.

The third possibility is hydrogen generation from biomass. In India, agricultural waste is a serious problem. The country sees a surplus of about 22 million tonnes of rice straw and 10 million tonnes of rice husk every year.[22] Similar quantities of agricultural waste are generated by other crops, such as wheat.[23] Rice and wheat straw, and sugar-cane bagasse, the pulpy residue after sugar cane is processed, is often burnt after the crop is harvested. The burnt crop is not only wasted, it also causes other environmental issues. Part of Delhi's air pollution is on account of crop burning in the neighbouring states. What if such biomass can be economically converted into hydrogen in a distributed manner? What if solutions are found to fix the burning of agricultural biomass, and this activity also generates another source of income for the poor farmer?

We believe the answer lies in generating hydrogen from biomass. This is an immensely exciting avenue—and not just technologically. Imagine, just like grain and milk flow from our rural hinterlands to our cities, creating a bridge of economic interdependence, energy through hydrogen could create another such bridge. If we can create hydrogen from biomass, rural India can provide energy for transportation for the entire country.

This can generate incomes for our rural brethren, cut down our fuel-import burden, and provide clean, pollution-free fuel. As cabinet minister Nitin Gadkari stresses, all fuels generated from biomass, including CNG, ethanol, methanol or hydrogen, has the potential to create 5 million jobs in the country.[24]

The biohydrogen solution can also provide renewable, carbon-neutral fuels from inexhaustible green resources.

If this appears incredible, then one should keep in mind that replacement of a single conventional bus by a bio-hydrogen bus can reduce diesel requirement by 25 tonnes, and carbon dioxide emissions by 48 tonnes, every year. The added advantage of using biomass to create hydrogen is that it would otherwise have been burnt, causing more pollution.

This is economically attractive not only at individual and city levels, but at the national fiscal-level too, because it will reduce the country's dependence on fossil-fuel imports, which today cost India $102 billion every year.[25]

Not only can 'biomass for hydrogen' solve issues of rural employment and urban pollution, it can also solve the problem of rural pollution.

We believe that Indian industry can take up this challenge. KPIT is certainly contributing in this area.

As our discussion so far shows, much is happening in the world of technology to ensure that our transportation is clean. We are sure that this problem will be solved in the next two decades; we will then wonder how we damaged our Mother Earth by the reckless burning of dirty fuel for over 200 years. We are looking forward to the day when we all have clean transportation as a matter of right.

As mentioned earlier, today technology is at play in three aspects of transportation—fuel, ownership and elimination of driving. We now turn to the other two aspects.

Sharing our rides

The solutions discussed so far can lead to clean and eco-friendly transportation, but neither BEV nor FC-EV can reduce the number of vehicles on the street, leaving the major issues of city congestion and the related social costs unresolved. Beyond the application of physics and chemistry as seen above, information technology is solving road transportation issues too.

Traffic congestion is being partly solved through the use of shared transportation, either by means of public transport or by sharing rides through mobile apps. An information cloud over a geographical area can solve problems of congestion, pollution and time loss. The Olas, Lyfts and Ubers of our times are a part of this solution.

In addition, a move to sharing our assets can lead to even more savings. An MIT study shows that New York City could potentially see a 75 per cent decline in taxis if everyone moved to ride-sharing.[26] Ride-sharing allows for movement of two to four people at a time instead of one person per taxi. The reduced traffic and reduced fuel usage will significantly bring down congestion on the road and toxins in the air, having a positive impact on both the economy and public health. This is estimated to save the city $160 billion, including savings from 3 billion gallons of fuel that won't be burned by vehicles waiting in traffic and 7 billion hours of time that won't be lost by people waiting in traffic.[27] All this with an average waiting time of less than three minutes for cabs.

Even more efficiencies are possible. Current technology allows route creation only after all requests are submitted. It is only a matter of time before software becomes self-learning and can reroute a vehicle on the fly, optimizing car size with the number of passengers on a given route. Other than e-hailing and car-pooling there are other transport-mobility innovations too, such as pay-per-use models and peer-to-peer car rentals. That these ideas attract funds is an encouraging sign.

Already, it is found that ride-sharing apps reduce the number of vehicles on the road in cities where such apps are well established. Moreover, they encourage multimodal, sustainable transport, which complements public and active forms of transport, such as cycling and walking. In addition, sharing rides has reduced car ownership. Each shared car added on the road replaces five to fifteen owned cars. And although long-distance car-sharing services compete with rail and coach services, they significantly increase car occupancy and reduce emissions per kilometre.[28]

No driving at all!

And what if none of the vehicles above needed a human driver? What we would have dismissed as science fiction is likely to happen sooner rather than later. If they satisfy regulatory requirements, autonomous vehicles (AVs) will be here to stay. The immediate advantage of AVs is far fewer accidents and congestion-free roads.

To begin with, AVs are already a reality in industrial fleets for transportation within industrial premises. As their application and capabilities move from industrial to personal use, the entire road transportation ecosystem will change. As a reminder of the potential changes that AVs can bring about alluded to in the chapter on 'Technology', here are a few more. Insurance companies will move their focus from individuals' health to cover manufacturers' technical failures; the entire aftersales service industry will see a shift which is difficult to even imagine right now; and car design will change to suit the passenger rather than the driver. As driverless cars increase in popularity, the time people would have spent in driving and in traffic jams will be freed up. Parking space too will be freed up for other civic uses. Accidents are estimated to reduce by 90 per cent.

Moreover, when the relatively latest ride-sharing innovations meet AVs, routing efficiencies and time saved will be taken to a whole new level. Shared transportation calls for connectivity devices and high-quality software powered by AI and machine learning—an area in which the Indian software industry can proudly boast significant strengths. However, public transportation is an area in which our cities and towns are woefully inadequate. Not only do we need better funding for bus transportation, we also need better technology. We need high data connectivity, better comfort and better route management to make our buses the preferred mode of urban travel. Some of KPIT's solutions in this area cover aspects of data connectivity as well as route management.

Our roads need to be made safer for drivers, passengers and pedestrians. The world is moving towards AVs which, when fully developed, will make for a safe world. We believe that in India we may not need fully autonomous vehicles, but we surely need appropriate driver-assist systems. KPIT is also working on technologies for driver assist systems that will reduce accidents. Currently, globally, driver assistance ranges from zero to the fully automated vehicle that doesn't need a driver at all. Each country needs different attributes in their assist systems, depending not only on their road rules and signages, but also on their road conditions, driving behaviour, and so on. For instance, a driver-assist system in India would have to accommodate for two-wheeler, three-wheeler and pedestrian behaviours that are specific to the Indian context. Our work on AI-based systems focuses on the Indian market. This system will learn from tracking driver behaviour and traffic and vehicular movement to completely connect and automate a vehicle.

In addition, all the technological experiments for AVs can be put to use in completely different fields too.[29] Of course, at present these developments are clearly out of reach of the common man. But that is only a matter of time, because the other STEP levers that make and break innovations are already in motion.

This brings us back to this book's core hypothesis: for any sustainable long-term change, all four levers— technology, social engagement, public policy and economic model—have to work together. Let us now consider how the other three levers currently operate to impact road transportation.

Economic sense is as plain as day. And where it is not, it is only a matter of time

With reducing battery prices, experts now believe that by 2025 there will be parity between the costs of ICE cars and EVs. As demand increases, costs will only reduce further. On the other hand, ride-sharing itself makes for a much cheaper alternative compared with owning a car, especially in cities, where parking and traffic congestion add to the economic and non-economic costs of owning a car. A back-of-the-envelope calculation shows that personal cars are more economical compared with cab-hailing only if a person drives more than 12,000 kilometres a year.[30, 31] But of course, the more expensive the owned car, the more kilometres it will have to run, to break even with hailing cabs.

We are highly optimistic about new technologies that will make road transportation more accessible and economically equitable. Of course, as with all things that are for public good, EVs too will need some degree of push from public policy. And this is already coming about around the world.

Policy—adapting to the shift, and yet more room for dynamism

Indeed, public policy has helped shift gears when it comes to creation of sustainable economic models for EVs. In time, almost every country will give right of way to electric cars, create infrastructure for free charging stations, subsidize EV infrastructure, penalize dirty vehicles through taxes and make it inconvenient to own ICE vehicles.

Worldwide, EVs are gaining support through one or more of the three policy tools of subsidization, public procurement and taxation. Non-economic policies have helped streamline transportation through the use of parking rules, speed lanes, etc. Countries are also working together to set worldwide standards for emissions, among other parameters.

Countries such as India, China, the US and Germany use subsidies for EVs. This serves the national good at various levels. First, of course, it directly reduces air pollution. Indirectly, it not only reduces the country's need for imports, but also brings benefits good enough to justify the subsidies.

Here again, as described in an earlier chapter, the principle of bonus-malus is used in France to tax cars with higher emissions. This revenue then finances tax credits to cars with more desirable emission standards. Eventually, when environment-friendly cars become the norm, targets for emissions can either be revised, or subsidies can be progressively eased out. Benefits to individual consumers as well as to society would be evident enough to encourage the use of such vehicles without any policy support. Getting to this point of critical mass, however, is where policy can be very helpful.

Policy can be even more proactive through procurement, which will go a long way in helping technologies reach the desired critical mass. What can be better than the government encouraging EVs for its own use and electric buses for public transport? This sends demand signals to the market too. These signals are further reinforced when EVs are provided to government staff for their use. Mandates and tenders from national and local authorities can foster EV uptake for large public fleets of vehicles, including service vehicles such as garbage trucks and public transport vehicles. Four cities in the United States—Los Angeles, Seattle, San Francisco and Portland—initiated mass-purchase of EVs for their public vehicle fleets, including police cruisers, street sweepers and trash haulers. This order was for 114,000 vehicles. To put things in perspective, 200,000 EVs were sold in all of the United States in 2017. Even in India, the government has set up an energy service company, EESL (Energy Efficiency Services Limited), which has made investments worth 2400 crore (~$370 million) in EVs for use by the government.[32]

Leading EV cities have shown that when backed by effective policy, they can popularize EV usage and reduce barriers to their uptake. Another way to use city policy is to make the public sector or the government the testing ground for nationwide application.

Policy can also grant financial incentives, fiscal advantages and other forms of monetary incentives to individuals, businesses and local authorities willing to invest in the installation of electric vehicle supply equipment (EVSE)—charging stations for EVs. China's central government supports municipalities deploying public charging infrastructure by subsidizing their construction. The government of the Netherlands contributes towards the joint deployment of publicly accessible EVSE with the municipalities and a third party. This is also accompanied by a tax incentive for businesses investing in EVSE deployment. In the United States, Colorado grants up to 80 per cent of the costs of an EVSE unit and installation.[33] These are just a few examples of state promotion of EVs. And the web of charging stations is only spreading.

Similar initiatives in India are taking shape through its National Mission for Electric Mobility. One such initiative, FAME (Faster Adoption and Manufacturing of [Hybrid &] Electric Vehicles), is working towards creating the infrastructure, such as charging stations, needed to make EVs operational.

Parking and zoning rules too are being used to encourage EVs. The city of Paris has mandated that all electric cars be permitted to use the chargers of its Autolib electric car-sharing programme and has allowed them free parking or dedicated parking spots. Amsterdam has deployed an EVSE network rather innovatively: citizens can sign up with the municipality to have a charger installed near their home when they buy an EV. This policy-led deployment of public charging infrastructure optimizes new charger installations only when there are new EVs circulating in the area.

International policy frameworks too can be used to get consensus on requirements and deployment strategies for EVs. One such example is that of support for the deployment of EVSE. These standard protocols allow for quicker policy action at the national level because some of the major technical decisions will already have been made internationally, freeing national policies to focus on implementation and enforcement. In alignment with these international protocols, China aims to deploy 4.3 million private EVSE outlets by 2020, France is set to deploy 7 million charging outlets by 2030, and South Korea upgraded its former target for fast public EV chargers from 1400 to 3000.[34]

This government push and availability of technology has led to increasing demand and use of EVs. In turn, taking their cue from regions that are encouraging EVs, those that are not are being pushed by their citizens to do so.

Social engagement—changing behaviour patterns, a cause and effect of the other levers

People participation has had a subtle impact on technology, economic model and policy, and these three levers have in turn captured the people's involvement. Along with the impact of technology and policy on reducing the costs of EVs or AVs, and the economic sense that ride-sharing makes, there has also arisen a lot of social awareness. Every urban citizen is conscious of the problems created by unclean vehicles. Citizens are rebelling against the pollution they are suffering in their cities. People don't want the status quo. That the next generation is moving away from traditional, personally owned transportation to shared transportation is already leading to the reduction of environmental and energy problems.

This trend is clearer among the young generation, especially in the western world. Over the years, in American and European cities, people don't want to own cars or drive a car themselves. Globally, the number of new driving licences issued every year is dropping. Many people now prefer to use public transport such as buses or rental cars.

A rise in ride-sharing is a clear indicator of the move away from owning a vehicle. From a status symbol that car ownership was, the day might not be far when it might be looked down upon because you are not being eco-friendly. This is because there is a social movement towards changing our 'objects of desire'.

By 2030, 25 per cent of road miles driven in the US are expected to be through ride-sharing.[35] Seattle has already seen a decline in car ownership—for the first time since 1970![36] And this is true of many developing countries too. In fact, like many other intermediary technologies, such as landline telephones and banking, transportation has also skipped a technological step in many developing countries. The bottom-of-the-pyramid population will not go through the step of owning a car before having to let go of it. They will directly move to using a mobile app that allows them to share a ride. This has been driven as much by the high cost of ownership of cars and increased traffic congestion as by an increase in data connectivity and the reach of the now ubiquitous mobile phone.

Uptake of EVs is also an indicator of change in people's behaviour. Tesla Model 3's successful advance booking is one such example. Tesla did not spend a single cent on advertising. The bookings came through word of mouth and from free media coverage.[37] We have to bear in mind that Tesla is only a fifteen-year-old brand and is not yet a profitable company from the shareholder's point of view. However, Tesla and its CEO, Elon Musk, have a huge social media presence. Whether or not their online presence and the advance bookings are connected is a matter of debate. But what is clear is that people are ready to be part of the EV revolution that will make their world 'clean'.

Given these developments across the world, the time is now ripe for the sector to change from deep within, especially in the developing world. We are excited to be active participants in this change at various levels, as mentioned in the chapter.

We believe that India missed out on the last automotive revolution, which happened in the aftermath of the Model T. Indian automotive manufacturing was a little too late to the party, beginning only in the 1950s and 1960s. However, we don't need to miss the wagon again. The industry is now at an inflection point in every aspect of EV and AV technology. This is our time to be ahead of the tide.

We are sure we will be able to play our role in making road transportation accessible to as many citizens as possible while keeping them safe and the planet clean. This is because our solutions fulfil the requirements of ASSURED Total Innovation. All the solutions enumerated above are affordable, by definition. With the right policy push, which will bring agencies together, the solutions can be scalable and sustainable in the long term—economically, socially and environmentally. The processes will include the marginalized farmer, and the bus and truck driver, so that the solution satisfies the requirement of universality. Again, with government backing there is nothing that can keep this solution from achieving scale with rapidity. This makes each of these solutions 'excellent', as we define it, because they are developed keeping in mind the bottom-of-the-pyramid producer and user. In totality, all these qualities make them distinctive solutions too.

A new green revolution of our times is certainly in the offing. Cohesive work on the STEP levers can take us into a very different world. It is not difficult to imagine converting India from a large importer to a net exporter of energy sources, similar to the change that the last century's green revolution brought about. Also, let us not forget that these technologies that bring meaningful employment, while solving critical issues related to transportation, are not problems that India alone faces. These are global problems.

India can truly be a global technological leader. After all, every nation wants better transportation that leads to cleaner air, self-reliance and fewer accidents, and every individual in the world wants less time spent in commuting, and better quality of life.

Towards a new world

Indeed, when the world comes together, it is not out of line to envision a new world. We acknowledge that, given the pace at which things are changing, predicting the future will be underestimating the potential of the next generation and new technologies. And yet, some of the predictions that make the ideal world not too far into the distant future are too thrilling not to mention.

From solar-powered EVs to on-demand, app-driven delivery of mobility—the predictions cover the entire chain of transportation in the next ten to twelve years. A few of those are an extrapolation of what we see today. The world tomorrow is expected to have a very competitive ride-sharing industry if AVs reach the market. This is because autonomous EVs will be cheaper than human-driven ICE vehicles. This competition will serve the customer better and be cheaper. As a result, Transport-as-a-Service, aka TaaS, will become the norm, owing just to its economic attractiveness. Each car bought will be used at least ten times more than an individually owned car today. These factors will come together to reduce the number of cars on the road. A more imaginative prediction—likely to be outsmarted—is that of recharging stations serving as community hubs, where recharging time will be used for meetings and meet-ups.[38, 39]

Other predictions have total savings on transportation costs in the US adding up to $1 trillion by 2030. These savings are expected to result in a permanent rise in annual disposable income. Productivity gains as a result of reclaimed driving hours are expected to boost the nation's GDP by another $1 trillion. On-road cars are expected to drop from 247 million to 44 million in the same period, opening up vast tracts of land for other, more productive uses.[40]

The TaaS disruption is also expected to reduce, if not eliminate, air pollution and the greenhouse gases attributable to the transportation sector. Energy demand from transportation is expected to reduce by 80 per cent, and tailpipe emissions by over 90 per cent. If combined with the use of solar and wind as sources of energy, a carbon-free road transportation system in the US can be expected by 2030.[41]

What is predicted for the US is likely to be similar to, if not be bettered by, what will happen in the rest of the developed world. The developing world will not be too far behind either, because they are likely to adopt some of these innovations quicker, if not skip a couple of them on the way.

We for sure look forward to living in cleaner cities and with healthier lungs. We also hope to see more people gainfully and dignifiedly employed in creating and maintaining new energy solutions for transportation. We certainly want to see an earth that doesn't need to be dug any more for us to move from place to place. And this is not too far away. Only a decade or so to go.

* * *

Urban solid waste management and mobility are only two illustrative examples of areas that are seeing the much-needed holistic transformation through use of the 'leapfrogging to pole-vaulting' model. Health, education, agriculture, water pollution, and many, many other areas of modern day-to-day life are in need of a complete overhaul. Indeed, we need a series of revolutions.

While absolutely possible, this dramatic change, which needs to happen quickly, will require an entire shift in mindset. Changing the mapping of our minds will have to begin with reshaping our thoughts on transformational solutions. This thought revolution is not just restricted to leadership. In fact, we contend that the current leadership—be it organizational or governmental—has to drive a conducive environment for creating many leaders rather than letting leadership just happen. This powerful concept warrants a discussion of its own, which we will dive into next.

TWELVE

Creating Pole-vaulting Leaders

The Janwani case of urban solid waste management was a telling illustration of how the STEP levers, when used in an integrated manner, can enable 'pole-vaulting', to achieve the seemingly impossible goal of making every municipal ward a zero-garbage ward. We also illustrated the potential of the STEP levers to drive a 'mobility' transformation which is radical yet sustainable. But these successes are not possible without a fundamental force—the people behind the success—the inspiring leaders. In this chapter we will discuss how organizations can build leaders who have a 'pole-vaulting mindset', who are capable of creating many leaders better than themselves, and who inspire their teams to develop a 'yes we can' mindset, no matter how impossible their task may seem!

This book is all about pole-vaulting to radical yet sustainable transformation. Let's focus on the radical part first. By this we mean change that is radically different, not just marginally different, from what existed earlier. An organization, be it a business or a government, has to first be dissatisfied with a 10 per cent increase in value or a

10 per cent reduction in price of a product or service. We have to shoot for 10x, that is 1000 per cent improvement—this is the pole-vaulting spirit. And this is an organizational aim that should seep in from the top management.

Such a transformative top management is beyond the dictionary definition of 'innovator'. Employees—that is, the future leaders—should be groomed in such a way that they will find a solution to a problem, no matter what; they see what everyone else sees but they think of solutions which no one else has thought of.

Pole-vaulting thinkers find opportunities where others see nothing. Their mindspace is largely devoted to future growth and the next big challenge. They have hindsight, foresight and insight. They drive discontinuity and encourage risk-taking.

This is a stark shift from the attitude of the everyday leader. An ordinary leader meets a new idea with either:

A cautionary 'Too risky! What if it fails?' or
A disbelieving 'Impossible! Never done before!' or
The know-it-all 'Been there, done that. It is old.' or
The non-confrontational 'Let me play devil's advocate . . .'

All in all, it is a 'can't be done' mindset, whereas what we need is a 'let's do it' one.

History of 'can't be done' mindset

As mentioned earlier, many major breakthroughs and 'game changers', as we know them today, were initially met with disbelief, cynicism and even ridicule. They were derided strongly by even business leaders and other top innovators! Sceptical CEOs of the time have mocked the then unheard-of ideas such as the iPhone and e-commerce, blockchain and what have you.[1] When a handheld Palm satisfied all your address book needs, where was the need for a phone to do it for you too? Why would an intimate act of browsing in a bookstore be replaced by online shopping? Why would anything other than government-approved currency be involved in monetary transactions?

The point is, the best of innovators have been guilty of being dismissive naysayers of breakthroughs that would have pole-vaulted society to a different future in an astoundingly short period of time. However, alongside them existed pole-vaulting innovation leaders too, who made the arrival of the new world possible.

In order to pole-vault, individuals, institutions, enterprises and governments need to have 'a healthy disrespect for the impossible', to borrow a phrase from a leadership training programme at Stanford. We have to look at being revolutionary, and not just evolutionary. Why? Because incremental improvement does not help in a world that is rapidly and non-linearly changing. We cannot sit marvelling at the move from email to instant messaging when wearable devices to read thought are being developed.[2] Can you even imagine the big pole-vault that will take place when communication by thought will no longer be sci-fi?

From Jeff Bezos to Larry Page, from Mukesh Ambani to Elon Musk, from Mark Zuckerberg to Nandan Nilekani, from Bill Gates to Steve Jobs—without these 'beyond-the-imagination' thinkers, the world wouldn't have reached this stage of progress. And yet there is room for more disruptive innovators. Many more.

How do we then uplift a seemingly 'common person' spirit from the self-satisfied state of leapfrogging to the urge to pole-vault?

Fuelling the pole-vaulting spirit

We believe the human mind needs to be challenged to achieve feats that appear impossible. Challenges that look grand tend to kindle, excite and inspire humans. We have witnessed such grand challenges down the ages.[3]

One of the earliest grand challenges was the Orteig Prize of $25,000, offered in 1919 by French hotelier Raymond Orteig for the first non-stop flight between New York City and Paris. While it took eight years for underdog Charles Lindbergh to win it, the challenge unlocked sixteen times the prize money, giving unheard-of impetus to the aviation industry![4] Nine teams spent a total of $400,000 in pursuit of the Orteig Prize.

US President John Kennedy's 'Man on the Moon' is another classic example of a grand challenge. In 1962, Kennedy announced that the country would land a man on the moon by the end of the decade.[5] Political will, the longing of the country's scientists and engineers to achieve something path-breaking, and public support coalesced into a well-rounded national effort to achieve the ambitious goal. Of course, all this was backed by heavy research investments made after World War II.

These challenges are clearly different from the Nobel Prizes or the Queen Elizabeth Prize in engineering. Grand challenges have a quantitatively defined 'finish line' rather than a selection committee discussing the relative merits of the nominees for a prize.

'Moonshot' ideas and projects

Inspired by the 'Man on the Moon' success, the technological world saw 'moonshot' projects being announced across the spectrum.[6] These are audacious ambitions, appearing to be almost on the borderline of reality and science fiction, without near-term profitability in vision.

In 1996, entrepreneur Peter Diamandis offered a $10 million prize to the first privately financed team that could build and fly a three-passenger vehicle 100 kilometres into space, twice within two weeks. The Ansari XPRIZE for Suborbital Spaceflight motivated twenty-six teams from seven nations to invest more than $100 million in pursuit of the $10 million purse.[7] Eight years later, a spacecraft designed by Burt Rutan, an aerospace engineer, and financed by Paul Allen, co-founder and former CEO of Microsoft, broke the 100-kilometre mark, internationally recognized as the boundary of outer space. A week later, Brian Binnie, a navy officer, completed the second part of the prize requirement.

Awards such as XPRIZE achieve three primary goals. They attract investment from outside the sector that takes new approaches to difficult problems. They create significant results that are real and impactful owing to the stretched targets. And most valuably, they encourage intellectual and financial investments that require breaking national and disciplinary boundaries.

XPRIZE has now spread its reach to exploration of space and oceans, the life sciences, energy and environment, education and global development.[8] The hope is that the prizes will help improve lives, create equity of opportunity and stimulate new, important discoveries.

Sometimes innovation can outpace the very incentive programmes that got it off the ground in the first place. The target for the Archon Genomics XPRIZE was sequencing of 100 human genomes in ten days or less, with less than one error per 100,000 DNA base pairs, covering 98 per cent of the genome at less than $10,000 per genome.[9] Fortunately or unfortunately, it became the first XPRIZE to be cancelled because market incentives outpaced those of the contest. The rapid R&D advances in industry, driven by the benefits of rapid sequencing, helped the world achieve XPRIZE's original target, and the prize was no longer required.

At its launch in 2006, the Archon Genomics XPRIZE sought to address the many market failures in the genome sequencing industry of the day, including its poor accuracy, high costs, low quality and long processing times. Over the next seven years, these performance issues were solved by the industry at a rate that outpaced all technological and economic expectations. By 2013, the Archon Genomics XPRIZE was no longer relevant for driving innovation in the market.[10] At the time of its cancellation, companies could sequence whole human genomes in a few days for around $1000 per genome. The XPRIZE can take some credit for providing this new industry the ignition it required. Even this discontinued contest can, and will, have lasting benefits for humanity.

The Google Lunar XPRIZE of 2007 was for the team that successfully launched, landed and operated a rover on the lunar surface for 500 metres and obtained high-definition images and video.[11] It offered a $20 million award for the first prize and $5 million for the second. This XPRIZE went unclaimed, and the contest had to be abandoned because success was elusive.

Does this mean that the goals set by Google Lunar XPRIZE will never be met? Unlikely. We believe that there is no limit to the human imagination and no limit to human achievement except the limits we put on ourselves.

In fact, the beauty of innovating lies in actively embracing failure.

The story of Indian grand challenges

An early pole-vaulting social innovator was Mahatma Gandhi. In 1929, Gandhi announced a 'Machine Contest' carrying a prize of £7700 (1,00,000).[12] The challenge was to create a machine that could produce yarn from raw cotton at the same speed as the European spinning mills did. The specifications he created for the grand challenge were impeccable. They belonged to the class of what we have referred to elsewhere as 'affordable excellence'. The challenge was the requirement of 'affordability', because the machine had to be produced in India, cost less than ₹150, and run for twenty years at least. In terms of 'excellence' in performance, the machine had to be able to run for hours together so that it could produce twelve to twenty threads of 16,000-foot yarn. Many machines were made; however, none satisfied all the performance parameters.

In today's times, we have made attempts to put up Indian challenges. One of us, Mashelkar, has created grand challenges in Indian science, technology and innovation, at the laboratory level (NCL), the institution level (Council of Scientific and Industrial Research, i.e. CSIR) and at the national level (NMITLI). With bold and innovating funding mechanisms, a daring spirit in Indian science and technology and innovation can be cultivated. National Chemical Laboratory (NCL) created a 'Kite-Flying Fund', which reserved a small budget for funding proof-of-concept studies on out-of-the-box ideas. The success rate could be as low as 1 per cent.

This created an air of excitement because failure was not going to be berated. Some top-class research publications emerged from this incentive, but no great technological breakthroughs came through.

Later, the CSIR, a chain of forty Indian national research laboratories, created the 'New Idea Fund', similar to the 'Kite-Flying Fund' at NCL. Scientists such as N. Chandrakumar, a CSIR scientist who owns early patents in spin computing, pursued risky ideas.[13, 14] But these ideas were ahead of their time. In fact, Chandrakumar was one of the earliest scientists to file US patents on spin computing.

In 2000, Mashelkar again conceived and operationalized the New Millennium Indian Technology Leadership Initiative (NMITLI) at a national level. The key word was 'leadership'. It was a bold public–private partnership.[15] The '10x' challenges here were different from those in the western world. The challenge was not to make something only ten times better but also make a 10-time cost improvement, because affordability was of the utmost relevance in India. For example, a globally competitive, extremely affordable, portable and versatile bioinformatics software package, Biosuite, was created by Tata Consultancy Services, jointly with as many as nineteen institutional NMITLI partners, in a record time of eighteen months!

Some other NMITLI grand challenges were: to create a liquid crystal display (LCD) device that was two orders of magnitude faster[16] than existing devices; a new molecule that would clear tuberculosis (TB) in two months' time, rather than take the conventional six to eight months;[17] a leather-processing technology that was biological (clean) and could replace the current chemical treatments which were polluting; and an indigenous fuel-cell technology.

Were all these challenges met? And if met, were they successful in the long run? No. Sometimes the ecosystem failed the innovation, at other times unforeseen developments led to failure. But that is what happens with '10x' thinking! What is important is that minds and mindsets from different spheres and geographies came together to work towards common goals. Even though the TB drug molecule couldn't go through its second phase of development, a new molecule for TB was created for the first time in forty years! An unheard-of scientific invention for India.

More importantly, these NMITLI challenges have been germane to some fresh Indian grand challenges. The Atal New India Challenge launched in April 2018 is a collaboration between five government ministries. Prospective innovators and start-ups have been invited to design market-ready products using cutting-edge technologies across several identified focus areas, such as climate change, smart agriculture, smart mobility, etc. And this is not just a grant of ₹1 crore (~$150,000) successful applicants will be offered mentoring, incubation and other support needed at various stages of commercialization of their inventions.

It is gratifying to see that Indian corporates, like the Googles of the world, are also trying to promote '10x' thinking. The Tata Group's 'Daring to Try' programme, for instance, awards the best 'try', irrespective of whether it succeeds or not. Reliance Industries Ltd's (RIL) 'Chairman's Grand Challenges' poses specific grand challenges which could move the organization from 'best practices' to 'next practices' or create next businesses. RIL also has an innovation leadership development programme, 'Beyonders', which aims to identify not only '10x' thinkers but '10x' doers.

Stop waiting for Godot[18]

The intention behind all grand challenges is to reduce dependency on a single mind or on even a handful of 'great' minds. These challenges seek to democratize the very process of transformation. Of course, great minds will take on leadership without any prompting. However, the rest of us should shake ourselves out of the mindset that waits for great minds to show us the way. We certainly need not wait for a messiah.

And when we imagine a world in which there are as many transformations as there are people, we will see a world that is a bright one for all.

Though it might come across as ideal even for Utopia, it is not really so. Just one small online news site in India has headlines such as these:

'Gurugram lady opens "crockery bank" for steel utensils to reduce plastic waste!'[19]

'This inflatable helmet by IIT-Roorkee could save biker lives in road accidents!'[20]

'Inspired by proactive citizen, Bengaluru takes up pothole challenge to fix its roads!'[21]

'Bengalureans build robotic chef who'll be able to cook 100+ Indian dishes!'[22]

'Water from thin air: this low-cost device can produce upto 1000 litres per day!'[23]

'In a first, you can now rent a self-drive e-car from metro station at just ₹40/hour!'[24]

'Waste to taste: TN researchers create edible plates from jackfruit skins, seeds!'[25]

'Blood-less, prick-free diabetes test? Chennai students' device does just that!'[26]

Are the innovators of these ideas not thought leaders without knowing that they are? That transformative ideas don't stay restricted in their scope is the aim of the 'leapfrogging to pole-vaulting' model. That not all these ideas will meet expectations is intrinsic to the model.

The next logical step is for these ideas to see how they fit into the ASSURED Total Innovation framework and take support from the STEP levers to keep satisfying the requirements of the framework. Most importantly, these examples give us immense hope. Yes, we can look forward to a world that we imagine—a world where progress doesn't leave some citizens behind; a world that doesn't constantly fear its own extinction; a clean, safe and enjoyable world for all.

THIRTEEN

Towards a New World

'There is a tide in the affairs of men. Which, taken at the flood, leads on to fortune. Omitted, all the voyage of their life is bound in shallows and in miseries. On such a full sea are we now afloat. And we must take the current when it serves, or lose our ventures.'

—William Shakespeare, *Julius Caesar*

We stand at such a juncture right now. Our actions today will determine whether we will lead humanity to good fortune or we could very well drown ourselves in misery and environmental apocalypse.

From where we see the world, we see human beings racing towards a better life for one and all. This is not optimism for the sake of optimism. Enzymes that degrade and digest PET plastic bottles are already in the laboratory stages of development.[1] This plastic takes hundreds of years to decompose, and in the meanwhile lies on our land and in our oceans. Suddenly, there is now the possibility that they could go back to their original building blocks such that they can be sustainably recycled. Of course, for this promise to turn into an industrially viable process, it will have to meet the ASSURED transformation criteria. It will also need further ecosystem support to become sustainable.

We also cannot forget that the rate of acceleration of technological change is itself accelerating. Therefore, it makes it even harder to predict the order and the structure of the new world. One of the World Economic Forum's 'Technology Tipping Points' predictions for 2025 was that an AI machine would become a member of a corporate board of directors.[2] Amazingly, this prediction for 2025 came true in 2014 itself! Deep Knowledge Ventures, a Hong Kong-based venture capital management fund, appointed an AI machine, VITAL (Validating Investment Tool for Advancing Life Sciences), to its board of directors—with voting rights in investment decisions too![3]

Enzymes that break down plastic and machines as board members are just a couple of illustrations of what the future holds for us. Even from what we see currently evolving around us, there is ample reason to enthusiastically look forward to a new world. If we were to address all our current problems, like cleaning our polluted rivers, changing our destructive methods of food production and wasteful industrial operations, this new world would emerge. What would such a world look like just a couple of decades from now?

Can we imagine a world in which the air in our cities is so clean that we would feel like we were amid mountains and forests? Can we think of a world where our rivers are so pristine that we do not have to worry about the effect of their waters on our health and our crops? Can there exist a world where ugly mines don't scar the face of our earth? Can we visualize a world whose diversity of animal and plant life is on the rise so that those of us who love nature can marvel at the vibrancy and profundity of life? Our answer is a resounding 'yes' to all these questions, for we are already seeing signs of these aspirations coming true.

Now, what would the situation of the 3Es be in this new world?

Conserving energy

The sun alone provides 5000 times more energy to the earth in a single hour than all of us—profligate as we are—use in a whole year.[4] So the problem is not scarcity of renewable and clean energy. We certainly have it in abundance. The question is whether we can make this energy available to all humanity whenever and wherever it is needed and whether we can create energy of the quality that is needed. The question is not about generating energy. It is about capturing, storing, distributing and consuming energy that already exists. The question is about making this abundant energy available to everyone in a cost-effective manner.

Renewable energy generation has been increasing very rapidly and has resulted in a quick decline in costs. Solar power generation capacity in the world was negligible about ten years ago. Today it is at 75,000 megawatts. In a fast-developing country like India, it was a mere 35 megawatts in 2011, against over 24,000 megawatts in 2018.[5, 6]

Increased renewable energy capacity, along with improved manufacturing processes, has lowered costs. In less than a decade, solar panel installation costs in the US have decreased by about 60 per cent to around $3 per watt.[7] The comparable installation costs in India are even lower on account of the scale obtained here, and stands at ₹35 per watt (~¢50).[8] This declining trend in price is occurring at an accelerating speed too. Consequently, the per-unit cost of electricity generated through solar energy has been dropping year after year. The cost of electricity in India was as low as ₹2.44 (~¢3) per kilowatt-hour in 2017, a 73 per cent drop since 2010. Clearly, in the very near future, solar energy will cost less than conventional energy.

Wind-power generation too is witnessing increasing capacities and declining costs. A government auction in the state of Gujarat in India for 500 megawatts received tenders that totalled to over 1500 megawatts. This implies that thrice the capacity tendered for is possible. More remarkably, none of the bids was above ₹3 per kilowatt (~¢4.5), and the lowest bid was only half a rupee lower than the highest. And we are talking about just one state in India.

Hydropower as a form of renewable energy is promising too, and despite achieving the targets set for it, its full potential has not been tapped completely.[9]

Safe nuclear energy is making a comeback too. The nuclear energy world is recovering from the Fukushima Daiichi disaster in Japan, which was caused by a tsunami and an earthquake. There is an attempt to restart nuclear energy efforts. A new and much safer nuclear plant is being set up. These developments are a step in the right direction for nuclear energy as a source of non-renewable energy.

And finally, there is hydrogen, the cleanest of all fuels. Hydrogen can be generated by reformation of methane, hydrolysis, thermolysis and photolysis—all new technologies, the costs of which will fall rapidly in the near future. Electricity generation from hydrogen through use of fuel cells can displace many other solutions for energy generation. This form of energy is conducive to being stored effectively too. Hydrogen has the largest energy content of all fuels. Also, hydrogen's relatively stable chemistry allows its storage for longer durations. This is an important feature that is missing in other renewable sources.

Moreover, we are making massive strides in energy storage.[10] Since storage is one of the biggest bottlenecks in the use of renewable energy, various energy storage systems, apart from batteries, are being considered. Expanding markets and increasing commercialization are going hand in hand to scale manufacturing of these systems.

'Sensible heat storage' is a system that uses heat capacity and temperature changes of a material to store energy. For instance, solar energy is stored at a high temperature using molten salts. Currently, this technique is used to store the heat created by solar towers or troughs. This heat is later used to create steam. Power plants in Spain use this method for energy storage. In 2016, the Gemasolar Thermosolar Plant in Spain produced continuous electricity for thirty-six consecutive days using this method. This is just one example of an alternative to batteries.

While technology is making renewable energy economically attractive, regulation is forcing users away from fossil fuel. Many countries in the world are putting an immediate or a prospective ban on mining for fossil fuel. Looking at the way the world is moving away from fossil fuels, in a couple of decades we will all be looking back on the current times and wondering in anguish and amazement why humanity dug up the earth for fossil fuel and burned it at all.

Saving the environment

We are convinced that our current way of life is damaging our environment almost irreparably. Almost each dimension of the environment shows significant decline in quality. We know of the damaging impact of air pollution, climate change and ozone-layer reduction on all things living. Freshwater availability is a serious cause of concern too. Plant and animal species are becoming extinct, and the world's stock of essential non-renewable minerals is depleting fast.

Let us now look at current trends and see how they impact the environment.

No more digging?

Renewable energy trends clearly show that the damage done to the environment because of the use of fossil fuels can significantly reduce and even be nullified in the near future. The burning of fossil fuels has the largest impact on carbon-dioxide content in the atmosphere, and therefore on our climate. We believe that the move from fossil fuels to renewable fuels in the field of transportation and in other industries will significantly dilute the negative impact of the burning of fossil fuels. Apart from substitution of dirty energy with renewable energy, there are many other factors that would also work towards repairing the environmental damage that humans have caused.

As we have seen earlier, there is a movement towards asset-light economies owing to the trend towards shared assets. In the MIT study, for example, we saw the potential of ride-sharing mobile apps to reduce taxis in New York by 75 per cent.[11] We also discussed how people are moving towards renting out their spare rooms and the impact this would have on the building of new hotels. Similarly, e-commerce is making an impact on brick-and-mortar stores. As a result, there is a reduction in construction of

new malls. All these trends point towards significantly
reduced creation of assets, especially in the developed
world. Even in the developing world, the rate of new asset
creation will be relatively low. Both these factors will
significantly reduce energy and material requirements.

These and other such trends will reduce environmental
damage in the years to come. Earlier in the book we
addressed the issue of pollution arising from the use of
non-biodegradable materials. We saw that using the STEP
levers significantly reduces such pollution all around us.

To recall the air pollution statistics, 25 per cent of
greenhouse gas emissions in the world can be attributed
to electricity and heat production, 21 per cent to industry,
24 per cent to agricultural and other land uses, 14 per
cent to transportation, and 6 per cent to buildings. The
remaining 10 per cent is produced by all other human
activities.

However, we are seeing reductions in these emissions
with every passing year, aided by the development of
energy-efficient machines and buildings, reuse of materials,
reduction of leakages, etc. Attempts are also being made
to minimize conversion of forest land for other purposes.
Improved grazing management and replantation too are
being done to reduce emissions.

On the transportation front, both public transportation
and better walking-cycling infrastructure are being
encouraged, even as transport vehicles and related
infrastructure are being made more energy-efficient.
Processes to reduce traffic or aircraft taxi-ing time at
airports are also being introduced to reduce the airline
industry's carbon footprint.

Recognizing that reversing the damage done to the
environment is not just about carbon emissions, equal

efforts are being made on other fronts too. From drip irrigation, irrigation scheduling and efficient water storage to growing drought-tolerant crops and dry crops that use only soil moisture as water input—all methods to reduce water usage in farming are being employed. On the soil conservation front, rotational grazing, use of soil-improving compost and plastic mulch are helping improve soil structure.

As we work towards reducing our mining activities and increase our efforts towards creating a circular economy (as described in the chapter, 'A Clean Revolution—Solid Waste Management') we are likely to benefit from drastically reduced costs and increased growth. At the same time we will continue to keep the environment safe. A concentrated effort, consisting of creating healthy food chains, reduction of food waste, efficient urban planning, sharing of assets, building of passive houses and other such activities, would have great potential to drastically reduce our adverse impact on the environment.

On this front, a peek into the future looks very heartening. For example, raw material currently makes up 40 to 60 per cent of total costs in European manufacturing companies. The European Union also imports 60 per cent of its fossil fuel and metal requirements. A move to a circular economy is one method to use resources to their maximum. Instead of linear production lines, where we make, use and dispose of goods, circular production looks at each product at the end of its life as raw material for another product. In effect, the basic resource is used to its fullest. In an analysis of the potential impact of a circular economy in three sectors—mobility, food and shelter—this use of primary materials was estimated to drop by a whopping 32 per cent by 2030 and by 53 per cent by 2050.[12]

While some companies must be pressured into changing the ways in which they produce goods, there are others such as Apple Inc. that proactively work towards relatively more conscientious production practices. The company is gearing towards making its products with 100 per cent recycled and renewable materials. They want to stop mining the earth altogether. Also, the prices are likely to be even higher and it isn't a foolproof method, but at least the thought process is headed in the right direction as far as digging the earth for minerals is concerned.[13]

Feeding humanity, judiciously

Agricultural as well as non-plant food consumption is going to witness a major revolution, as is necessary. As we move towards synthetic food and science-based, technology-enabled agriculture, our footprint on natural resources can be substantially shrunk. If we move to synthetic meat, for instance, our requirement for water and land will reduce dramatically. Seventy per cent of agricultural land is currently used to feed animals that make it to our dinner plates.[14] Moreover, this shift will still allow us to enjoy the taste, flavour and nutrition of animal-based proteins, but we will have got rid of the strain and damage that animal husbandry currently thrusts on our environment. This change is also coming through a huge social wave away from meat-based diets and towards vegetarianism and veganism.

Reversing damage

Change in each aspect of urban life will start our process of redeeming the havoc we have wrought on our environment.

Our examples of the changes in strategy in the area of mobility are a mere indicator of how such redemption is possible. Hydrogen and other new sources of energy will change the way industries consume energy, making manufacturing environmentally benign.

This recovery is not just for our cities. Entire countries, deep down to the remotest villages, can significantly alter their impact on the environment through better practices in every sphere of activity. India could benefit from a circular economy path to development. A study of just three focus areas—cities and construction, food and agriculture, and mobility and vehicle manufacturing—anticipates annual benefits of ₹40 lakh crore (~$615 billion) by 2050 for India, if it shifts its current development path. That is an impressive 30 per cent of the nation's current GDP. Economic benefits aside, this study estimates that greenhouse gas emissions can be reduced by 44 per cent by moving to a circular economy.[15] This drop doesn't account for the better quality of life that will accrue to citizens through the easing of congestion and pollution.

We can look at construction as an example to understand this better. Buildings account for 34 per cent of the country's energy consumption, and only 20 per cent of this energy can be assigned to the initial construction of the building itself. About 80 per cent of this energy is consumed when a building is used over an estimated life of fifty years. A circular economy would involve the rethinking of building design in such a way that buildings do not use a lot of non-renewable energy. This would mean using rooftop tiles that generate solar electricity and using the insides and outsides of building walls to grow vertical gardens. These solar panels and vertical gardens would use nutrients from waste water generated in the building.[16]

Similarly, every human activity can be reimagined. From something as omnipresent as growing food to something as inconspicuous as doing laundry—each activity can seek innovation to use very little energy, water and other sources. To bring about these actions, businesses will have to lead the way, with a simultaneous enabling environment created by the policymakers. Organizations such as universities and non-profits can support the efforts through local, collaborative initiatives.[17]

The endeavours highlighted in this book are only the tip of the iceberg. There is a lot we can do—not just to reduce or stop our future impact on the environment but to even reverse the damage we have done. We can turn the needle substantially, if we focus on making land and manpower available for activities that preserve nature. Reforesting, river preservation, developing diversity of flora and fauna and eco-tourism are all steps in that direction. Such actions will turn the tide of denudation of the earth.

Elusive employment

Of the three core problems we talked about, that of employment—generation of income for everyone in a dignified and absorbing manner—is probably the toughest to solve. It is also a problem with the highest potential to damage life as we know it, and is probably the most urgent one to solve too. Many of the current events—the problems of terrorism across the world, the instability of political systems in the developed and developing world, all the way to the farmer suicides in India's hinterlands—have their roots in this problem. This is also a problem that is exercising the minds of social thinkers, political leaders, cutting-edge technologists and economists alike.

The last few decades have only deepened economic disparity across the world, and it threatens to only get worse. Such is the state of affairs that the very survival of the contract behind the free enterprise and the propriety of capitalism as a way to organize human activities are being questioned. This, in turn, leaves the merit and future of globalization on questionable grounds too.

The situation is bleak in the developed countries. Yes, in develop'ed' countries. One in five Americans have no pension or savings, and almost 30 per cent of households are headed by a person who is fifty-five or older.[18] On the other side of the globe, in another developed country, a significant part of Japan's working population is actually engaged in non-temporary, full-time work. This has been a direct result of changes in labour laws that made use of temporary and contract workers cheaper for organizations.[19]

We cannot repeat this enough—we believe that what is true of developed countries will be true of developing countries as they are on their path to development unless we do things drastically differently. The population which is on the developing-to-developed path is much larger than the entire population of the current developed world. And the change is going to happen sooner rather than later, as developing countries rush towards progress, skipping a few steps in technological and other innovations along the way, because they are directly moving to where the developed world is right now.

Given that most societies are in a precarious situation, it is important to deliberate on one question—would a new world that is so beneficial from energy and environmental perspectives be able to successfully reduce income disparity, or would it simply aggravate the situation? Let us take a holistic view of the expected impact of new technologies on the creation or decimation of jobs.

Will new technologies displace all human labour? This is one of the biggest debates of our times. Some economists and technologists believe that AI will destroy many of the current jobs, while some others believe that this may only be a temporary phase, after which new jobs will shortly emerge. There are very valid arguments at both ends of the spectrum.

The robots are coming. Coming fast

Technology-induced income inequality has always existed, but it seems like the divide is growing wider and faster. Study after study has brought out the magnitude of this problem. Nine out of ten jobs lost in manufacturing between 2000 and 2010 were owing to automation, not job transfers or globalization.[20] Bear in mind that output is at an all-time high today, while employment peaked in 1980 and has declined since 1995.[21] New-age companies that use cutting-edge technology are making national and global incomes even more diverse.

There is reason to be wary of this trend. The coal mining industry has declined for most of the last century. However, in the last twenty years the slowdown has been accelerating. The good news is that new jobs were generated in industries that produced other forms of energy. These new jobs were also far greater in number than those eliminated. The not-so-good news is that many who lost their coal jobs were not equipped to find jobs in the alternative industries. The new jobs were not taken up by the ones who lost their jobs but by other people. More jobs have been created, but for a different set of people.

There were 168,000 workers in the US coal industry in 1990; today there are 81,000. This drop was considered huge. Now consider this—3.4 million Americans work as cashiers today and another 3.5 million as truck drivers— what happens when robots and drones take over these jobs?

The apprehension is that another 10 million people employed as cooks, janitors, warehouse workers or in similar roles, are at risk of losing their jobs in the next five to ten years. Yet another 5 million retail workers are at a medium risk of losing their jobs.[22] It is estimated that a telemarketer's job is at 99 per cent risk of being automated, a loan officer's 98 per cent, and a paralegal's 94 per cent. The job of the healthcare worker is among the safest— an occupational therapist's job is at 0.35 per cent risk of automation and the surgeon's, 0.42 per cent.[23]

Knowing what we know so far, this isn't surprising. However, what should make us take a step back and ponder is that one of the jobs that appears least in danger of automation—that of a surgeon—isn't far from being automated. The number of robo-surgeries have increased from 1000 in the year 2000 to 570,000 in 2015.[24] And this when only 10 to 18 per cent of developed countries have digitized overall operations so far.[25]

Again, jobs in developing countries will be hit harder and sooner than in developed countries—69 per cent of jobs in India and 77 per cent of jobs in China are at high risk of automation, as against 47 per cent in the US and 57 per cent in OECD countries.[26] The problem cannot be resolved by telemarketers and paralegals retraining themselves. The rate of change we are witnessing is getting faster. Therefore, new skills will need to be learnt continuously. Else, we are looking at a new class of people—the unemployable class.[27]

Will bits and bytes really leave no jobs for humans?

However, all these stark projections are met with undying optimism by thought leaders and people at large. We, the authors, strongly believe that not many of us would like to be unemployable. The current fears are overrated because this phenomenon has repeated often enough over the centuries. In many areas we want to see a human in action. Tennis matches and movies are watched because Serena Williams or Leonardo DiCaprio are doing what they do so well. A robot will not do in their place. We are likely to see more people in jobs they are passionate about.

Certainly, those who lose their jobs as loan officers or insurance agents might not be able to cope with new technology. However, how many of them actually enjoy their jobs? Many of the jobs that are likely to be replaced are either dull, dirty and dangerous. While we worry about truck drivers losing jobs to automated trucks, the average age of commercial drivers in the USA is rising, like that of farmers in Japan. Truck driving is a monotonous, dissatisfying job that has few takers among the next generation.[28] The same can be said of a range of jobs from manufacturing and mining to retail and food-servicing.

Instead, automation can be credited with making jobs more interesting. A renowned anthropologist, Benjamin Shestakofsky, spent nineteen months in a US company that uses technology to connect buyers and sellers. Contrary to his expectations, he found that the complex computing systems needed more humans to analyse the data. So sure, an old type of job was replaced by digitization, but a new type of job was created too.[29]

To take another example, when we see digital teaching tools or online courses, we are bound to assume that the classroom teacher is slowly being eliminated. On the contrary! Another anthropologist, Shreeharsh Kelkar, observed that human educators used the digital medium to be more effective.[30] Similarly, radiologists are relieved with the help they get from their digital counterparts because their job is not being replaced but simply being made easier because of better diagnosis.[31] Thus emerges a new pattern of humans and machines working together harmoniously.

This shift will be similar to us using the Internet instead of the encyclopedia or the library for research; or us using our phones to listen to music instead of playing a gramophone or hearing a live orchestra. Some libraries might have closed down but there could be more people at work in companies that provide news and collate information on the Net. Live orchestras may or may not have reduced in number, but the music industry has more employees than it did earlier.

Lower income, but lower cost of living too

Another argument in favour of automation is that it lowers the cost of products and services, thus lowering the cost of living for the common man. Tianyuan, a Chinese apparel company which supplies to Adidas, Armani and Reebok, has moved operations to the US because robots make their apparel cheaper and faster. A T-shirt at a cost of 33¢ and in twenty-six seconds. With rising wages in China and the lower distribution costs in moving production closer to the market, Tianyuan's decision makes business sense.[32] It is also good for the consumer, as selling prices go down too. We have witnessed many examples of lowered production costs leading to more competition, reducing the cost to consumers.

We are only likely to see more of this and on a larger scale too. Online retail aggregator Amazon expanded its business to physical stores by buying Whole Foods, an American supermarket chain. They are likely to use automation and data analysis to bring customers to the stores by turning the stores into delivery hubs and pick-up centres. On the other hand, Whole Foods could cut costs, and perhaps prices.[33]

You can see examples of lower costs and prices all around. Our basic needs, and some luxuries too, are indeed getting cheaper.[34] The cost of groceries has dropped in the US in recent years. With virtual reality and autonomous cars, living in less expensive areas outside the city will become practical. This will also reduce the demand on urban housing. As mentioned in the chapter 'Transforming Mobility', cab services might eliminate the very need to own cars, even autonomous cars.

Another big-ticket expense item for an average household is education. The cost of education might be on the rise right now, but it is only a matter of time before the marginal cost of that one extra student taking on an online Coursera course will reduce. More importantly, quality education will now be available to those in the deepest corners of the world, who didn't have access to it earlier.

And any time you doubt whether the cost of living is actually reducing, you just have to look at your mobile-phone service bill and compare it against your usage. Your phone has reduced not only your communications bill, but also your photography and banking expenses, to name a few of the common expenses. Twenty years ago, a well-off American owned a camera, a camcorder, a CD player, a stereo, a gaming console, a mobile phone, a watch, an alarm clock, an encyclopedia and an atlas—all of which added up to around $900,000.[35] Today, with your smartphone, the marginal cost of these assets is closing in on zero.

This is true across the social classes. With the lower costs of data and the phone itself, people in the lower-income brackets can easily avail of education or audio and video entertainment, which was earlier way out of their reach. Similar drops in costs of living will come about in healthcare, energy and other spheres of life.

Drops in costs lead to increase in savings, which opens up lifestyle choices for us. This is a qualitative change in terms of happiness and satisfaction, which cannot be reduced to numbers.

Moving from city to nature—not fad, but lifestyle choice

To start with, technology is said to improve the quality of life because of the time it saves people. While we might not stand and stare, we can choose to if we want to. That social media marketeers are told to push content during daytime on weekdays implies that people are taking time off during working hours. In that sense they are working fewer hours every day.[36]

Also, new avenues of employment are being generated in recreation, entertainment and other spheres, which was not common even fifteen or twenty years ago. Nowadays there are more openings for event managers, pet fashionistas, communication stylists and social media managers, to name a few professions. Many people who do these jobs are driven by passion.

Successful careers at MNCs that are dropped for pursuit of personal passions are not anecdotal any more. People who have accumulated finances are choosing to have had enough of the rat race and are moving on to farming or starting entrepreneurial ventures in the lap of nature. What's more, they are selling or providing unique experiences.

In the US, there are many well-educated first-time farmers who have left their lives in the cities to take advantage of the demand for local, eco-friendly, healthy food. Their numbers are large enough to impact the food system, as grocery chains want to carry their produce in their stores. The number of farmers under thirty-five years of age is increasing, with 69 per cent of the young farmers having college degrees. In some states, the number of first-time farmers has grown by as much as 20 per cent. This is a significant shift. And indeed, this younger generation believes in growing food organically with minimal use of pesticides and fertilizers.[37]

In countries such as India too, there is a breed of successful executives that is moving to the mountains and beaches to start boutique hotels. They offer small but high-end rooms that have a local flavour and offer personalized services. Such experiences are seeing traction, and there is a growing demand for non-touristy vacations.[38] Following this track, we envision entirely new professions becoming commonplace, even though we might not know what they will be.

Even though robots, AI and the like are here to stay, the doomsday predictions can be refuted by the argument that entire new professions will be created. We didn't know that virtual-world designing would be a career a decade ago; in the same way, we don't know what types of jobs will be created over the next decade. The only concern is that the thirty-five-year-old telemarketer, like the coal mine worker in the 1990s, might not be able to keep pace with and adapt to the demands of these new jobs; and especially because these new jobs will involve more creativity while offering greater flexibility, which will require initiative.

It is a balancing act—more now than ever before

'The machines will leave us unemployed and poor.'

vs

'The machines are here only to help us.'

As with anything in life, the solution lies between these two extremes. The problems related to automation cannot be wished away. We must acknowledge that we truly don't know the extent to which technologies such as AI can change various aspects of human life. However, there is something that technology is unlikely to change—the importance of striking a balance:

> A balance between exploiting to the fullest the abundant range of innovations such as genetics, blockchain and virtual reality, and ensuring that they do not endanger people while they are being used to address human flaws;
>
> A balance between increasing productivity and distributing the wealth that results among many rather than among a handful;
>
> A balance between controlling data from misuse and decentralizing ownership so that a few don't gain power over the many;
>
> A balance between micro-production, decentralized distribution and economies of scale.

The good news is that, thematically, none of this is new to us. Sweeping, dramatic changes have come earlier, and we have thrived. From the industrial revolution in the 1770s to the invention of the steam machine in the 1830s, through the introduction of steel, electricity and heavy engineering in the 1870s, and right till the oil, automobile and automation revolution in the early 1900s—we have made it through the turbulence each of these disruptions brought.

We have seen production using steam, production using electricity, production using 'simple' digitization and we are on the brink of beginning production using 'complex' digitization—Industry 4.0. In each of these shifts, technology-led destruction and creation of jobs has been rather cyclical.

The economics historian Carlota Perez sees this cycle of bubbles and golden ages—with one cycle lasting about seven decades—as a part of mankind's process of innovation. All these revolutions reveal a pattern. In the first phase of this pattern, new technologies lead to dramatic changes in production and even daily life. It takes about two to three decades for the new wave of technological changes to establish itself.

During the period of overlap, in a given category of job, one technology can be a creator as well as a destroyer. Using a current example, Uber has created a renewed demand for drivers. However, it has destroyed the conventional cab industry.

A key concern of this wave is job displacement. The resultant income disparity grows so intense that the bubble bursts, leading to a crisis phase that could range from two to seventeen years. This is when policy kicks in to check financial excesses and stimulate employment, leading to some form of stability. This phase lasts a good thirty years. This stable period is the cause and effect of reduced income inequality, because economies are funded by production capital rather than by speculation and uncertainty. But, as is true of all good things, this golden age too is temporary. Opportunities stagnate and so do markets, sparking off a restlessness to bring about a new wave of change.

However, there is a period of adjustment, which could be long and painful. We took 200 years to arrive at the modern, social welfare state from the industrial revolution of the 1800s. This period included two major communist revolutions that involved a death toll of 100 million. This means today's wage stagnation is likely to get worse before it gets better. How long will that be? One century? Two?

While we recognize that history won't necessarily repeat itself, we can prepare ourselves so that we do not have to suffer the trough of this known pattern. As per this pattern, we are at the peak of the current cycle. Specific to this age of 'complex' digitization, we are on the brink of innovation which will lead to democratization of both demand and supply.

We cannot let go of technology or globalization because of the immense value they bring to us. But, we can collectively brace ourselves to face them so that they cause minimal collateral damage. The main advantage we have on our side is hindsight. The last time we saw a crisis of this magnitude was after World War II. At the time, governments and business leaders came together as stimulants of change. Concentrated efforts from European countries and Japan to rebuild themselves, international aid to ailing countries and world trade pacts were actual actions that got us through that disaster. We don't see such cohesion today, but we are certainly making attempts to arrive at solutions.

To make sure we don't fall into the downside of the pattern, we need global economic and political consensus. Global trade will require global policies. While technology will not take care of all human flaws, we are at a stage where it was never more possible. At this point of human evolution, we can establish a positive-sum game across countries if we apply ourselves to it collectively.

If global leaders looked at the lessons of history, they would realize they have a pivotal role to play. Leaders from all spheres of life need to come together to make sure that 'complex' digitalization doesn't bring World War III in its wake.

Our definition of 'free enterprise' might need a tweak. As proponents of the free economy, we want to increase productivity, increase the number of new goods produced and generate new wealth. As humans we want to devise systems that distribute this wealth among many rather than a few.

That jobs are under threat is more naked to the eye today than the possibility of positive change. It will therefore take great visionaries to see us through this apparent threat. There is no option but for all agencies—businesses, governments and consumers—to work together.

Creative solutions—UBI?

A coming together of all stakeholders will require a multi-pronged, creative approach. From the wages angle, what if we didn't have to worry about being employed? Universal basic income (UBI) is a concept that is being seriously considered across the globe.

UBI can be thought of as a government welfare scheme, where every citizen, irrespective of their current income, wealth, education or even age, is regularly given a basic sustenance amount. In most cases, this is in lieu of current welfare schemes such as child support, unemployment insurance, etc. Income over and above UBI is, of course, taxed. In the context of potential loss of paying jobs, provision of UBI to the unemployed or underemployed is an attractive and humane proposal.

The government of Switzerland recommended payment of 2500 Swiss Francs ($2578) a month as UBI. The plan fell through as voters rejected it, mainly because this payment was over and above the current welfare schemes. Nevertheless, it brought the concept of UBI into public discourse.[39]

Those in favour of UBI consider it a tool to pull the impoverished out of their misery. UBI systems are usually set up to make the payout smooth and immediate. Since the systems destigmatize unemployment benefits, those engaged in unpaid work, such as stay-at-home parents, would not be averse to accepting the extra income. Businesses can become leaner and more efficient— without the emotional burden and bad press of laying off people, because UBI can take the ugly edge off firing employees.[40]

Those who aren't poor but aren't affluent either could benefit by using the money to get a better education or to escape from jobs they don't like. People, it is claimed, would be free to write poetry and design new art. The UBI concept sounds like a legitimate attack on economic inequality and a means to lift the happiness and satisfaction levels among citizens. The basic income is also likely to foster the economy since it is likely to be spent.

On the flip side though, for any economy to prosper, merely money changing hands from government to citizens is not enough. Goods and services have to be created. So this utopian world, in which people will be free to write poetry and create art, will also need buyers for this poetry and art. In such a situation no one would want to produce goods and services needed by the society. In that world, we would need robots to completely take over all production of goods and services. Since we are not close to either of these situations, UBI as a solution is a few decades from being practical. In the meantime, if adopted, UBI will only be a means to buy the forced satisfaction of dissatisfied citizens. This is the opinion many experts have about the pilot efforts by corporates such as Y Combinator to try out UBI—their attempt to reduce their guilt of having earned disproportionately high incomes while many were left behind.[41]

Some others who oppose the idea hold that money is not everything. People work because it brings them joy and a sense of dignity. Moreover, not all countries can afford to pay UBI. Saudi Arabia has had a UBI in place in the form of guaranteed government jobs. However, the Saudi government can afford to pay UBI only while it has oil reserves, or for as long as those reserves have value.[42] Also, this system has not fostered their economy because it hasn't increased production.

Other than affordability to the state, we should also consider the impact of giving people money that they have not earned. As tempting and humane a solution as UBI may seem, is it worth considering if it makes citizens indolent?

These back-and-forth arguments about UBI reveal why this attractive solution is flawed—it is over-simplistic.

Its unintended consequences could be far worse than the expected benefits. We believe that in a world where so much work is yet to be done—rivers must be cleaned, denuded lands are waiting to be be afforested, heritage needs preservation; plant and animal diversity needs restoration; a whole new agricultural, energy and industrial infrastructure is calling for attention—handing out unworked-for income to citizens seems hardly the right solution. We need to work out a system whereby human energies and public money are directed towards building a cleaner and sustainable world. This would ensure, at least in the developing economies, that the problems of environment and employment are simultaneously addressed.

Building skills to create this new, sustainable world would not be automatic—it would need learning and relearning throughout one's life.

Relearning and adaptation—the new skill of the 21st century

App developer, social media manager, Uber driver, cloud architect, big data analyst, drone operator, 3D-printing engineer, AI research scientist—ten years ago, we had not even heard of these jobs, but they are amongst the most sought after today.

To cope with the advent of technology, if there is one life skill our children need to learn, it is to learn how to keep learning. While super-specializations will certainly have their place for decades to come, they will benefit only a select few. The rest of the population can best take care of itself by learning how to adapt to a constantly changing environment.

Some communities are taking an initiative in this direction already. In Massachusetts, New Jersey and Illinois, teacher unions and educationists are expanding support systems for teacher development through online courses. The aim is to help workers refresh their skills in a fast-changing world.[43] Our engineers, scientists and mathematicians will also need to learn—or to be around people who are adept at—behavioural skills such as leadership and teamwork.[44] On the other hand, professionals, such as doctors, nurses and risk managers, will need to know how to use new technologies. In turn, this is why we have to look at making college education affordable again. Online resources will be key to making skill upgradation affordable.[45]

We have to bear in mind that we are following the trajectory identified by Perez. We are therefore in for a major upheaval before we can look forward to a long period of prosperity. The last time humanity was at this stage, we had a world war. We certainly don't want another one. With large sections of society facing unemployment, we have to be equipped to retrain them in time, before time. The current system of learning needs a complete rehaul. By the time a student can apply the knowledge they have learnt in graduate school, the applications in the real world have changed. We have to rethink ways in which learning can be scaled.[46]

Maybe the answer to income inequality is not in handing out free cash but in empowering lower-income households by giving them access to high-quality education. Maybe the answer lies in providing these fresh graduates with better opportunities to find themselves better-paying or more meaningful jobs.[47]

Rethinking every aspect of human activity

Not just education and employment, every aspect of human activity needs a complete change in our outlook towards it. We will have to begin with how we define 'success' and 'progress'.

Since World War II, a key indicator of national success has been growth in the GDP. However, the GDP has always measured quantity, not quality. Producing durable goods of low quality so that they break down and make it necessary for new goods to be produced increases the GDP. It says nothing about the damage done to the earth. It says even less about customer dissatisfaction. Just digging, building and redigging a road can increase the GDP because of the materials and human resources used. Wasteful efforts can add to the GDP. On the other hand, the GDP doesn't take into account highly productive efforts, such as the time parents spend raising children. Neither does the GDP accommodate desirable parameters such as good health, reduced inequality and available leisure time—aspects of life that have now grown in importance.

The GDP might have been a necessary tool in the 1940s, for a world that was just coming out of recession. But we have seen the consequences of using this system of measurement. It is now time for us to use a combination of indices such as the Human Development Index and the Happiness Index. These indicators, combined with the GDP, would then represent the well-being of a country. We already do that in some measure today. Every time we enforce a work safety norm or a pollution cess, we are reducing the rate at which businesses, and thus the GDP, can grow. We ought to do this with more vigour for the planet to survive longer.[48] We are hardly the torchbearers of this idea. Nobel Prize–winning economist, Joseph Stiglitz, has for years been asking us to take a relook at how we measure success.

Again, the starting point is a change in mindset. Much like the new breed of entrepreneurs who have begun enterprises such as boutique hotels, countries could focus on the quality of life of their population, even if it means less income. The GDP is only a fifty-year-old concept. We can change it as a measure of success. In fact, we should. We should redefine the bottom line. We should redefine social responsibility—both individual and corporate.

An individual, a company, a nation could instead work on other, more meaningful indices, such as safety and crime rates, working hours and resource usage. What if shareholder-driven companies were also held accountable for employee satisfaction and environmental damage?

Out of their own sense of duty, corporates are taking it upon themselves to be accountable not only to their shareholders but to all stakeholders, including the planet. The focus is ever so slowly moving from profit-based bottom lines to people-planet-profit-based bottom lines, known as the triple bottom line. Countries such as Australia are trying to make it national policy.[49]

Such rethinking is imperative in every walk of life. It is believed that the food wasted by the richer countries is enough to feed the entire sub-Saharan Africa. Could we create an AI-based supply chain that feeds the world without growing more food? On the education front, instead of teaching all subjects to all students in school, we could have customized learning programmes to make our teaching and learning systems more productive. On the products front, marquee brands could be made eco-friendly so that people are willing to pay an even higher price for them—a rethinking that will bring proper balance between energy, the environment and employment.

It is keeping this in mind that we have presented our framework for transformation, which also ensures responsibility towards other humans and the environment. This framework can help us consider our problems holistically. We sincerely believe that the framework can be a good first step in deliberating any change to make the world a better place and to act on it.

It is heartening to see the seeds of change all around us. We see them in the Chloe Maxmins of our world—the youth who are turned towards sharing economy. We see them in long-term investors who hold their investee companies accountable for more than just their dividends. We see them in our billionaires who are compassionate capitalists. Political leaders across the world can also sense the rumblings of change in the ground beneath their feet. All of us, together, can become a part of this movement. We would like to close our book with a prayer for the world—a prayer for this togetherness. This prayer, from the ancient Indian scriptures, usually a communication between a teacher and a student, embodies a philosophy of universal peace. We see this prayer equally applicable to the universe and its beings.

ॐ सह नाववतु।
सह नौ भुनक्तु।
सह वीर्यं करवावहै।
तेजस्वि नावधीतमस्तु
मा विद्विषावहै।
ॐ शान्तिः शान्तिः शान्तिः ।।

Om, may we both [teacher and student] be protected
May we both be nourished
May we work together with energy and vigour
May our study be enlightening
And not give rise to hostility
Om, peace, peace, peace[50]

We pray for your well-being as we do for our own. May together—you and I—be protected, may we be nourished. May we work together with renewed energy, may our intellect only sharpen with effective practice and study. May there be no animosity between us.

May there be peace within and without.

NOTES

CHAPTER ONE

THE WORLD AT A CROSSROADS

1. Jeffrey R. Immelt, Vijay Govindarajan and Chris Trimble, 'How GE Is Disrupting Itself', *Harvard Business Review*, October 2009, https://bit.ly/2nxbuii.
2. 'Om Sarve Bhavantu Sukhinah: In Sanskrit with meaning', GreenMessage.org, https://bit.ly/2OjrkXT.

CHAPTER TWO

THE 3Es: TODAY'S IMPOSING CHALLENGES

1. Javier Blas, 'Crude's top hedge fund manager says oil at $300 not impossible', *Economic Times*, 30 April 2018, https://bit.ly/2MxLTOV.
2. 'Icebergs could be tugged from Antarctica to drought-hit Cape Town to ease water crisis: experts', *Japan Times*, 1 May 2018, https://bit.ly/2NHjoTm.
3. Paul Davidson, 'Automation could kill 73 million U.S. jobs by 2030', *USA Today*, 28 November 2017, https://usat.ly/2AIg0l9.
4. Jeff Tollefson, 'Brazil's lawmakers renew push to weaken environmental rules', *Nature*, 30 April 2018, https://go.nature.com/2FJ9AQD.

5. 'Solar PV and wind are on track to replace all coal, oil and gas within two decades', *Conversation*, 6 April 2018, https://bit.ly/2muXDHf.

6. Arpita Sharad, 'Around 6,000 Aurangabad villages being trained to tackle drought', *Times of India*, 25 February 2018, https://bit.ly/2NNKvvU.

7. Tom Barfield, 'German government predicts one million new jobs for next year', *Local*, 25 April 2018, https://bit.ly/2KujaKT.

8. Neil Yeoh, 'Solar Startup Brings Renewable Energy to Haitian Businesses', *Forbes*, 30 April 2018, https://bit.ly/2x9RjL2.

9. Nidhi Sharma, 'One fourth of armed conflicts in ethnically divided countries coincide with climatic problems: Study', *Economic Times*, 20 May 2017, https://bit.ly/2p5G0Px.

10. Elizabeth Winkler, 'How the climate crisis could become a food crisis overnight', *Washington Post*, 27 July 2017, https://wapo.st/2DKt2iK.

11. Country insights—India, BP Energy, https://on.bp.com/2EVisaZ.

12. BP Statistical Review of World Energy, June 2017, https://on.bp.com/2DPTw2X.

13. 'Venezuela's worst economic crisis: What went wrong?', *Al Jazeera News,* 4 May 2017, https://bit.ly/2xbxFyi.

14. Google Public Data: World Development Indicators: Population (India and China), World Bank, 6 July 2018, https://bit.ly/2DOPlDU; Google Public Data: World Development Indicators: Energy use per capita (India and China), World Bank, 6 July 2018, https://bit.ly/2AzcRBM.

15. 'Electric power consumption (kWh per capita)', World Bank, https://bit.ly/2D4cdwL; and 'GDP per capita (current US$)', World Bank, https://bit.ly/2igrmkD.

16. Ken Caldeira, 'Stop Emissions!', *MIT Technology Review*, 29 November 2015, https://bit.ly/2xgi9jN.

17. 'Ozone depletion', Britannica.com, https://bit.ly/2v338Se.

18. 'A Comparative Risk Assessment of Burden of Disease and Injury Attributable to 67 Risk Factors and Risk Factor Clusters

in 21 Regions, 1990–2010: A systematic analysis for the Global Burden of Disease Study 2010, https://bit.ly/2qmvzru.

19. Nicholette Zeliadt, 'QnAs with Kirk R. Smith', *Proc Natl Acad Sci USA* 109 (22) (29 May 2012): p. 8357, https://bit.ly/2yJGJI.t.

20. Soutik Biswas, 'India cities dominate world air pollution list', BBC.com, 2 May 2018, https://bbc.in/2NiH5lx.

21. Shankkar Aiyar, 'Air pollution: two deaths per minute and politicos in denial', *New Indian Express*, 26 February 2017, https://bit.ly/2qntbR3.

22. 'State of Global Air/2017', Institute for Health Metrics and Evaluation's Global Burden of Disease Project and the Health Effects Institute, https://bit.ly/2lkLfdK.

23. '9 out of 10 people worldwide breathe polluted air', World Health Organization, https://bit.ly/2KsYUtf.

24. A twist on a quote by Samuel Taylor Coleridge.

25. 'Water Scarcity', UN Water, https://bit.ly/2Re5uXv.

26. Katherine Boerher, 'This Is How Much Water It Takes To Make Your Favorite Foods', *Huffington Post*, 13 October 2014, https://bit.ly/2F5DWlB.

27. Siobhan Norton, 'The environmental impact of our hunger for Valentine's roses', *Independent*, 13 February 2015, https://ind.pn/2CVbmAH.

28. Christopher Lloyd, 'Rose', in *What on Earth Evolved? . . . In Brief* (London: Bloomsbury, 2013).

29. 'Drinking-water: Key facts', World Health Organization, 7 February 2018, https://bit.ly/2L1GjHE.

30. Hannah Ritchie, 'Is organic really better for the environment than conventional agriculture?', *Our World in Data*, 19 October 2017, https://bit.ly/2xcA9dt.

31. Julian Lee, 'The Plastic Fantasy That's Propping Up the Oil Market', 10 September 2017, BloombergQuint.com, https://bit.ly/2PAWePm.

32. Pimm et al., 'The Biodiversity of Species and Their Rates of Extinction, Distribution, and Protection', *Science* 344 (6187) (30 May 2014): p. 124675, https://bit.ly/2zgbx5X.

33. Mark C. Urban, 'Accelerating extinction risk from climate change', *Science* 348 (6234) (1 May 2015): pp. 571–73, https://bit.ly/2O9Mo6B.

34. Damian Carrington, 'Oceans suffocating as huge dead zones quadruple since 1950, scientists warn', *Guardian*, 4 January 2018, https://bit.ly/2lURl3N.

35. Sajai Jose, 'Debate: India Is Not "Self-Destructing", It's Being Destroyed Systematically', *Wire*, 26 January 2018, https://bit.ly/2LkhGCs.

36. Richard Black, 'Nature loss 'to hurt global poor', BBC News, 29 May 2008, https://bbc.in/2DLJOhn.

37. Thomas Friedman, *Thank You for Being Late: An Optimist's Guide to Thriving in the Age of Accelerations* (New York: Macmillan, 2016), p. 172.

38. David Rotman, 'Hotter Days Will Drive Global Inequality', *MIT Technology Review*, 20 December 2016, https://bit.ly/2h5094T.

39. Ibid.

40. David Paul, 'Food Matters: Commodity Prices and the Egyptian Revolution', *Huffington Post*, 9 February 2011, https://bit.ly/2FKSjvM.

41. 'IEA raises its five-year renewable growth forecast as 2015 marks record year', International Energy Agency, IEA.org, 25 October 2016, https://bit.ly/2dFeAaY.

42. Katrin Bennhold, 'For First Time Since 1800s, Britain Goes a Day Without Burning Coal for Electricity', *New York Times*, 21 April, 2017, https://nyti.ms/2oviXvy.

43. Morgan McCorkle, 'Nano-spike catalysts convert carbon dioxide directly into ethanol', 12 October 2016, Oak Ridge National Laboratory, https://bit.ly/2dN8Tvg.

44. 'Inspirational environmental leaders from Chile, China and United States win UN's top environmental honour', UN Press Release, 5 December 2017, https://bit.ly/2AyCdyW.

45. Bob Davis, 'Barely Half of 30-Year-Olds Earn More Than Their Parents', *Wall Street Journal*, 8 December, 2016, https://on.wsj.com/2DfgKiY.

46. Tim Worstall, 'Millennials Earn 20% Less Than Boomers—Not As Important As You Might Think', *Forbes*, 14 January 2017, https://bit.ly/2ADy1zz.

47. Peter S. Goodman and Jonathan Soble, 'Global Economy's Stubborn Reality: Plenty of Work, Not Enough Pay', *New York Times*, 7 October 2017, https://nyti.ms/2y6GcmP.

48. Connolly, 'Angela Merkel.' And 'Guaranteed to Fail'.

49. Jon Hilsenrath and Bob Davis, 'America's Dazzling Tech Boom Has a Downside: Not Enough Jobs', *Wall Street Journal*, 12 October 2016, https://on.wsj.com/2F3ilKa.

50. Digital history, and compiled from many other sources.

51. 'Politicians cannot bring back old-fashioned factory jobs', *The Economist*, 14 January 2017, https://econ.st/2CRvy6q.

52. Eric Brynjolfsson and Andrew McAfee, *The Second Machine Age: Work, Progress, and Prosperity in a Time of Brilliant Technologies* (New York: W.W. Norton & Company, 2016); and Eric Brynjolfsson and Andrew McAfee, *Race Against the Machine* (Digital Frontier Press, 2011).

53. Jennifer Alsever, 'Will Cheap Robots Prevent a Comeback in Jobs?', *Fortune*, 14 March 2017, https://for.tn/2n6FRvX.

54. Ibid.

55. 'Technology At Work v2.0: The Future Is Not What It Used to Be', Citi GPS: Global Perspectives & Solutions, January 2016, https://bit.ly/2KhYfyg.

56. Umesh Chandra Sarangi, 'Changing Agricultural and Rural Employment Scenario in India', abstract of paper submitted to PIC conference (9 December).

57. A quote by William Gibson.

58. Johan Norberg, *Progress: Ten Reasons to Look Forward to the Future* (London: Oneworld, September 2016).

59. Moshe Y. Vardi, 'What the Industrial Revolution Really Tells Us About the Future of Automation and Work', ACM.org, 5 September 2017, https://bit.ly/2gD5Vtn.

60. Eric Brown, 'Building a future in which good jobs still matter', Institute for Work and Employment Research, MIT, 13 June 2017, https://bit.ly/2E02uL5..

61. Natasha Lomas, 'MIT study shows how much driving for Uber or Lyft sucks', 2 March 2018, TechCrunch.com, https://tcrn.ch/2FPl5rC.

62. Anna Ratcliff, 'Just 8 men own same wealth as half the world', Oxfam.org, 16 January 2017, https://bit.ly/2jOcybW.

63. T.S.R. Subramanian, 'Country of a chosen few', *Indian Express*, 16 September 2017, https://bit.ly/2DhJirT.

64. 'India's missing middle class', *The Economist*, 11 January 2018, https://econ.st/2LFWNkQ.

65. Peter S. Goodman and Jonathan Soble, 'Global Economy's Stubborn Reality: Plenty of Work, Not Enough Pay', *New York Times*, 7 October 2017, https://nyti.ms/2y6GcmP.

66. Surjit S. Bhalla, 'Piketty has got it wrong', *Indian Express*, 20 January 2018, https://bit.ly/2CWL5Sd.

CHAPTER THREE

ASSURED TOTAL INNOVATION

1. Brad King, 'The Day the Napster Died', 15 May 2002, Wired.com, https://bit.ly/2sLfrjh.

2. C.K. Prahalad and R.A. Mashelkar, 'Innovation's Holy Grail', *Harvard Business Review*, July–August 2010, https://bit.ly/2sENaP3.

3. Tony Seba, 'Clean Disruption—Energy & Transportation', YouTube Presentation, 8 June 2017, https://bit.ly/2utYPxG.

4. C.K. Prahalad and R.A. Mashelkar, 'Innovation's Holy Grail', *Harvard Business Review*, July–August 2010, https://bit.ly/2sENaP3.

5. Ibid.

6. '2017 Winner: Dr. Navin Khanna for "Dengue Day 1" test', Anjani Mashelkar Foundation, 1 December 2017, https://bit.ly/2PX00ni.

7. '2016 Winner: Mihir Shah for "iBreastExam" Device', Anjani Mashelkar Foundation, https://bit.ly/2lkr3Y9.

8. C.K. Prahalad and R.A. Mashelkar, 'Innovation's Holy Grail', *Harvard Business Review*, July–August 2010, https://bit.ly/2sENaP3.

9. Satty Bhens, Ling Lau and Shahar Markovitch, 'Finding the speed to innovate', McKinsey.com, April 2015, https://mck.co/2CSlUQZ.

10. Nicolas Bry, 'Is there a model for fast innovation?', *Paris Innovation Review*, 29 February 2012, https://blt.ly/2F0uUWN.

11. Wyatt Urmey, 'Innovation at speed—Are you making it happen, or just skating along?', IBM.com, 13 June 2017, https://ibm.co/2Djuklr.

12. Tekla S. Perry, 'China's Big Tech Advantage Is Speed, Not Cost', Spectrum.IEEE.org, 27 June 2017, https://bit.ly/2SEsqjG.

13. 'A tale of two file-sharers', *The Economist*, 13 September 2013, https://econ.st/2DiQKmy.

14. '10 Startups that Failed but Should Have Succeeded', Complex.com, 13 July 2013, https://bit.ly/2Rs0gH6.

15. Brad King, 'The Day the Napster Died', 15 May 2002, Wired.com, https://bit.ly/2sLfrjh.

16. Vlad Savov, 'BlackBerry's success led to its failure', TheVerge.com, 30 September 2016, https://bit.ly/2P8VBgQ.

17. Sam Gustin, 'The Fatal Mistake that Doomed BlackBerry', *TIME*, 24 September 2013, https://ti.me/1o74iUi.

18. Mathew Miller, 'Crash of the Mobile Titans', Zdnet.com, 26 September 2013, https://zd.net/2Rtq45O.

19. Dan Worth, '6 reasons BlackBerry crumbled in the smartphone market', 7 October 2016, *Inquirer*, https://bit.ly/2PCZj1i.

20. 'The 10 Biggest Tech Failures of the Last Decade', *TIME*, 14 May 2009, https://ti.me/2zlRIKt.

21. Chris Ziegler, 'Pre to postmortem: the inside story of the death of Palm and webOS', TheVerge.com, 5 June 2012, https://bit.ly/2PCG0Fv.

22. Aaron Brown, 'Here's the story behind GM's revolutionary electric car from the 90s that disappeared', *Business Insider*, 17 March 2016, https://bit.ly/2P5j3v5.

23. 'GM, Chevron and CARB killed the sole NiMH EV once, will do so again', 2016, https://bit.ly/2SCpiVk.

24. James Woudhuysen, 'The Electric Car Conspiracy . . . that never was', TheRegister.co.uk, 1 Jan 2008, https://bit.ly/2DiFlmX.

25. Jeff Cobb, 'Tesla Model S Is World's Best-Selling Plug-in Car For Second Year In A Row', HybridCars.com, 26 January 2017, https://bit.ly/2SELG0z.

26. 'Rise and Fall of Netscape Browsers', Inst.EECS.Berkeley.edu, https://bit.ly/2CWzra3.

27. Ellio Zaret, 'The Rise and Fall of Netscape', Zdnet.com, 9 March 2000, https://zd.net/2yUGVI3.

28. Michael Calore, 'Netscape: The Browser That Started It All Dies A Quiet Death', Wired.com, 1 January 2008, https://bit.ly/2CSmVsh.

29. John Naughton, 'Netscape: the web browser that came back to haunt Microsoft', *Guardian*, 22 March 2015, https://bit.ly/2BMNGOX.

30. Damien Scott, 'The 50 Worst Fails In Tech History', Complex.com, 29 April 2011, https://bit.ly/2AGmobo.

31. Scott McNulty, 'Behind the scenes of the ROKR failure', EnGadget.com, 26 October 2005, https://engt.co/2Px3YCd.

32. Michael Mace, 'Motorola ROKR Instant Failure', *Mobile Opportunity* (blog), 23 September 2006, https://bit.ly/2qmLztk.

33. Frank Rose, 'Battle for the Soul of the MP3 Phone', Wired.com, 1 November 2005, https://bit.ly/2CWSTn9.

34. Luke Dormehl, 'Today In Apple History: Steve Jobs Unveils Rokr E1, the First Itunes' Phone', 7 September 2018, CultofMac.com, https://bit.ly/2P28b1c.

35. Elizabeth Kartini, 'The Apple Products That Totally Failed In The Market', 2 October 2015, Technobezz.com, https://bit.ly/2P5DKHw.

36. Adam Hartung, 'The Reason Why Google Glass, Amazon Fire Phone and Segway All Failed', *Forbes*, 12 February 2015, https://bit.ly/2OhGtrT.

37. Paul Sloane, 'A lesson in why did the Segway fail', InnovationManagement.se, May 2012, https://bit.ly/1QjsEV3.

38. Jordan Golson, 'Well, that didn't work: The Segway is a technological marvel. Too bad it doesn't make any sense', Wired.com, January 2015, https://bit.ly/2Px4a4p.

39. Carlos Guevara and Hitendra Patel, 'What the most innovative organizations are doing to speed up innovation?', GimInstitute. org, 9 May 2017, https://www.giminstitute.org/index. php/2018/05/01/speed-up-innovation/.

40. Chris Foster and Richard Heeks, 'Innovation and Scaling of ICT for the Bottom-of-the-Pyramid', *Journal of Information Technology* 28 (4) (December 2013): pp. 296–315, https://bit. ly/2PVhDDY.

41. 'A Twenty Year Odyssey 1997-2017', Telecom Regulatory Authority of India, https://bit.ly/2Df8gZf.

42. Ibid.

43. Kul Bhushan, 'Reliance Jio subscriber base reaches 186.6 million', *Hindustan Times*, 28 April 2018, https://bit.ly/2Q8LS6q.

CHAPTER FIVE

LEVER 1 OF 4: TECHNOLOGY—NOTHING IS IMPOSSIBLE

1. R.A. Mashelkar, 'Technology 2050: A Potential Global Landscape', in *The World in 2050*, ed. Harinder Kohli (New Delhi: Oxford University Press, 2016), pp. 243–72, https://bit. ly/2BIC3av.

2. 'Life expectancy at birth, total (years)', World Bank data, https://bit.ly/2xXI77g.

3. 'Fact Sheet: Measles', WHO, https://bit.ly/2MBMsbb.

4. Afshan Yasmeen, 'India's child mortality rates declining: Lancet', The Hindu, 23 September 2017, https://bit.ly/2JzLAms.

5. 'Healthy life expectancy (HALE): Data by WHO region', Global Health Observatory data repository, World Health Organization, https://bit.ly/2P8Wcdj.

6. Paul Cresswell, 'Indian airport passenger traffic continues to grow', SteerGroup.com, 9 June 2015, https://bit.ly/2CSnLoV; and compiled from various Directorate General of Civil Aviation (GOI) reports, https://bit.ly/1f8aQPP..

7. Chris Dixon, '11 reasons to be excited about the future of technology', *Business Insider*, 19 August 2016, https://bit. ly/2QiZXlf.

8. Lauren Covello, 'US cities where you can find driverless cars or buses right now', *Fortune*, 24 January 2017, https://for. tn/2k0Glls.

9. Catherine Clifford, 'Billionaire CEO of SoftBank: Robots will have an IQ of 10,000 in 30 years', CNBC.com, 25 October 2017, https://cnb.cx/2yLNDBj.

10. Chris Dixon, '11 reasons to be excited about the future of technology', *Business Insider*, 19 August 2016, https://bit. ly/2QiZXlf.

11. 'Internet Transit Prices: Historical and Projected', DrPeering. net, https://bit.ly/1qkWz5A.

12. 'Technology At Work v2.0: The Future Is Not What It Used to Be', Citi GPS: Global Perspectives & Solutions, January 2016, https://bit.ly/2KhYfyg.

13. Ben Gaddis, 'How Sensors Will Revolutionize Service Businesses', Wired.com, May 2013, https://bit.ly/2CSnPoF.

14. Chris Dixon, '11 reasons to be excited about the future of technology', *Business Insider*, 19 August 2016, https://bit. ly/2QiZXlf.

15. Clouds Over Sidra: An Award-Winning Virtual Reality Experience, UNICEFUSA.org, 18 December 2015, https://bit. ly/2EWUdZH.

16. 'Virtual Human Interaction Lab', Stanford University, https:// stanford.io/2CUsPZU.

17. 'Amikasa 3-D Room Designer', http://www.amikasa.com/.

18. Abha Bhattarai, '"A new extreme" for the sharing economy: Shoe rentals', *Washington Post*, 5 October 2017, https://wapo. st/2OlhNPs.

19. 'Fact Sheet: Road traffic injuries', WHO, 19 February 2018, https://bit.ly/2qo1Kqr.

20. Chris Dixon, '11 reasons to be excited about the future of technology', *Business Insider*, 19 August 2016, https://bit. ly/2QiZXlf.

21. Paul Barter, '"Cars are parked 95% of the time". Let's check!', ReinventingParking.org, 22 February 2013, https://bit. ly/2FO9wkr.

22. '24 Industries Other Than Auto That Driverless Cars Could Turn Upside Down', *CB Insights*, 31 July 2017.

23. '10 Breakthrough Technologies 2018', *MIT Technology Review*, March–April 2018, https://bit.ly/2ERYs7V.

24. Eric Brynjolfsson and Andrew McAfee, *The Second Machine Age: Work, Progress, and Prosperity in a Time of Brilliant Technologies* (New York: W.W. Norton & Company, 2016).

25. 'William Lee', Britannica.com, https://bit.ly/2QoOnVB.

26. Jon Hilsenrath and Bob Davis, 'America's Dazzling Tech Boom Has a Downside: Not Enough Jobs', *Wall Street Journal*, 12 October 2016, https://on.wsj.com/2F3ilKa.

27. Ibid.

28. Neil Irwin, 'To Understand Rising Inequality, Consider the Janitors at Two Top Companies, Then and Now', *New York Times*, 3 September 2017, https://nyti.ms/2wuNn7v.

29. Jon Hilsenrath and Bob Davis, 'America's Dazzling Tech Boom Has a Downside: Not Enough Jobs', *Wall Street Journal*, 12 October 2016, https://on.wsj.com/2F3ilKa.

30. David Goldman, 'Facebook claims it created 4.5 million jobs', Money.CNN.com, 20 January 2015, https://cnnmon.ie/2QnKlwz.

31. Clifford Krauss, 'Texas Oil Fields Rebound From Price Lull, but Jobs Are Left Behind', *New York Times*, 19 February 2017, https://nyti.ms/2lxfZI6.

32. Claire Cain Miller, 'The Long-Term Jobs Killer Is Not China. It's Automation', *New York Times*, 21 December 2016, https://nyti.ms/2pbg17j.

33. Grace Donnelly, 'Robots Have Been Taking Jobs at a Blistering Pace in China', *Fortune*, 23 August 2017, https://for.tn/2wFL41S.

34. 'World Bank President: Automation Threatens 77% of Chinese Jobs', *Talent Daily*, 5 October 2016 https://goo.gl/4i14yC.

35. 'Robots, not humans: official policy in China', *New Internationalist*, 1 November 2017, https://goo.gl/pRRqAm.

36. R.A. Mashelkar, *Exponential Technology, Industry 4.0 and Future of Jobs in India* (New Delhi: SAGE publications, 2018), https://bit.ly/2r9I8qx.

37. Karl Flinders, 'Highly skilled professionals at risk of being replaced by computers', *Computer Weekly*, 9 May 2017, https://goo.gl/uADcqb.

38. Malcolm Foster, 'Aging Japan: Robots may have role in future of elder care', Reuters.com, 28 March 2018, https://reut.rs/2pKxkP8.

39. Leonid Bershidsky, 'Machines Can Replace Millions of Bureaucrats', Bloomberg.com, 9 February 2017, https://goo.gl/9WbN23.

40. David H. Autor, 'Why Are There Still So Many Jobs? The History and Future of Workplace Automation', *Journal of Economic Perspectives* 29 (3) (Summer 2015): pp. 3–30, https://goo.gl/paUjuJ.

41. Danny McCance, 'Demand for accountants rockets 21%', *Economia*, 26 July 2017, https://goo.gl/74BAkJ.

42. Oscar Williams-Grut, 'Lord Turner: "We may be at a turning point in the nature of capitalism"', *Business Insider*, 5 November 2016, https://goo.gl/P8WQYY.

43. R. Gopalakrishnan, 'Reboot manufacturing policy to benefit from digitised industrial revolution', *Economic Times*, 5 June 2016, https://bit.ly/2RfqFZe.

44. James Vincent, 'DeepMind's Go-playing AI doesn't need human help to beat us anymore', TheVerge.com, 18 October 2017, https://bit.ly/2yT4liv.

CHAPTER SIX

LEVER 2 OF 4: PUBLIC POLICY—A DELICATE BALANCING ACT

1. Vijay Kelkar, 'Reflections on the Art and Science of Policymaking', C.D. Deshmukh Memorial Lecture, 27 January 2017, https://goo.gl/VwVbxH.

2. Robert VanGiezen and Albert E. Schwenk, 'Compensation from before World War I through the Great Depression', *Compensation and Working Conditions* (Fall 2001), 30 January 2003, https://goo.gl/NvcqtZ.

3. 'New Deal', History.com, https://goo.gl/r3q416.
4. Philippe Grangereau, 'La Chine Creuse Ses Trous De Mémoire', *Liberation*, 17 June 2011, https://bit.ly/2SiZZXl.
5. Wayne Whipple, Michael Kerr and Troy Strock, 'Improving confidence in the TO 15 Atmospheric Analysis at Trace Concentrations', US EPA R5 CRL, https://bit.ly/2E73UUj (p. 19).
6. Fred Pearce, 'Thirty Years After Montreal Pact, Solving the Ozone Problem Remains Elusive', *Yale Environment 360*, 14 August 2017, https://goo.gl/J5ZsZJ.
7. 'Montreal Protocol assessment reveals healing ozone, untapped potential for climate action', World Meteorological Organization, Press Release Number: 05112018, 5 November 2018, https://bit.ly/2D59R2U.
8. 'India's UJALA Story: Energy-efficient Prosperity', IndiaEnergy. gov.in, https://bit.ly/2DYDeVT.
9. Debjoy Sengupta, 'Clean energy cess collections rise, but spending low', *Economic Times*, 15 February 2017, https://bit. ly/2Si4eCG.
10. Dibyendu Mondal, 'No detention policy has hit quality of education', *Sunday Guardian*, 17 September 2016, https://goo. gl/W23YJG.
11. Sanjay Bakshi, 'Heard of cobra effect? Be Careful what you Ask for', *Economic Times*, 28 September 2017, https://goo.gl/SPxKjY.
12. *Malpe Vishwanath Acharya & others Vs State of Maharashtra*, Supreme Court, 19 December 1997, https://bit.ly/2P9z2nn.
13. 'Political Economy of rent control—case of greater Mumbai', a Tata Institute of Social Sciences (TISS) study.
14. Walter Block, 'Rent Control', *The Concise Encyclopedia of Economics*, https://goo.gl/MTLjTf.
15. Rebecca Diamond, Timothy Mcquade, Franklin Qian, 'The Effects of Rent Control Expansion on Tenants, Landlords, and Inequality: Evidence from San Francisco', NBER Working Paper No. 24181 (January 2018), https://goo.gl/hrysHF.
16. Steve Schaefer, 'Forbes Flashback: How George Soros Broke The British Pound And Why Hedge Funds Probably Can't Crack The Euro', *Forbes*, 7 July 2015, https://bit.ly/2DNWbcJ.

17. John Donohue and Steven Levitt, 'The Impact of Legalized Abortion on Crime', NBER Working Paper No. 8004 (November 2000), https://goo.gl/j1ZB7i.

18. Rajeev Chawla and Subhash Bhatnagar, 'Online Delivery of Land Titles to Rural Farmers in Karnataka, India', Case Study for the World Bank, https://goo.gl/78uo72.

19. 'Deep Shift: Technology Tipping Points and Societal Impact', Survey Report by World Economic Forum, September 2015, https://bit.ly/1KlN8ZR.

CHAPTER SEVEN
LEVER 3 OF 4: SOCIAL ENGAGEMENT—THE POWER OF PEOPLE

1. Chloe Maxmin profile, *Nation*, https://goo.gl/3Cfcuy.

2. 'Harvard Undergraduate Arrested As Students Blockade the President's Office Calling for An Open Dialogue on Fossil Fuel Divestment', Divest Harvard, press release, 1 May 2014, https://bit.ly/2TOwbDT.

3. 'Britain's LSE to reduce investments in coal, tar sands', Reuters.com, 26 November 2015, https://reut.rs/2DNPibB.

4. Subhash Mehta, 'Bhoodan-Gramdan Movement—50 Years: A Review', Gandhi Sevagram Ashram, https://goo.gl/pCQ6ma.

5. '[Land Reforms] Bhoodan, Gramdan, Vinoba Bhave: Achievements, obstacles, limitations', Mrunal.org, https://goo.gl/GAJ897.

6. Richard Mahapatra, 'Where's Bhoodan Land?', *Down to Earth*, 28 June 2015, https://goo.gl/sQLJLQ.

7. Greg Satell, 'What Successful Movements Have in Common', *Harvard Business Review*, 30 November 2016, https://goo.gl/sR1dZ3.

8. 'Critical Mass and Tipping Points: How To Identify Inflection Points Before They Happen', *Farnam Street* (blog), https://bit.ly/2KCmlAv.

9. Ibid.

10. Greg Satell, 'What Successful Movements Have in Common', *Harvard Business Review*, 30 November 2016, https://goo.gl/sR1dZ3.

11. Ibid.

12. Anand Karandikar, 'चळवळी यशस्वी का होतात, का फसतात?', *Aisi Akshare* (blog), 13 October 2014, https://goo.gl/CmSbxT.

13. Greg Satell, 'What Successful Movements Have in Common', *Harvard Business Review*, 30 November 2016, https://goo.gl/sR1dZ3.

14. Greg Satell and Srdja Popovic, 'How Protests Become Successful Social Movements', *Harvard Business Review*, 27 January 2017, https://goo.gl/mFcbPc.

15. 'Number of monthly active Facebook users worldwide as of 3rd quarter 2018 (in millions)', Statista.com, https://bit.ly/2daz7Yr.

16. 'Number of monthly active WhatsApp users worldwide from April 2013 to December 2017 (in millions)', Statista.com, https://bit.ly/2j0uHH6.

17. 'Number of monthly active Twitter users in the United States from 1st quarter 2010 to 3rd quarter 2018 (in millions)', Statista.com, https://bit.ly/2y0NSEb.

18. Emily Steel, 'Ice Bucket Challenge has Raised Millions for ALS Association', *New York Times*, 17 August 2014, https://goo.gl/cyU7i8.

19. Matt Petronzio, 'ALS Wikipedia Page Views Up 18-Fold Since Ice Bucket Challenge', Mashable.com, 6 September 2014, https://goo.gl/R6whMr.

20. 'The ALS Association Expresses Sincere Gratitude to Over Three Million Donors', ALSA official website, https://goo.gl/xufy7s.

21. Andrea Park, '#MeToo reaches 85 countries with 1.7M tweets', CBSNews.com, 24 October 2017, https://goo.gl/vcyaty.

22. Nadia Khomami, '#MeToo: how a hashtag became a rallying cry against sexual harassment', *Guardian*, 20 October 2017, https://goo.gl/jSby7T.

23. Rebecca Seales, 'What has #MeToo actually changed?', BBC News, 12 May 2018, https://bbc.in/2NaKAdO.

24. Molly Redden, '#MeToo movement named Time magazine's Person of the Year', *Guardian*, 6 December 2017, https://goo.gl/w4PkSs.

25. Sandra E. Garcia, 'The Woman Who Created #MeToo Long Before Hashtags', *New York Times*, 20 October 2017, https://goo.gl/UJaFXC.

26. Yara Rodrigues Fowler and Charlotte Goodman, 'How Tinder Could Take Back the White House', *New York Times*, 22 June 2017, https://goo.gl/BmABKD.

27. Ryan Browne, 'Cambridge Analytica whistleblower says Facebook users' data could be stored in Russia', CNBC.com, 9 April 2018, https://goo.gl/h4n7sk.

28. Matt Peckham, 'Foldit Gamers Solve AIDS Puzzle That Baffled Scientists for a Decade', *Time*, 19 September 2011, https://bit.ly/1cxO52p; and Firas Khatib, Frank DiMaio et al., 'Crystal structure of a monomeric retroviral protease solved by protein folding game players', *Nature Structural & Molecular Biology*, 18 September 2011, https://bit.ly/2TRdbo7.

29. Google Public Data on Life Expectancy, 11 January 2017.

30. Jeanne Sahadi, 'They work harder for the money', CNN.com, 7 June 2007, https://goo.gl/Qdfoon.

31. Tania Ellis, 'The era of compassionate capitalism', TaniaEllis.com, https://goo.gl/WBftSQ.

32. The Giving Pledge, official website, 11 January 2017, https://goo.gl/Roqm8h.

33. Michael Thomas, 'The Giving Pledge List Reaches $365 Billion', 22 April 2016.

34. 'Forbes releases list of 7 most powerful rural Indians', *Economic Times*, 14 November 2010, https://goo.gl/eoQ52k.

35. Anil K. Gupta, *Grassroots Innovation* (New Delhi: Penguin Random House, 2016).

CHAPTER EIGHT

LEVER 4 OF 4: ECONOMIC MODEL—DOING WELL BY
DOING GOOD

1. Ashok Gadgil, Andree Sosler and Debra Stein, 'Stove Solutions: Improving Health, Safety, and the Environment in Darfur with Fuel-Efficient Cookstoves', *Solutions* 4 (1) (January 2013): pp. 54–64, https://goo.gl/kALf8V.

2. Rajeev Chawla and Subhash Bhatnagar, 'Online Delivery of Land Titles to Rural Farmers in Karnataka, India', Case Study for the World Bank, https://goo.gl/78uo72.

3. Marcia Stepanek, 'Exploring Failure', *Stanford Social Innovation Review*, 3 November 2010, https://goo.gl/cow1Ih.

4. Christian Seelos and Johanna Mair, 'Innovate and Scale: A Tough Balancing Act', *Stanford Social Innovation Review*, Summer 2013, https://goo.gl/dZVmZd.

5. 'The Procurement of Innovation Platform', https://bit.ly/1kevCtm.

6. Ibid.

7. 'Sustainable investment joins the mainstream', *The Economist*, 25 November 2017, https://goo.gl/j7y9ki.

8. Ramesh Mangaleswaran and Ramya Venkataraman, 'Designing philanthropy for impact', McKinsey.com, October 2013, https://goo.gl/werQjc.

9. 'Sustainable investment joins the mainstream', *The Economist*, 25 November 2017, https://goo.gl/j7y9ki.

10. R.A. Mashelkar, '2018 K.R. Narayanan Oration: Dismantling inequality through ASSURED innovation', Mashelkar.com, https://bit.ly/2rbmBOd.

11. Barbara Kiviat and Bill Gates, 'Making Capitalism More Creative', *Time*, 31 July 2008, https://bit.ly/2PVXOwl.

12. Michael Porter and Mark Kramer, 'Creating shared value', *Harvard Business Review*, https://goo.gl/xyrN14.

13. Tania Ellis, 'The era of compassionate capitalism', TaniaEllis.com, https://goo.gl/WBftSQ.

CHAPTER NINE

LEAPFROGGING TO POLE-VAULTING: CREATING RADICAL YET
SUSTAINABLE TRANSFORMATION

1. 'Milk production and per capita availability of milk in India', National Dairy Development Board, https://bit.ly/2FJNOBF.

2. 'Amul: 1966 Operation Flood is India's most successful revolution since Quit India Movement', *India Today*, 18 August 2003, https://goo.gl/ZEtdV1.

3. Amrita Patel, 'Women and the White Revolution', *Co-op Dialogue* 8 (1) (Jan–June, 1998): pp. 20–25, https://bit.ly/2DNTRm4.

4. National Dairy Development Board Website, https://www. nddb.coop/about/genesis/flood.

5. Ibid.

6. Kenda Cunningham, 'Connecting the Milk Grid: Smallholder dairy in India', DairyKnowledge.in, https://goo.gl/H6JsMm.

7. Harish Damodaran, 'Chilling technology: White Revolution – Part II', *Indian Express,* 30 November 2017, https://goo.gl/ Y6BVpa.

8. Amrita Patel, 'Women and the White Revolution', *Co-op Dialogue* 8 (1) (Jan–June, 1998): pp. 20–25, https://bit. ly/2DNTRm4.

9. Kenda Cunningham, 'Connecting the Milk Grid: Smallholder dairy in India', DairyKnowledge.in, https://goo.gl/H6JsMm.

10. D. Narasimha Reddy, 'The story of White Revolution', *The Hindu,* 17 May 2011, https://goo.gl/YCSVWC.

11. Kenda Cunningham, 'Connecting the Milk Grid: Smallholder dairy in India', DairyKnowledge.in, https://goo.gl/H6JsMm.

12. Sumit Chakraborty, 'On World Milk Day, a look at how India became the largest producer and why it continues to be so', *Financial Express*, 1 June 2017, https://goo.gl/4uk6r7.

13. The UIDAI website: https://uidai.gov.in.

14. 'Understanding the UID Aadhaar project and IT's role in its success', ComputerWeekly.com, September 2011, https://goo. gl/7tRAvo.

15. Shelley Singh, 'Benefits of Aadhaar are real but so are fears of biometric theft. Here's why', *Economic Times*, 13 April 2017, https://goo.gl/y1JKEz.

16. 'Aadhaar helped Indian govt save $9 billion: Nandan Nilekani', *Indian Express*, 13 October 2017, https://goo.gl/gLPyCZ.

17. '31.20 crore accounts opened under Pradhan Mantri Jan-Dhan Yojana (PMJDY) with aggregate deposit balances ₹75,572.09 crore as on 28.2.2018', Press Information Bureau, 22 March 2018, https://bit.ly/2BBgdpw.

18. Aadhaar enrolments: 1131.3 million (UIDAI website 27 March 2017).

19. Somesh Jha, 'Almost every household has a bank account: Labour Bureau', *The Hindu*, 28 September 2016, https://goo.gl/K7wH6f.

20. 'Mobile internet users in India seen at 478 million by June: IAMAI', *Times of India*, 29 March 2018, https://goo.gl/GPwBEs.

21. Shweta Banerjee, 'Aadhaar: Digital Inclusion and Public Services in India', Background Paper: Digital Dividends, World Development Report 2016, World Bank, https://goo.gl/JrjDKp.

22. Amrit Raj and Upasana Jain, 'Aadhaar goes global, finds takers in Russia and Africa', LiveMint.com, 9 July 2016, https://bit.ly/2r8LcmE.

23. Aman Sharma, 'Savings from direct benefit transfer pegged at ₹83,000 crore', *Economic Times*, 23 March 2018, https://goo.gl/cXsWRE.

24. Reetika Khera, 'Impact of Aadhaar on Welfare Programmes', *Economic & Political Weekly* 52 (50) (16 December 2017), https://bit.ly/2zovHf1.

CHAPTER TEN

A CLEAN REVOLUTION: SOLID WASTE MANAGEMENT

1. 'Urbanization and Development: Emerging Futures', World Cities Report 2016, UN-Habitat, https://goo.gl/yMbW37.

2. Sunita Narain and Swati Singh Sambyal, *Not in My Backyard: Solid Waste Management in Indian Cities* (New Delhi: Centre for Science and Environment, 2016).

3. 'Solid Waste Management Rules Revised After 16 Years; Rules Now Extend to Urban and Industrial Areas: Javadekar', Central Monitoring Committee Under Environment Secretary to Monitor Implementation, Press Information Bureau, Government of India, 5 April 2016, https://goo.gl/iHGfKb.

4. Bibi Farber, '7 Ways to Launch Your Own Anti-Plastics Movement', 25 December 2017, EcoWatch.com, https://bit.ly/2BRYBU8.

5. Ashley Coates, 'Ocean plastic cleanup: A 23-year-old's mission to take rubbish out of our seas', *Independent*, 7 August 2017, https://ind.pn/2IsFFOG.

6. 'Great Pacific Garbage Patch: Pacific Trash Vortex', NationalGeographic.com, https://bit.ly/2qfM22v.

7. 'Himalayan littering leading to brown-bear habit changes', *Business Standard*, 2 January 2018, https://bit.ly/2AIJ1vE.

8. Mithun Ray and Mijanur Rahman, 'An overview of legal framework for waste management system in india with special allusion to SWM rules, 2016', *International Journal of Interdisciplinary and Multidisciplinary Studies* 4 (1) (2016): pp. 13–19, https://bit.ly/2DZeFYV.

9. Sunita Narain and Swati Singh Sambyal, *Not in My Backyard: Solid Waste Management in Indian Cities* (New Delhi: Centre for Science and Environment, 2016).

10. Raghu Karnad, 'Scavengers Are India's Real Recyclers', *New York Times*, 29 July 2015, https://nyti.ms/2zmNv9l.

11. Suparna Dutt D'Cunha, 'Mumbai's $13B Waste Management Market and the Startup that's Tapping Into It', *Forbes*, 24 August 2016, https://bit.ly/2zoEPPP.

12. Going by Janwani's experience, every community of 800–1000 people needs two waste collectors. India's population is 1.32 billion;
    required employees: 2.64 million;
    average members per family: 5;
    lives touched: 13.2 million.

13. Hari Pulakkat, 'With new technologies and knowledge of segregation, India is fast learning how to manage its waste', *Economic Times*, 21 May 2017, https://bit.ly/2F0SbYM.

14. 'Indore cleanest city, Jharkhand emerges best-performing state', *Business Standard,* 17 May 2018, https://bit.ly/2QkSZMB.

15. India's population: 1.32 billion;
    Urban:Rural population: 34:66 ('Urbanisation on the rise in India', *The Hindu*, 18 May 2018, https://bit.ly/2AJauNS);
    professionals needed in urban areas: ~45,000;
    professionals needed in rural areas: ~87,000;
    monthly salary: urban – ₹25,000;
    rural – ₹15,000;
    total cost: ₹28.52 billion (2850 crore) per year.

16. India's population: 1.32 billion;
    average members per family: 5;
    number of families: 300 million;
    total cost: ₹28.52 billion (2850 crore) per year;
    cost per family: ₹110 per year.
17. Bibi Farber, '7 Ways to Launch Your Own Anti-Plastics Movement', EcoWatch.com, 25 December 2017, https://bit.ly/2BRYBU8.
18. Ibid.
19. 'The Declaration of the Global Plastics Associations for Solutions on Marine Litter – Progress Report', May 2016, https://bit.ly/1OSzzc5.
20. Assuming a waste collector covers 200 households collecting approximately 30 kilograms of dry waste and 50 kilograms of wet waste, he collects ₹6000 ($91) in user fees, ₹9000 ($136) from the sale of dry waste and ₹1500 ($23) from the sale of wet waste.
21. Commercial LPG price, Pune, April 2018.
22. '3rd National Conference on Sustainable Infrastructure with Plastics', Knowledge Paper on Plastic Industry for Infrastructure, FICCI, February 2017, https://bit.ly/2TTDeLi.
23. 'Swachh Bharat: PM Modi ropes in nine people including Tendulkar, Salman Khan, Baba Ramdev', *Economic Times*, 2 October 2014, https://bit.ly/2OpazKp.
24. Christine Cole, 'Four Tough Actions to Help Fight the Global Plastic Crisis', *Wire*, 15 January 2018, https://bit.ly/2AJ2lZJ.
25. Farber, '7 Ways to Launch Your Own Anti-Plastics Movement'.
26. 'All India Installed Capacity (in MW) Of Power Stations', report by Central Electricity Authority, India, 31 January 2018, https://bit.ly/2EY2Cw9.
27. 'India Waste to Energy, EAI Catalyzing Cleantech & Sustainability', EAI.in, https://bit.ly/2PF4IoG.
28. Chander Kumar Singh, Anand Kumar and Soumendu Shekhar Roy, 'Quantitative analysis of the methane gas emissions from municipal solid waste in India', Nature.com, 13 February 2018, https://go.nature.com/2RsrSMi.

29. Going by Janwani's experience, every community of 800–1000 people needs two waste collectors. This will work out to 2.4 million employees for India. Taking an average of five people per family, 12 million lives will be touched.

CHAPTER ELEVEN
TODAY'S GREEN REVOLUTION: TRANSFORMING MOBILITY

1. 'India's Trade: Back on Track', Annual Report, 2017–18, Department of Commerce, Ministry of Commerce & Industry (page 44, table 3.2), https://bit.ly/2BBN5hQ.
2. 'The Hidden Cost of Fossil Fuels', Union of Concerned Scientists, 30 August 2016, https://bit.ly/2rglMnB.
3. Ibid.
4. Id.
5. Rajat Kathuria and Nicholas Stern, 'Take a Deep Breath', *Indian Express,* 10 April 2015, https://bit.ly/2JB0mtk.
6. India Energy Statistics 2018, Ministry of Statistics and Programme Implementation, India, https://bit.ly/2RwTYGa.
7. R.K. Shrivastava, Neeta Saxena and Geeta Gautam, 'Air Pollution Due To Road Transportation In India: A Review On Assessment And Reduction Strategies', *Journal of Environmental Research and Development* 8 (1) (July–September 2013), https://bit.ly/2Pafiof.
8. Soutik Biswas, 'India cities dominate world air pollution list', BBC.com, 2 May 2018, https://bbc.in/2NiH5lx.
9. Neema Davis, Harry Raymond Joseph, Gaurav Raina and Krishna Jagannathan, 'Congestion costs incurred on Indian roads: A case study for New Delhi', Arvix.org, https://bit.ly/2Nmjkcx.
10. Aparajita Ray, '10 million Bengalureans lose 60 crore hours, ₹3,700 crore a year to road congestion', *Times of India,* 6 January 2017, https://bit.ly/2Irk6yz.
11. 'Transportation of the Future discussed at World Government Summit in Dubai, BusinessWire.com, 14 February 2017, https://bit.ly/2KEfNBJ.

12. Dipak K. Dash, '2017 saw 3% decline in road accident deaths', *Times of India*, 8 February 2018, https://bit.ly/2P5on1R.

13. 'Road accidents in India, 2016: 17 deaths on roads every hour, Chennai and Delhi most dangerous', *Indian Express*, 11 September 2017, https://bit.ly/2yNzORo.

14. 'Automotive Sector: Achievements Report', Department of Industrial Policy and Promotion, 24 November 2016, https://bit.ly/2AvA6fN.

15. 'Making India a world class automotive manufacturing hub', EY and Confederation of Indian Industry, 6 February 2016, https://go.ey.com/2RA9QYL.

16. 'Automotive Sector: Achievements Report', Department of Industrial Policy and Promotion, 24 November 2016, https://bit.ly/2AvA6fN.

17. 'India's logistics sector to reach USD 215 bn by 2020: Survey', *Economic Times*, 29 January 2018, https://bit.ly/2EjyLtT.

18. 'Transportation of the Future discussed at World Government Summit in Dubai, BusinessWire.com, 14 February 2017, https://bit.ly/2KEfNBJ.

19. Anthony King, 'Battery builders get the cobalt blues', Minerals.usgs.gov, 12 March 2018, https://bit.ly/2QfPZ0E.

20. Brian W. Jaskula, 'Lithium', U.S. Geological Survey, Mineral Commodity Summaries, January 2018, https://on.doi.gov/2yNFzyF.

21. Anthony King, 'Battery builders get the cobalt blues', Minerals.usgs.gov, 12 March 2018, https://bit.ly/2QfPZ0E.

22. S. Werner Siemers, 'Technical and Economic Prospects of Rice Residues for Energy in Asia', FAO.org, 2 June 2011, https://bit.ly/2OjLj81.

23. A.K. Misra, K.K. Singh, T.A. Khan and Gh Pailan, 'Estimates of Wheat Straw Availability and Variation in Straw Quality', *Range Management and Agroforestry* 34 (1) (2013): pp. 112–18, https://bit.ly/2zvaQXf.

24. Union Minister Nitin Gadkari's address at the National Legislators Conference, 11 March 2018, https://bit.ly/2JBNQtN.

25. 'India's Trade: Back on Track', Annual Report, 2017–18, Department of Commerce, Ministry of Commerce & Industry (page 44, table 3.2), https://bit.ly/2BBN5hQ.
26. Adam Conner-Simons, 'Study: carpooling apps could reduce taxi traffic 75%', MIT Computer Science & Artificial Intelligence Laboratory, 1 December 2016, https://bit.ly/2DiEFOl.
27. Adam Conner-Simons, 'Study: carpooling apps could reduce taxi traffic 75%', 1 December 2016, MIT Computer Science & Artificial Intelligence Lab, https://bit.ly/2DiEFOl.
28. Barbora Bondorová and Greg Archer, 'Does sharing cars really reduce car use?', TransportEnvironment.org, June 2017, https://bit.ly/2A8z7jY.
29. Michele Bertoncello and Dominik Wee, 'Ten ways autonomous driving could redefine the automotive world', McKinsey.com, June 2015, https://mck.co/2AjEPjh.
30. M. Allirajan, 'Drive 12,000 km a year? Cheaper to call cab', *Times of India*, 9 August 2017, https://bit.ly/2yMvzFB.
31. Joel Diffendarfer, 'Is it Cheaper to Own a Car or Use a Taxi?', ToughNickel.com, https://bit.ly/2zlbfuC.
32. 'EESL To Buy 20,000 Electric Vehicles By March 2019; Invest ₹2,400 Crore', Auto.NDTV.com, 3 April 2018, https://bit.ly/2yR33CT.
33. Global EV Outlook 2017, International Energy Agency, https://bit.ly/2rz3sZb.
34. Ibid.
35. Tim Higgins, 'The End of Car Ownership', *Wall Street Journal*, 20 June 2017, https://on.wsj.com/2sz3gq5.
36. Gene Balk, 'Seattle has reversed a decades-long trend of rising car ownership—and millennials are the reason', *Seattle Times*, 12 May 2017, https://bit.ly/2QekZhq.
37. E.J. Schultz, Tesla Still Doesn't Need Paid Advertising to Make Sales', Adage.com, 3 August 2017, https://bit.ly/2DkbLxy.
38. Nikolas Badminton, 'The Future of Fuel and Transportation in 2030 and 2050', NikolasBadminton.com, 13 April 2016, https://bit.ly/2OmnRa8.
39. James Arbib and Tony Seba, 'Rethinking transportation 2020–30', May 2017, https://bit.ly/2pL0cZV.

40. Ibid.
41. Id.

CHAPTER TWELVE
CREATING POLE-VAULTING LEADERS

1. 'Foot In Mouth: 43 Quotes From Big Corporate Execs Who Laughed Off Disruption When It Hit', CBInsights.com, 13 September 2018, https://bit.ly/2BvOZCE.
2. Arnav Kapur, 'Fluid Interfaces', MIT Media Lab, https://bit.ly/2DkCry6.
3. 'Prizes', XPrize.org, https://bit.ly/2AwnmFX.
4. 'The Orteig Prize', NESTA.org.uk, https://bit.ly/2yOG3nZ.
5. 'John F. Kennedy Address at Rice University on the Space Effort', Rice University, 12 September 1962, https://bit.ly/1gaqFOM.
6. Eric Griffith, '5 Moonshot Projects Just Crazy Enough to Work', PCMag.com, 18 February 2014, https://bit.ly/2TTmTXd.
7. 'Launching a New Space Industry', Ansari X Prize, https://bit.ly/2P7fmQR.
8. 'Let's Change the World Together', X Prize, https://bit.ly/2E8aOWy.
9. 'Outpaced by Innovation', Archon Genomics X Prize, https://bit.ly/2r8jsyJ.
10. Peter Diamandis, 'Outpaced by Innovation: Canceling an XPRIZE', *Huffington Post*, 22 August 2013, https://bit.ly/2rbluy4.
11. 'The New Space Race', Lunar X Prize, https://bit.ly/2SjEmXd.
12. 'Mahatma Gandhi's Announcement of Machine Design Contest', 24 July 1929, https://bit.ly/2E23oqH.
13. Chandrakumar Narayanan, Logic device, US Patent 5,847,565, filed 31 March 1997, https://bit.ly/2BByxP8.
14. Chandrakumar Narayanan, Device for excitation and detection of magnetic resonance using orthogonal transmitter probe coils, US Patent 5,719,499, filed 4 March 1996, https://bit.ly/2RqNmJK.

15. R.A. Mashelkar, 'What will it take for Indian science, technology and innovation to make global impact?', *Current Science* 109 (6) (25 September 2015), https://bit.ly/2rhSdlr.

16. V.N. Raja, S.K. Prasad, Sivaramakrishna, C.V. Yelamaggad and U.S. Hiremath, An improved liquid crystal display device, Indian Patent Number 206304, filed 18 February 2000, https://bit.ly/2KGC1mr.

17. Arora Sudarshan Kumar, et al., US Patent Nos US 7763602B2, US 7691889B2, US 7491721B2, US 2004497615A and US 2004844992A.

18. 'Waiting for Godot', Wikipedia.org, https://bit.ly/2qwdB42.

19. Jovita Aranha, 'Gurugram Lady Opens "Crockery Bank" for Steel Utensils to Reduce Plastic Waste!', TheBetterIndia.com, 28 June 2018, https://bit.ly/2KsZslG.

20. Rayomand Engineer, 'This Inflatable Helmet By IIT-Roorkee Could Save Biker Lives in Road Accidents!', TheBetterIndia.com, 26 June 2018, https://bit.ly/2qWoJsP.

21. Tanvi Patel, 'Inspired by Proactive Citizen, Bengaluru Takes up Pothole Challenge to Fix Its Roads', TheBetterIndia.com, 25 June 2018, https://bit.ly/2OUAXfa.

22. Rayomand Engineer, 'Bengalureans Build Robotic Chef Who'll Be Able to Cook 100+ Indian Dishes', TheBetterIndia.com, 25 June 2018, https://bit.ly/2DzexOA.

23. Rayomand Engineer, 'Water From Thin Air: This Low-Cost Device Can Produce Upto 1000 Litres Per Day!', TheBetterIndia.com, 25 June 2018, https://bit.ly/2DxBzoW.

24. Rayomand Engineer, 'In a First, You Can Now Rent a Self-Drive e-Car from Metro Station at Just ₹40/Hour!', TheBetterIndia.com, 23 June 2018, https://bit.ly/2OZG26c.

25. Tanvi Patel, 'Waste to Taste: TN Researchers Create Edible Plates From Jackfruit Skins, Seeds!', TheBetterIndia.com, 22 June 2018, https://bit.ly/2tAGhMi.

26. Ahmed Sherrif, 'Blood-Less, Prick-Free Diabetes Test? Chennai Students' Device Does Just That!', TheBetterIndia.com, 22 June 2018, https://bit.ly/2FIAiOS.

CHAPTER THIRTEEN

TOWARDS A NEW WORLD

1. Harry P. Austin, Mark D. Allen wt al., 'Characterization and engineering of a plastic-degrading aromatic polyesterase', *Proc Natl Acad Sci USA* 115(19) (8 May 2018): E4350–E4357, https://bit.ly/2BgBh4z.

2. Deep Shift: Technology Tipping Points and Societal Impact, Survey Report September 2015, World Economic Forum, https://bit.ly/1KlN8ZR.

3. Rob Wilemay, 'A Venture Capital Firm Just Named An Algorithm To Its Board Of Directors – Here's What It Actually Does', *Business Insider*, 13 May 2014, https://bit.ly/2RkiURE.

4. Peter Diamandis, 'Why the Cost of Living Is Poised to Plummet in the Next 20 Years', 18 July 2016, SingularityHub.com, https://bit.ly/2OVdV8a.

5. 'Renewables 2017: Global Status Report', REN21, 2017, https://bit.ly/2ghNrlA.

6. 'All India Installed Capacity (in MW) of Power Stations', Central Electricity Authority, Ministry of Power, Government of India, https://bit.ly/2E1ZGgw.

7. Sara Matasci, 'How solar panel cost and efficiency have changed over time', 16 March 2017, https://bit.ly/2yR3Fsb.

8. India Solar Handbook 2017, *Bridge to India*, https://goo.gl/E8xFsF.

9. All India Installed Capacity (in MW) of Power Stations, Central Electricity Authority, Ministry of Power, Government of India, https://goo.gl/T4ChbY.

10. Energy Storage Association, http://energystorage.org/.

11. Adam Conner-Simons, 'Study: carpooling apps could reduce taxi traffic 75%', MIT Computer Science & Artificial Intelligence Laboratory, 1 December 2016, https://bit.ly/2DiEFOl.

12. 'The circular economy: moving from theory to practice', McKinsey and Company, October 2016, p. 9, https://goo.gl/HYMrxs.

13. Nick Whigham, 'Apple exec on making a completely green iPhone and tackling child labour concerns in supply chain', News.com.au, 20 November 2017, https://goo.gl/kGcRZk.

14. Katherine Boehrer, 'This Is How Much Water It Takes To Make Your Favorite Foods', *Huffington Post*, 13 October 2014, https://goo.gl/PUA49m.

15. 'Circular Economy in India: Rethinking Growth for Long-term Prosperity', Ellen MacArthur Foundation, 5 December 2016 (p. 59), https://bit.ly/2h3wPJM.

16. Ibid., p. 30.

17. Circular economy in India: rethinking growth for long-term prosperity, https://www.ellenmacarthurfoundation.org/publications/india

18. Michael Batnick, 'The Price of Progress', TheIrrelevantInvestor.com, 10 October 2017, https://bit.ly/2RrOblK.

19. Alana Semuels, 'The Mystery of Why Japanese People Are Having So Few Babies', *Atlantic*, 20 July 2017, https://bit.ly/2eCJxmc.

20. Ingram Pinn, 'How robots are making humans indispensable', *Financial Times*, 22 December 2016, https://on.ft.com/2R1VbW7.

21. Moshe Y. Vardi, 'What the Industrial Revolution Really Tells Us About the Future of Automation and Work', TheConversation.com, 2 September 2017, https://bit.ly/2ey6PdG.

22. 'Deep dive on impact of AI and intelligent machines on jobs', CBInsights.com, 6 October 2017, https://bit.ly/2y8dMJJ.

23. Arwa Mahdawi, 'What jobs will still be around in 20 years?', *Guardian*, 26 June 2017, https://bit.ly/2tM3DOd.

24. Victoria Stern, 'Doing the Math: Can the Robot Be Cost-Effective for General Surgery?', GeneralSurgerynews.com, 22 May 2015, https://bit.ly/2TSbhnm; and 'Robotic Surgery', ECRI.org, 2015, https://bit.ly/2AuvjLA.

25. Heather McGowan and Chris Shipley, 'Future Of Work: Learning To Manage Uncertainty', LinkedIn.com, 28 August 2017, https://bit.ly/2x3AfHk.

26. 'Technology At Work v2.0: The Future Is Not What It Used to Be', Citi GPS: Global Perspectives & Solutions, January 2016, https://bit.ly/2KhYfyg.

27. Yuval Noah Harari, 'The meaning of life in a world without work', *Guardian,* 8 May 2017, https://bit.ly/2pq4jWY.

28. 'Deep dive on impact of AI and intelligent machines on jobs', CBInsights.com.

29. Ingram Pinn, 'How robots are making humans indispensable', *Financial Times,* 22 December 2016, https://on.ft.com/2R1VbW7.

30. Ibid.

31. Greg Ip, 'How Robots May Make Radiologists' Jobs Easier, Not Redundant', *Wall Street Journal,* 22 November 2017, https://on.wsj.com/2BfIRKw.

32. Alex Beall, 'Chinese factory sets up in Arkansas to make t-shirts using U.S. robots', TheRobotReport.com, 25 September 2017, https://bit.ly/2xG9KaQ.

33. Anick Jesdanun, 'Amazon Deal for Whole Foods Could Bring Retail Experiments', NWHerald.com, 16 June 2017, https://bit.ly/2A8va0c.

34. Peter Diamandis, 'Why the Cost of Living Is Poised to Plummet in the Next 20 Years', 18 July 2016, SingularityHub.com, https://bit.ly/2OVdV8a.

35. Ibid.

36. Alex York, 'Best Times to Post on Social Media: A Complete Guide', 9 January 2017, SproutSocial.com, https://bit.ly/2qL761F.

37. Caitlin Dewey, 'A growing number of young Americans are leaving desk jobs to farm', *Washington Post,* 23 November 2017, https://wapo.st/2DvlWhT.

38. Malini Goyal, 'Five entrepreneurs redefining the boutique hotel landscape', *Economic Times,* 5 June 2016, https://bit.ly/2zlDJFw.

39. Catherine Clifford, 'Elon Musk: Robots will take your jobs, government will have to pay your wage', CNBC.com, 4 November 2016, https://cnb.cx/2QgzXac.

40. 'Switzerland's voters reject basic income plan', BBC.com, 5 June 2016, https://bbc.in/2xYi0CJ.

41. David H. Freedman, 'Basic Income: A Sellout of the American Dream', *MIT Technology Review,* 13 June 2016, https://bit.ly/1Yl0Wxu.

42. Dan Nidess, 'Why a Universal Basic Income Would Be a Calamity', *Wall Street Journal*, 10 August 2017, https://on.wsj.com/2vQ4m3K.
43. Thomas Kochan, 'Election rage shows why America needs a new social contract to ensure the economy works for all', *Huffington Post*, 23 November 2017, https://bit.ly/2DEhMEH.
44. Eric Brown, 'Building a future in which good jobs still matter', Institute of Work and Employment Research, MIT, 13 June 2017, https://bit.ly/2qVwDD4.
45. Ibid.
46. Heather McGowan and Chris Shipley, 'Future Of Work: Learning To Manage Uncertainty', LinkedIn.com, 28 August 2017, https://bit.ly/2x3AfHk.
47. Bob Davis, 'Barely Half of 30-Year-Olds Earn More Than Their Parents', *Wall Street Journal*, 8 December 2016, https://on.wsj.com/2DfgKiY.
48. Alana Semuels, 'Does the Economy Really Need to Keep Growing Quite So Much?', *Atlantic*, 4 November 2016, https://bit.ly/2f8g8fx.
49. 'Triple Bottom Line Reporting in Australia: A Guide to Reporting Against Environmental Indicators', Department of the Environment and Heritage, Australia, June 2003, https://bit.ly/2TvMIwk.
50. 'Om Sahana Vavatu – In sanskrit with meaning', GreenMesg.org, https://bit.ly/2S8vHqx.

Get Better at Getting Better
Chandramouli Venkatesan

From the bestselling author of *Catalyst*, which has sold over 60,000 copies

What makes people succeed? Why do some people succeed, while others struggle despite working hard?

This book is based on the insight that success is not about how good you are but how powerful a model you have to improve how good you are. Chandramouli Venkatesan calls it the Get Better Model or GBM. Successful people are those who are able to build a powerful GBM to continuously improve themselves and this book will show you how to do it.

A GBM is made up of four key components and these must be practised deliberately for getting better—getting better by yourself; getting better by leveraging others; making others get better; and making and implementing a get-better plan.

This powerful and life-changing book shows you how you can constantly get better to unlock your potential at work and in life.

The Tata Group: From Torchbearers to Trailblazers
Shashank Shah

With over 100 companies offering products and services across 150 countries, 700,000 employees contributing a revenue of US$ 100 billion, the Tata Group is India's largest and most globalized business conglomerate.

The Tatas are known for salt, software, cars, communications, housing, hospitality, steel and gold. But how did they come so far? How did they groom leadership, delight customers, drive business excellence and acquire global corporations? How did they maintain a brand and corporate values that are considered the gold standard?

A deep dive into the Tata universe, the Tata Group brings forth hitherto lesser-known facts and insights. It also brings you face-to-face with the most intriguing business decisions and their makers. How did Tata Motors turn around Jaguar Land Rover when Ford failed to do so? Why wasn't TCS listed during the IT boom? Why wasn't Tata Steel's Corus acquisition successful?

This definitive book tells riveting tales and provides insider accounts of the adventure and achievement, conflict and compassion, dilemmas and decisions of dozens of Tata companies.

The result of over a decade of rigorous research and interviews with more than a hundred leaders at Tata, this book decodes the Tata way of business, making it an exceptional blend of a business biography and management classic.